Spoiled Rotten

SPOILED ROTTEN

Affluence, Anxiety, and Social Decay in America

BRIAN GOFF

ARTHUR A. FLEISHER III

Westview Press

A Member of the Perseus Books Group

Published in 1999 in the United States of America by Westview Press, 5500 Central Avenue, Boulder, Colorado 80301-2877, and in the United Kingdom by Westview Press, 12 Hid's Copse Road, Cumnor Hill, Oxford OX2 9JJ

Library of Congress Cataloging-in-Publication Data
Goff, Brian.
  Spoiled rotten: affluence, anxiety, and social decay in America /
Brian Goff, Arthur A. Fleisher III.
     p.   cm.
  Includes bibliographical references and index.
  ISBN 0-8133-3618-X (hc)—0-8133-9757-X (pb)
    1. Wealth—United States.   2. Income distribution—United States.
3. United States—Economic conditions.   4. United States—Social
conditions. I. Fleisher, Arthur A.   II. Title.
HC110.W4G58   1999
339.2'0973—dc21   99-17259
                                                                                 CIP

The paper used in this publication meets the requirements of the American National Standard for Permanence of Paper for Printed Library Materials Z39.48-1984.

10   9   8   7   6   5   4   3   2   1

For Julia, Merritt, and Dana
—B.G.

For my parents,
Arthur A. Fleisher II and
Francine Q. Fleisher
—A. A. F. III

CONTENTS

TABLES AND FIGURES

Tables

Figures

PREFACE

According to commonly repeated reports, wages and personal incomes have stagnated in the United States over the past thirty years. The upsurge in the stock market and the low level of unemployment in the mid-1990s have tempered these reports slightly, but a great deal of pessimism still persists. As a corollary, the combination of flat living standards for the masses and rising standards for a privileged few has received substantial blame for a variety of social ills.

The pessimism about American living standards struck us as odd. When looking at the things that average people own and use, drastic improvements over the 1960s and 1970s seemed apparent. As we contemplated the disparity between common reports about living standards and the seemingly obvious improvements, we began to develop the simple but contradictory theses discussed in the following chapters: Properly measured standards of material well-being have grown dramatically for practically all U.S. residents since 1970, and this fantastic growth is responsible for many of the negative social consequences usually attributed to economic stagnation and disparity in wealth. To be a little more specific, affluence and its resulting benefits have reached such enormous levels that the United States has become a nation full of poorly motivated, self-obsessed individuals who have enough money and leisure time to create imaginary problems, indulge fanciful whims, and outsource important responsibilities—in short, to behave like overindulged children.

Although our title and subject matter may seem destined for little more than polemics, our main intent is to steer away from the usual debates about whether capitalism is better or worse than other kinds of economic systems. Instead, we have tried to take the economic system for what it is and examine its consequences. Many readers may view our main points as supporting a conservative or limited-government agenda, but, in fact, our beliefs transcend political philosophies. Social commentators of all stripes—liberal, conservative, populist, socialist—have succumbed to the temptation to underplay the tremendous economic growth of the past thirty years. As a result, their views of the causes and consequences of social problems in the United States, though diverse, have shared one thing—a misunderstanding of the role that rapidly improving living standards have played in contributing to these social problems.

In developing our ideas about wealth and its influence, we look for grassroots-level explanations. The problems we attribute to the growth in wealth include employment issues such as job selection and security, family issues such as illegitimacy and divorce, rising crime trends and tepid punishment, educational issues such as sluggish SAT scores, and others. Further, we discuss how wealth has allowed Americans to create problems out of thin air or turn molehills into mountains. Examples include many of the supposed environmental dangers, health and medical care expenditures, safety regulation, income inequality, and other issues that capture so much attention.

Although we do not try to make this a "balanced" book in the sense of including one statement about wealth's positive consequences for every negative statement, we make clear what wealth's many beneficial contributions to societal outcomes have been. In fact, the many benefits of wealth lead to our analysis of the final question posed in the book: What can we do about wealth's negative effects without destroying its positive impacts? In the final chapter, we try to illustrate some basic insights from economics about offsetting incentive structures. Every attempt has been made to write this book to make it accessible to those outside the economics profession, combining basic insights from economics and easy-to-understand statistical evidence (mainly in terms of simple figures and tables) with historical anecdotes, quotations, and citations of more technical works.

We owe thanks to several colleagues and friends who assisted us in bringing this project to completion by reading the manuscript, helping us locate materials, or offering valuable criticisms and suggestions about the topics. These include Bill Borders, Mel Borland, Wayne Brough, Julia Goff, Roy Howsen, Shigeto Naka, Bob Pulsinelli, Beth Skinner, Larry Smith, Bob Tollison, John Wassom, Tom Wisely, and an anonymous reviewer. Karen Braun and several student workers helped us considerably in developing the manuscript. We also thank Marcus Boggs and the staff associated with Westview Press for their assistance. Of course, we alone are responsible for any errors.

Brian Goff and Arthur A. Fleisher III

Spoiled Rotten

ONE

AFFLUENT THINKING

You gotta be rich in the first place to think like that.
—Buck, in *Platoon*

In Oliver Stone's 1986 movie, *Platoon*, Charlie Sheen's character, Taylor, finds himself on latrine duty in a Vietnam army base with a California surfer and a poorly educated but world-wise black man from Tennessee named Buck. As these three soldiers discuss the time left on their tours of duty in Vietnam and their lives back home, Taylor reveals that unlike the other two, he volunteered for service. He explains, "I figured, why should only poor kids go off to war," to which Buck, with a stunned look, responds, "You gotta be rich in the first place to think like that."

Borrowing from Buck's insights about the effects of material affluence on thinking and action, we underscore in this book how the swell of material living standards for most Americans has muddled and altered both thinking and behavior. Like Taylor, social critics, politicians, and common citizens now think in ways that their poorer ancestors could not afford to, tilt at windmills too expensive for their predecessors to worry about, and engage in actions that are at the very root of the decay so prevalent in society. And because most Americans have little to guide them in evaluating gains in material living standards, they are just like Taylor in that they have little notion of the role that the surge in U.S. living standards has played in adjusting their attitudes and actions.

On the contrary, public opinion polls in the 1990s, which we cite in the next chapter, have consistently exhibited Americans' sweeping discontent not only with social problems such as crime or family breakups but explicitly with economic fortunes. The specific complaints vary from person to person and writer to writer. For one person, wages are not keeping pace with inflation. For another, leisure time is far too scarce. For others, anxiety about current and future job security hovers over them. For many, the gains by the very wealthy seem excessive and unjust, and on and on.

In supporting roles, newspaper columnists and talk show hosts regularly pump up the anxiety and discontent levels with close-ups and features on specific people and families whose lives and enjoyment have been weighed down by the economic crush. The media and entertainment industries, though, have gone far beyond merely monitoring the bad mood about the economy and have offered consolation to the haggard masses as well as prescriptions for improvements. The prescriptions are usually spiced with plenty of recriminations for the alleged culprits behind the angst in America—Ronald Reagan's White House, Newt Gingrich, the Clintons, the Japanese, big corporations, the North American Free Trade Agreement (NAFTA), consumer credit, and other contemptible characters and institutions.

Political figures such as Pat Buchanan, Ross Perot, and Richard Gephardt continue to feed off the discontent and fuel its fires by citing all kinds of instances that demonstrate America's economic decay. In 1992, Perot vaulted to the most impressive showing of any third-party candidate in modern U.S. presidential elections by packaging the economic misery message with a "plain-talk" presentation, down-home humor, and plenty of bravado about his experience in running big operations. One of the most detailed histories of the whole 1992 campaign, in fact, summarized the essence of the economic discontent in its title: *Mad as Hell*.[1]

Even though almost all of the usual data used to track the economy looked better in 1996 than during the 1992 primary season, Pat Buchanan unabashedly sought out those voters who felt most deeply connected to the "we've-got-it-so-bad" theme, for example, those who had been dislodged by foreign workers. He proposed a 15 percent tariff on each product imported into the United States whenever a similar good is produced domestically, both as a means of stemming the outflow of American jobs and as a cross-country wage-equalization plan.[2] His efforts won him an early and unexpected victory in

Louisiana. Even though Perot's backing weakened considerably after 1992, he still received what was a historically large percentage for a third-party candidate by continuing to sell his message of economic trouble in America.

Economic Despair and Affluence: Perception Versus Reality

What might have started as a whisper and a "little secret" about stagnation in the late 1980s had come to be accepted offhandedly as fact. Although the message of economic despair became commonplace in the 1990s, its backers continued to write as if they were exposing subtle truths that had been hidden within the typical economic facts and figures. They thought they were exposing the bed of sand underneath the foundation of a palatial estate.

The evidence that supposedly supports the dismal situation for working America might better be termed elusive rather than subtle. Except for those unfortunates living in the country's worst crime-infested neighborhoods and housing projects, people who might want to take a commonsense look at society as it really is—free from the doomsayers' biases—will struggle to detect the economic blight allegedly draining America. People searching for the truth of the matter might be arrested by various problems pressing on society—teenage pregnancy, crime, broken homes, poor educational attainment, lack of contentment—but if the issue were purely one of material success, then the economic misery that is touted to hold large numbers of middle-class families in its grip would hardly be impressive.

Whether one observes the largest metro areas, mid-sized towns, or rural communities, the crowds supposedly battered by economic misfortune drive late-model, stereo-laden cars, $20,000 Dodge Ram pickup trucks, and all kinds of four-wheel-drive sport-utility vehicles with such names as Explorer, Passport, Trooper, Rodeo, 4-Runner, and Blazer, and the granddaddy of them all—the Suburban. They live in houses nearly twice as large as their parents' and appointed with color television sets, microwave ovens, VCRs, Nintendo software, stereo equipment, and related tapes and gadgets. They not only own but chew up minutes on cellular phones as if their survival depended on it.

American living spaces illustrate the improvement as well as anything. The amenities inside these houses have also improved, making the luxuries of bygone decades now standard. As children growing up in middle-class neighborhoods in the 1960s and 1970s, we remember houses of the time as containing two bathrooms, and sometimes only one; a house with more than two bathrooms was rare. Now, in the late 1990s, nearly 50 percent of all houses contain 2.5 bathrooms or more. Game rooms, guest bedrooms, and the like were formerly also limited to only the more exclusive neighborhoods. And the data on these changes also back up our experience: The average house in 1970 contained less than 1,500 square feet, whereas by 1996, the average size had risen to around 2,000 square feet. Central air-conditioning began to become common only during the 1970s.[3] The appointments that have become routine in so many houses today— crown molding, multicar garages, fireplaces—were mainly for the rich and famous of the 1960s.

Material success for Americans extends far beyond living rooms and bathrooms. The same middle-class families portrayed as being in dire straits spend billions of dollars purchasing and hours of time using their boats, mountain bikes, camping equipment, golf clubs, court shoes, and softball bats, and along with this, there is a long list of expenses related to using such recreational equipment. They have pushed purchases of merchandise related to professional and college sports teams to record highs and have flocked to games in record numbers: The Colorado Rockies and Toronto Blue Jays have drawn more than 4 million fans to their parks in a single year; the Texas Rangers drew nearly 3 million, with a losing record; college football teams like those at the Universities of Michigan and Tennessee draw 100,000 people per game, who pay at least $30 per ticket.[4] The children of these households drive Barbie jeeps, fill cabinets full of Disney videos and Sega cartridges, buy out stocks of Beanie Babies, and wear $70 court shoes along with "authentic" team jerseys and caps.

Beyond these kinds of expenditures, which would appear to reflect relatively high affluence, just about all of these working-class families, said to be held down by stagnant or declining living standards, utilize daily conveniences that were unknown to past generations but that Americans now view as life's "necessities": hot tap water, flush toilets, refrigerators and freezers, cooktops, electric and gas ovens or ranges, microwave ovens, telephones, and thermostat-controlled air-conditioning systems. Except for those living in such high-density cities where not having a car can be an advantage, they almost all have at least one family car and usually more. In short, the American families enduring the "economic hardships" and stirring so much attention among editors and politicians enjoy living standards that would make most monarchs of bygone eras envious. In his book *The Good Life and Its Discontents, Newsweek* economic columnist Robert Samuelson refers to this contrast between the widespread discontent with economic well-being and the observable conditions of American lifestyles as a paradox.[5] Whether a paradox or outright delusion, the gap between the "economic chaos" and the reality of living standards is wide.

To resolve the imbalance between the subjective perception of economic progress and the more blatant contradictions in the expenditures and assets of Americans, it is necessary to regard the obvious facts about material well-being as poor indicators, to regard the perceptions about living standards as errors, or some of both. Samuelson chooses the last option, explaining the "paradox" as based partly on misperceptions and partly on genuine slowdowns—not in actual living standards but in the rate of their growth since about 1970.

In our view, as we discuss in detail in Chapter 3, the imbalance between perception and actual economic progress cannot be laid in any way at the feet of economic stagnation. Whether one considers purchases of recreational "toys" or freedom from concerns about basic needs for life, both anecdotal evidence and detailed, careful analysis of living standards discredit the idea of declining or flat living standards in the United States since 1970. Even the more temperate claim of a thirty-year slowdown in the rate of progress does not hold up against the evidence. The burden for the discrepancy in perception versus reality then rests squarely on perceptions about economic prosperity rather than on the reality of prosperity.

If perception of prosperity is the culprit, then what explains perceptions that are so out of step with reality? The answer to this question is illustrated by the bluntness of the metaphor in our title: Americans are spoiled rotten by their affluence. Ironically, rising prosperity has helped to shape these erroneous perceptions about economic prosperity and has contributed to several other negative social outcomes covered in Chapters 5, 6, and 7. We discuss the contribution of prosperity to negative perceptions of prosperity more thoroughly in Chapter 6. For now, suffice it to paraphrase *Platoon*'s Buck and say that people must enjoy a substantial level of affluence and have their thinking obscured by that affluence in order to build or accept a story of widespread economic blight in a nation so full of plenty.

Naturally, in using a title as loaded as *Spoiled Rotten* for this volume, we risk stirring plenty of suspicion that our book contains

merely ranting and ravings about Americans and their complaining
about economic fortunes. But the title merely borrows a common
phrase used to denote the discrepancy between "having things so
good" and thinking things are so bad. We describe a nation filled
with complaints about economic misfortune, reluctant to take personal responsibility for the consequences of choices, and troubled by
social problems in spite of enjoying creature comforts beyond the
imagination of most of the world's population. We analyze a society
of people unable to appreciate the home appliances and recreational
toys that their ancestors would have considered luxuries and extravagant indulgences. In this context, what metaphor could better express the divergence between economic advantages and the lack of
appreciation for these advantages?

In using the "spoiled rotten" metaphor, we are not alluding to
changes in the most basic aspects of individual psychology. At the
most fundamental level, we do not claim that Americans today differ
from their ancestors—contemporary Americans just have much
greater access to material means to pursue many ends that their ancestors could not. The effects of extremely high wealth, though not
completely unavoidable, are the predictable consequences of life- and
incentive-altering aspects of much higher standards of living. If past
generations had been plugged into the current level of affluence, we
would not be surprised to observe that, at least after a generation or
two, they exhibited attitudes and behavior similar to those that are so
common today.

Key Issues and Questions

Rather than making wild ideological accusations about Americans
and their ways, we propose two dispassionate theses: (1) Material
well-being in the United States is not only historically high but has
surged even over the past quarter century, the "era of economic stagnation," and (2) this progress in material affluence rather than its
stagnation or decline has brought with it many valuable results but
has also played a major role in creating many of the problems threat-
ening American society.

We put forward the first point about rising affluence not just as
conjecture but as fact, which can be soundly substantiated with existing evidence. The second point about the contributions of rising affluence to negative trends in society is more conjectural, and we con-

sider it using both intuition and evidence. We do not intend to suggest that enough hard data exist to ground all of the claims about the effects of affluence in concrete; yet the evidence that does exist is compelling enough to offer a credible alternative to the usual explanations for social decay.

A few aspects regarding trends in U.S. affluence are not controversial. Practically all informed observers would admit that U.S. standards of living are very high in comparison to living standards in more distant U.S. history and in comparison to the conditions found in many contemporary settings in the world. However, many of these observers would attribute the overflowing spring of goods and services that most consumers enjoy in this country to economic advances achieved before 1970. As a case in point, we would refer readers to *The Good Life and Its Discontents*, which is largely critical of the discontent about economic well-being.[6] That book views the discontent as a natural consequence of the unsustainably high growth rates following World War II. In this way of thinking, Americans need to ratchet down their expectations to well below the material gains made during the "golden era" of 1945 to 1970.

The controversial aspect of *Spoiled Rotten*, insofar as its claims about American affluence go, centers on the direction and magnitude of growth in living standards since 1970. As we discuss in detail later in this book, according to widespread published reports and statements, including those generated for mass appeal as well as many offered by professional economists, the economic well-being of average households flattened out after 1970. Some go further than this, claiming that living standards for most households have actually regressed since 1970. Public opinion polls and the path of inflation-adjusted wages over the past twenty years are two of the more frequently cited claims used to back up the stagnation thesis. Also, the critics of U.S. living standards point to the number and severity of noneconomic social ills themselves as evidence of fundamental economic problems. Without apology, we feature an opposing and seldom discussed conclusion: Living standards have jumped upward since 1970 for almost all segments of society and rival the kinds of economic gains made from 1945 to 1970.

Our evidence also rejects the class-driven rhetoric that tries to link rising economic fortunes with only the very wealthy. Although the improvements in living standards may not have been proportionate for every household in the country, all income classes have felt substantial impact from the rising tide of national affluence. More will be said about the income inequality dogma in Chapter 4.

The second major point of the book takes the facts about rising U.S. standards of economic well-being and utilizes Buck's dictum about riches: Affluence causes people to think and act differently. The difference arises not because wealth brings about higher basic intelligence or changes the most fundamental desires of people. Instead, just as affluence makes nicer homes and automobiles more affordable, it also makes certain ways of thinking and alternative ways of using one's time more affordable.

Over the past twenty-five years, the standard of living has improved significantly for American households, rising from an already high starting point in worldwide comparison. By 1970 and beyond, even middle-income Americans possessed the economic wherewithal to pursue objectives with their time and money that average citizens from any other society in mankind's history would never have been able to afford. A number of these objects of desire resulted in great achievements and improvements in society—organ transplants with long-term survivability, food in the stomachs of hungry children, and cleaned-up rivers and streams, just to name three. On the other side, though, the uptick in America's wealth has made other kinds of activity affordable, and these, in the aggregate, present severe problems for the country, resulting in the decline in moral standards, family breakups, rising litigation, the birth of environmental radicalism, and the stimulus for the politics of discontent, to name a few of the more general problems. Later chapters in the book pursue these in their specifics.

In the process of developing the two main theses about wealth's rising tide and the effects of that tide, a number of detailed questions are addressed in subsequent chapters. Chapter 3 focuses on issues related to measuring and assessing living standards, providing answers to several questions, including the following:

- Why don't the numbers show that incomes have not been keeping pace with inflation?
- Why don't the typical measures of national output, income, productivity, and prices show the true gains in living standards?
- What kind of picture of living-standard changes emerges when expenditures and assets are considered in addition to the usual measures such as gross domestic product (GDP)?

- How much income do households have left over after meeting basic necessities, compared with households of twenty and thirty years ago?

Chapter 4 considers the arguments of last resort used by the stagnation writers to attempt to shoot down the evidence presented in Chapter 3. A few of the questions addressed there include:

- Are the rich getting wealthier while middle- and lower-income households are treading water?
- What about the cases of family economic troubles brought on by corporate downsizing?
- Have living standards in other countries caught up with those in the United States, or are they, at least, catching up quickly?
- Isn't the era of high unemployment and high inflation in the 1970s and early 1980s obvious evidence of economic decline in the post-1970 era?
- Do rising shares of income spent on medical care clearly illustrate embedded problems in the U.S. economy?

Chapters 5, 6, and 7 examine the effects of rising affluence on a variety of societal outcomes. Some of the main questions are:

- If affluence is growing by leaps and bounds, why has leisure time not seemed to keep up?
- Are reductions in working hours the only avenue for more leisure time?
- What do employment trends and educational performance trends have in common with each other and with affluence?
- Why does the wealthiest country in the world have education troubles?
- Why would all of the anxiety about employment exist if living standards were so great?
- What is the link between the family-depleting effects of the welfare system and problems experienced by nonwelfare families?
- If living standards are really so great and improving, why is America subject to so much violent crime?
- How could increases in affluence lead to more teenage and unwed pregnancies?

- Contentment levels may not rise with affluence, but why would they fall?
- How is rising affluence related to the massive growth in government regulation in the past quarter century?
- Why would a society switch from killing dangerous animals to putting people in jail for killing dangerous animals?
- How does the United States export the effects of its own affluence?

Chapter 8 dives into the murky waters of possible remedies for the affluence-driven effects. The discussion asks:

- Is it even possible to benefit from affluence while limiting its negative effects?
- What are the bases for material gains and happiness, more broadly defined?
- To what extent are public-sector initiatives needed and feasible?

Voices in the Wilderness

We are by no means the first writers to propose that living standards have been improving since 1970. Over the years, a few writers have advanced the idea, some before the stagnation message really got its legs underneath it. The doomsayers have buried those who have dared to emphasize economic gains in more recent years under an avalanche, barely considering the idea of rising living standards worthy of serious debate. To the extent that they have responded at all, the critics of American living standards have usually offered little more than fleeting acknowledgment to the most obvious technological advances such as personal computers or microwave ovens. We review this in Chapter 2.

Perhaps the precursor for modern works proposing a rising tide of economic prosperity for the masses is John Kenneth Galbraith's widely read *The Affluent Society,* published in 1958.[7] In it, he claimed concerns about life's necessities and basic survival had become a thing of the past for most Americans, freeing them to make most decisions based on preference and luxury. Of course, much of the support for the book, as well as the criticism of it, pertained to its conclusions about affluence leading to growing indifference by the affluent masses toward the few Americans still stuck at or near subsistence levels—a topic to which we return in Chapter 7. However, the main message of the book centered on widespread affluence rather than on political consequences or prescriptions, although these generated much of the discussion about the book.

In an ironic twist, a number of the people devoted to the stagnation message in the 1980s and 1990s are of the same intellectual heritage as Galbraith—Ivy League–trained intellectuals often with strong views about the shortcomings of private markets. Yet if Galbraith could claim in 1958 that the overwhelming majority of Americans had attained income and wealth levels high enough to eradicate life's most pressing economic problems, then how could things have degenerated so much by the late 1990s? Surely, given all of the kinds of products sitting in American homes of the late 1990s that were not present in homes of the 1950s, a person could hardly make the case that economic fortunes have deteriorated since the 1950s. One must suspect that the accolades given Galbraith's book, especially by the members of the political left who now embrace the stagnation message, may have been due more to the book's political prescriptions than to its main economic premise.

Written on the heels of a host of doomsday economic prophecies following the recessions of 1979–1982, Ben Wattenberg's 1984 book, *The Good News Is the Bad News Is Wrong*, offered the most comprehensive and forceful exposition of the improving living standards thesis up to that date.[8] His contribution is especially interesting in that the stagnation idea had seemingly gained credibility at the time because of the stagflation of the 1970 and early 1980s. Wattenberg's entire book is devoted to showing that if one looks beyond just one or two figures related to gross domestic product and surveys a wide swath of data related to living standards, one would conclude that Americans were living quite extravagant lifestyles. Wattenberg's substantial and wide-ranging evidence comes just after the worst recessionary period since the Great Depression, which raises serious questions about the legitimacy of thinking things have deteriorated greatly since 1984—a period of sustained economic growth interrupted by only one short recession in 1990–1991.

Another author whose work has had bearing on the direction of living standards is the late Julian Simon, a University of Maryland economist.[9] Beginning before the stagnation message became chic in mainstream circles, he attempted to straighten out the errors of the zero-growth and population-problem literature that arose in the 1960s. Since that time, in the areas of economic growth and population dynamics, he forcefully and eloquently showed how technical progress overcame what were thought to be insurmountable obstacles to continued economic growth. He not only explained but actually predicted declines in the inflation-adjusted prices of important raw materials—winning a bet with no-growth guru Paul Ehrlich in doing so. Simon's work was directed both at living standards in themselves and at explaining the mechanisms by which living standards increase with limited raw materials and growing populations. An important question resulting from Simon's works is this: If the prices of critical materials used to produce the most basic kinds of goods and services have been falling, then how can it be that American living standards have stagnated or fallen over the past thirty years?

In *The Seven Fat Years,* contributing editor Robert Bartley of the *Wall Street Journal* highlights many of the economic advances that paralleled the Reagan-Bush administrations of 1984–1990.[10] Also, as we have already mentioned, Robert Samuelson's 1994 book *The Good Life and Its Discontents* questioned at least some aspects of the stagnation idea. Although Samuelson does buy into the idea of a slowdown in the rate of improvement since 1970, his work definitely takes a view contrary to the dismal economic outlook that may have reached its zenith around the time his work was published.

Although their work did not receive circulation nearly as wide or as much attention as the books just mentioned, reports generated by two economists at the Federal Reserve Bank of Dallas, Michael Cox and Richard Alm, provide plain but unrelenting evidence contradicting the stagnation premise.[11] Instead of relying solely on typical summary figures, Cox and Alm dig more deeply into hours spent to purchase specific items, asset ownership, home characteristics, employment growth, medical advances, and other more specific measures of household standards of living. Anyone who thinks that systematic data and anecdotal evidence line up squarely behind the stagnation message should consult these reports, which present some of the most devastating evidence against the class-driven demagoguery that exists, as well as relaying several "success" stories of ordinary people who elevated themselves from the most meager economic circumstances to very successful positions as professionals and business owners.

Most recently, University of California–Irvine economics professor Richard McKenzie tackles the subject of misunderstood economic progress in his *Paradox of Progress*.[12] He relies heavily on Cox and Alm's data to support his claim that U.S. living standards have never been higher. He blames much of the misunderstanding about the true course of the economy on a failure to understand its fundamental shifts. In sum, he calls for Americans to grasp the abundant opportunities around them, build their education, and stop complaining.

Although these references indicate that we are not the first to attempt to set the record straight about living standards, there is also no tidal wave of support for the idea. Beyond these sources, most of the other challenges to the negative view of living standards have surfaced only as infrequent newspaper articles or editorials, but these works have largely been ignored.[13]

The Ubiquity of Affluence-Induced Effects

Although these authors and possibly a few others have ventured to overturn the misinformation about economic conditions in the United States, the second of our two main propositions—the link between the rise in affluence and numerous social ills—has received even less attention. An article here and there, in addition to Daniel Bell in his *Cultural Contradictions of Capitalism*, have steered in the direction we are heading with our argument.[14] Yet the intuition underlying the link between growing economic affluence and social decay that we discuss here is simple. Furthermore, it draws from a standard economic insight, one based in common sense: Affluence makes more items affordable. Many, if not most, of these items improve the American lifestyle. However, a few contribute to undesirable consequences.

Part of the allure of the stagnation message is seemingly its unique ability in the minds of many to account for the kinds of social ills experienced by Americans. Problems such as violent crime are real and serious. If these problems do not stem from economic stagnation, then what is their origin? A better understanding of the far-reaching influence of rising affluence can demonstrate how it can account for some of the problems so frequently attributed to dismal economic conditions and may help to diminish some of the appeal of the stagnation dogma.

Of course, affluence can mean different things to different people. Chapter 3 delves into some of the nuances of measuring living standards and the precise measurement of income, consumption, and wealth. For now, we broadly define a higher living standard as one that allows for greater consumption over an indefinite period of time, whether consumption is directed toward the purchase of long-lived goods, perishable goods, or services.

Although simple, this ability-to-consume definition of material success is critical to clear thinking about trends in affluence. For one thing, it explains that income in any given year is not always a reliable indicator of consumption ability. If one person reports an income of $50,000 but does not own a house, a car, or very many other assets, we cannot unambiguously state that the person's standard of living is higher or lower than someone who reports an income of $35,000. The person with the lower income may own a house, a car, a stereo, and a boat and as a result is able to "consume" by using these assets rather than purchasing new items.

Income is converted into wealth through purchases of financial assets like bank accounts, money market accounts, stocks, or bonds or through purchase of nonfinancial assets such as houses and cars. Other consumer durables such as televisions, cars, trucks, stereo equipment, and the like also reflect the conversion of income into tangible wealth. Wealth often provides for both consumption now and in the future, as is clear from items such as houses or most consumer durables. The kinds of income changes that are typically converted into wealth most frequently are those that are either permanent in nature or are very large in nature, so that whenever a permanent change in income is under consideration, it is equivalent for practical purposes to a change in wealth.[15]

With these few points in mind about the definition of affluence, we can easily illustrate the commonsense nature of affluence-driven effects. Consumer demand for most goods and services increases whenever consumers experience permanent boosts in their incomes. Many goods tend to keep pace with, and in a few cases even exceed, the growth of general purchasing power. Items such as new cars, boats, and home entertainment products often fall into this category, as would purchases of certain kinds of medical care services such as elective surgery. The purchase of other goods and services increases with wealth but does not keep pace with income growth. Most daily foodstuffs could be lumped into this group. Although the consumer purchases of most goods increase whenever consumers experience increases in income or wealth, exceptions occur with some degree of frequency. For example, in New York City, the very wealthy are much less likely to use the subway and buses, preferring more private transportation modes such as cabs and limos. College students with limited incomes are frequent purchasers of items such as Ramen noodles and peanut butter. Purchases of these items often decline as students find permanent employment and experience substantial increases in current income and expected future income and wealth.

Other kinds of increases in living standards and resulting changes in behavior stem from more subtle sources. For instance, if the discovery and use of new, cheap oil fields lowers the price of gasoline, purchases of gasoline will rise as long as other influences on gasoline purchases remain unchanged. The additional gasoline purchases really represent two separate effects. People purchase more, in part, because gasoline is now cheaper in relation to other products like food and housing. Additionally, purchases increase because consumers are now relatively wealthier—the oil discovery and subsequent price reductions have raised purchasing power for households. The increase in purchasing power will spill over and affect household purchases of other products also. For example, the same $100 of income can buy the same basket of goods (including gas) with money left over. If the cost of the identical basket of goods is now only $95 because of the lower gas prices, people are in a real sense $5 richer.

College freshmen and sophomores sitting in their first economics class must usually endure a lecture or two that centers on these very kinds of affluence-driven effects. In those classes, the term "income elasticities" is applied to measures of the responsiveness of purchases to changes in the income of consumers. Goods such as basic foodstuffs exhibit only small responses to income changes. Purchases of goods such as gasoline tend to go up in about the same proportion as income increases. Other goods like recreational equipment are highly responsive, sometimes showing as much as a 30 percent increase in units sold for every 10 percent increase in income.

Beyond these most simplistic notions of income and wealth effects, the economics profession makes wide-ranging application of the same notions in slightly more subtle ways. We know, for instance, that income and wealth play an important role in the decision about the percentage of household financial assets held in cash or checking accounts, versus those in stocks and bonds. A person's typical decisions about spending more than current income when in young adulthood and in late adulthood but building up savings during the middle period of adulthood follow from the expectations of income and wealth over a lifetime.

This brings us right to the brink of the link between affluence and the realities of social decay, which forms the second main thesis of our book. The critical point in jumping from the more common examples of income and wealth effects to our discussions in later chapters merely requires a person to understand that tradable goods and services like gasoline and medical care are not the only kinds of desired items linked to wealth changes. The influence of income and wealth extends into situations where money is never exchanged for a tradable good or service. For instance, job-related decisions such as whether to work more hours or decisions on whether to hold out longer when unemployed and looking for a new job are in part influenced by income and wealth considerations. Here, leisure is the item influenced by income and wealth, even though leisure does not have an explicit price tag attached to it.

Nonmarket and even nontradable objects of desire for households are just like market-traded goods and services, becoming sometimes more and sometimes less affordable as living standards rise and fall. The leisure decision helps to emphasize this point. In short, leisure—an object of desire but not a marketable good like cassette tapes—became much more affordable because of the economic gains made over the first part of the twentieth century. As a result, typical work-week length and annual hours worked have declined. The source of the reduction in working hours was not a fundamental difference in individual psychology—one would be hard-pressed to make the case that the nineteenth-century worker laboring more than fourteen-hour work days, six days per week did not desire shorter hours. Rather, the source of the change was the ability to reduce work time and still consume at a relatively higher level.

In this same vein, increases in income and wealth over the past half and even the past quarter century have altered decisions about many other nonmarket goods. These items may well have been desired by preceding generations, but they were simply too expensive. Chapters 5, 6, and 7 detail how income and wealth have made various objects of desire more affordable—and these objectives range from the political through the work-related, the educational, the sexual, the recreational, and so on, within the economic grasp of everyday citizens.

However, because these objectives have sometimes carried with them undesirable baggage, the rising affluence has also led to many problems plaguing society today. For instance, increased sexual activity may be directly influenced by increased income or wealth, bringing about increased births to unwed mothers as an indirect and undesirable consequence.

The idea that income and wealth can influence objects of desire even down to the point where it can be difficult to distinguish whether it is affluence that is the motivating influence or whether basic preferences have changed was first broached by Gary Becker and George Stigler, two Nobel Prize–winning economists from the University of Chicago. Their academic article with the Latin title "De Gustibus Non Est Disputandum" (in translation, "There's No Accounting for Taste") offers an economic-based rationale to account for preference formation and change.[16] Their point is simple: Prices and incomes alter the affordability of various kinds of preferences. Additionally, people build up more skill in consuming some kinds of items rather than others through childhood experiences and other social interactions. Taken together, these insights offer an explanation for preference formation and change, in which the traditional economic factors of price and income play a role in addition to biological forces or inexplicable whims of consumers. Our proposition about the relationship between rising affluence and social consequences applies this insight. Increasing wealth brings many more options into play for consumers, and some of these, at least indirectly, have serious downsides to them.[17]

Missing the Point

Writing a book in which we not only turn the view of economic misery on its head but also use increases in economic prosperity as the explanation behind the fretting about economic status and other problems is no simple task, given the widespread acceptance of the misery doctrine. It is a bit like saying the emperor is, indeed, wearing a handsome new suit of clothes when reports have exposed his nakedness. Even more damaging to the serious consideration of our points is that the message of economic stagnation supports many diverse political agendas, leaving plenty of people with an outright stake in keeping it going. For these and other reasons, we are likely to come under fire not just for what we say but for what some might perceive our motivation to be.

One charge that might crop up is that we are taking a rose-colored, Pollyanna view of America's affluence and the trends in this affluence. This has been a favored tactic of stagnation writers to attack the isolated author or two who dared to point out the material abundance within the United States. These kinds of critics may admit that evidence contrary to the stagnation view may not be wholly false but feel that the viewpoint focuses in on a few highly visible economic achievements while ignoring a faltering society. Americans may have CD players, VCRs, and microwaves, but highlighting such facts merely ignores the more substantial economic decay in society as well as the noneconomic social problems.

These critics commonly employ such comebacks when insisting on the stagnation story, but they are shallow rebuttals. Far from ignoring the many serious problems that not only persist but are on the rise in American society, we devote a large part of the book to analyzing the way in which U.S. material progress has contributed to noneconomic, societal problems. Rather than using society's problems as prima facie evidence of economic decay, we show how many of the failings of society arise because of the tremendous standards of living and their growth. Observed in this light, the seeming imbalance between impressive gains in material wealth and widespread discontent is not a paradox but an irony—the same increases in economic well-being that have made American lives so comfortable in many ways have simultaneously helped to foment some of society's most dangerous dilemmas.

A second charge likely to be thrown our way is that we are merely right-leaning apologists for Ronald Reagan or that we have imbibed of too many "Rush Room" conversations about America's ills. Even if this charge were true, it hardly addresses the validity of the data and arguments that we present. Unfortunately, the level of debate in this society about serious issues often degenerates into little more than name-calling and guilt by association. Although we strongly disagree with the stagnation message, we have steered away from assuming it is wrong merely because it has been utilized by people with a particular political ideology or questionable motives.

More to the point, though, the stagnation message cuts across and has been used by writers and politicians with very diverse backgrounds and agendas. One would hardly lump Al Gore and Pat Buchanan into the same political category, yet both of them have tied their wagon to economic stagnation at one point or another. We do not think that writers for the news pages of the *Wall Street Journal* are in league with the editorialists of the *New York Times*, yet the stagnation message has appeared in both papers. In criticizing the idea that America is mired in the economic doldrums or sits on the precipice of an economic decline, we espouse a position divorced from a particularly liberal or conservative ideology or agenda. Finally, on this point and to set the record straight, we are not on the dole from any political group or cause. We reject the idea of public policy as a panacea for problems, and we are skeptical of the notion that public policymakers always or even usually have the motives and information necessary to improve on private sector decisions. Yet in instances where the mix of information and incentives for government decisionmakers is clearly better than it is for private decisionmakers, we view government involvement as beneficial.

A third charge that might emerge is that our book is little more than moral philosophy and personal views about the "good life" and its disappearance. Throughout the book, we do describe some kinds of societal outcomes as "bad" or "negative," and by doing so, we have obviously taken implicit moral or ethical positions. Still, we do not parade ourselves as moral philosophers—not in this book, anyway. The things we describe as "bad" are outcomes that we would expect most people, though certainly not all, to view as undesirable, even if they might be unavoidable. We hardly think a case must be made for describing murder, assault, and theft as undesirable events. Maybe some people would not see anything grossly negative in the family-related problems of divorce, unwed pregnancy, and teenage pregnancy, but we would think that except for mitigating circumstances, most Americans deem these events less than desirable. Concerning the discussion of political outcomes in Chapter 7, we might collect a number of dissenters who really do not see much "bad" in ream upon ream of regulatory edicts, interest-group-driven legislation, and exports of U.S. economic regulation. In this case, even if someone does not view these as negative results, our analysis still helps to explain the outcomes.

In particular, even when outlining our suggestions for remedying all of these problems in Chapter 8, we do not try to generate guilt among Americans over affluence or try to turn the clock back to an earlier, poorer time. We cannot go back, and besides, Americans would not want to give up the many positive aspects of higher living standards—longer life spans, lower infant mortality, material wealth, and other highly valued features of American life. This last chapter offers suggestions about enjoying wealth's advantages while trying to limit its negative influences.

In stating how little we are trying to expound upon our own moral or ethical viewpoints, we are drawing a contrast to much of the stagnation literature, which is ripe with personal moral agendas and paternalism. Some of the contributors to that literature reject parts of the rising living standard evidence solely because the evidence does not fit their own very individual views of consumer behavior. To them, CD players cannot show rising standards of living because, after all, they are just CD players—mere playthings, and not goods or services of substance.

As far as our interests are concerned, we are neither for nor against material gains even if some choose to pursue them as ends in themselves. We readily go along with anyone who wants to draw a clear distinction between growth purely in terms of economic prosperity and gains in broader notions of happiness and contentment. Material affluence does not necessarily raise contentment. Nonetheless, the ability and desire to use money to purchase playthings to the exclusion of other goods or services does indicate material affluence. If some people want to purchase CDs and home videos instead of buying books by Faulkner and Hemingway or sending money to citizens of Bangladesh, we hardly think it appropriate to view those expenditures as not qualifying as affluence. In contrast, it is within elements of the stagnation literature and not in our book that terms such as "consumerism" and "conspicuous consumption" appear—and this language is intended to reflect a paternalistic and condescending view of those people caught in a buying-spending cycle and unable to smell the roses of a better life. Even if such an "anticonsumerist" mentality were appropriate, it hardly qualifies as a rebuttal of advances in economic prosperity.

Finally, because of the surge in the economic statistics in the past couple of years, especially as typified by the rise in the stock markets, some may think our refutation of the stagnation message is muted— who, after all, thinks the economy is stagnant anymore? As clearly as we can state it, this book is not about the short-term direction of the economy, either in the past or in the future. With the exception of a devastating economic depression like the 1930s with unemployment around 25 percent, whether the economy keeps moving up or undergoes a decline for a year or two does not change what we have to say. Our book is about trends over the past thirty years, beliefs about those trends, and the effects of those trends.

TWO

THE MESSAGE OF
ECONOMIC DESPAIR

*Yet despite all of these differences, I think we have been going
through a depression much like that of the 1930s.*
—Robert Heilbroner, "Anti-Depression Economics"

The economic doomsayers cling to the following belief, stated here
in its simplest and most direct terms: The standard of living for a large
segment of working-class American families has either stagnated or
declined since 1970. For many promoting this message and its many
corollaries, it is no mere assertion about reality; instead, it represents
nearly indisputable truth, supported by a devotion approaching religious zealotry. Suggestion that the evidence has been distorted is
damnable heresy. Dissenting from this "wisdom" or presentation of
contradictory evidence risks their ridicule and contempt on various
counts—for being an apologist for the Reagan administration, an im-
perceptive bean counter, a Pollyanna, or a flat-out fool. To paraphrase
the sentiments expressed, the decline is all around us, can't you see?

If only out-of-office or minority party politicians, their cronies, and
a few cranks accounted for all of the people spouting off about economic decay, we might easily pass over the whole statement about
stagnant living standards as merely political rhetoric employed to gain
advantage. But the team of true believers and advocates of the message extends far beyond a few politicians, their associates, and a few
back-to-nature relics from the 1960s. Even outside the core of the

most zealous promoters of the stagnation message, the basic premise has so thoroughly penetrated the thinking of analysts and average citizens that it has become part of American culture in the 1990s. Stagnation thinking and its vocabulary have forged their own reality, a particular mental outlook on the world that creeps into thought, conversation, print, and the airwaves in insidious and subtle ways, often when the topic under discussion may be far afield from economic well-being.

On our college campuses, for instance, we have been party to various discussions about the lack of student motivation or performance among seemingly capable students. On more than a few occasions, someone has referred to the strains and pressures on students who must not only keep up with their studies but also work long hours because of economic hardship as a prime rationale for the halting performance and absence of motivation. Or in a variation of the same line of reasoning, someone may add that these students are so dismayed with their job prospects that they have little motivation for educational success.

Looking at more systematic and broader evidence, survey after survey appears to confirm the bad news suggested by the anecdotal evidence. When asked in a January 1996 NBC/*Wall Street Journal* poll if they thought that their children's living standards would meet their own, two-thirds of the households responded negatively. When asked to rate their satisfaction with their own income relative to the cost of living, 52 percent said they were somewhat or very dissatisfied. In assessing the results of the poll, *Wall Street Journal* writers David Wessel and Gerald Seib concluded, "The poll provides fresh evidence that stagnant incomes, rather than widely cited worries about job loss, are behind much of the middle class's anxiety."[1]

A December 1995 survey of Connecticut residents commissioned by the state General Assembly and conducted by a policy institute at Fordham University reported that most thought the state's living standards had worsened in the previous five years. Seventy-one percent rated their chances of finding a satisfactory job as poor. Eighty percent said that it was difficult to provide for themselves and their families. In summarizing the results, the report's author stated, "Here you have a perception by residents that things are not improving and that in fact most things are worsening."[2] Similar responses appear on the West Coast as well. The *Los Angeles Times* reported on a survey conducted in the Los Angeles area in which 40 percent of families and 80 percent of mothers felt "haunted" by anxiety about spending too little time with their children and wished they could quit their jobs.[3]

It might be easy to dismiss numbers gathered on the heels of the 1990–1991 recession as being tainted by the recession, but the evidence of economic gloom in public opinion preceded and followed years beyond the fringes of the last recession. An October 1996 NBC/*Wall Street Journal* poll demonstrates just how ingrained the gloom is, reporting only a slim margin of respondents as viewing their economic situations as better than four years before.[4]

The heart of the stagnation message is not just tied to New England troubles or Orange County, California, home prices or to job slowdowns in 1990 but instead encompasses the economic fortunes of a large percentage of the population over a twenty-to thirty-year time frame. The message gained nearly as much attention leading up to the 1996 campaign as it did in 1992, shortly after the recession. A few of the polls showing economic anxieties may pertain to problems more or less related to specific geographic areas or very short-term downturns in economic performance and expectations, but this is the exception rather than the rule. Broadly surveyed, the polls are based on nationwide samples, cover both recession years and nonrecession years, and are so numerous that we can only conclude that those advancing the stagnation message are at least correct in assessing the national mood about economic matters.

Whether everyday Americans are more pessimistic about their economic fortunes than those who observe and comment upon their misery is not altogether clear. One point, though, is crystal clear: Americans have not been left to themselves to wallow in their misery. All kinds of purveyors of American life have been more than willing not only to monitor this misery but to go to great lengths to propagate the message.[5] Below, we present a mere sampling of the economic pessimism and despair, drawn from the writings of reporters and editorialists in newspapers, popular books, academic books and reports, and political debate.[6] Many other examples could be used, but these consider some of the most visible sources of the message and reveal some of the more detailed aspects. At the end of the chapter, we collect and summarize the main threads of this message of economic despair.

Newspapers, Magazines, and Television

Among the several groups important in providing a seemingly undeniable basis for the creed of economic despair, nobody peddles the
philosophy with more zeal or regularity than the print and television
media. The leading newspapers in the country probably lead this
pack. In any given week and probably on any given day, it would be
difficult to pick up the *Boston Globe*, the *Washington Post*, the *New
York Times*, the *Chicago Tribune*, the *Los Angeles Times*, or the *Wall
Street Journal* and not find an article or editorial about stagnating or
declining economic fortunes for large numbers of Americans. The articles sometimes emphasize the "facts" about diminishing income and
purchasing power (which we discuss later on), sometimes the hardships these circumstances impose on families, sometimes the special
plight of a segment of society—the poor, young families with both
parents working, middle-class families, the aged—and sometimes the
political forces behind the difficulties. Whatever the point of emphasis, the basic proposition of flat or declining living standards is not at
issue. So popular has this theme become that the deluge of articles
has built up to a deafening roar.

One of the most outspoken contributors to the creed, Robert Kuttner, has sprinkled columns across various papers, fomenting the message of economic problems.[7] In a 1994 *Washington Post* article entitled "Fewer Fruits for Our Labors," he lays out the charter statement
of the despair message: "The electorate is unhappy, I submit, mainly
because living standards for most people have been slowly declining
for a generation."[8] In a later *Boston Globe* article covering much of the
same turf, he adds, "What to do about the paradox of a rising economy and falling living standards ought to be at the heart of political
debate this Labor Day."[9] He then echoes one of the other fundamental themes of the stagnation club: Income gains find their way mostly
to the wealthiest 5 percent of Americans.

In fairness to Kuttner, he does not completely sweep aside all economic gains over the past twenty years, noting a few advances like the
new products available. Still, in his mind, benefits like this hardly
carry the day; he goes so far as to accuse political conservatives of
cooking government statistics in attempts "to obscure what most
people know from their household budgets."

Pat Buchanan's early successes in the 1996 Republican primaries
opened the door for a minifrenzy among the media to develop re-

ports about the despair message. Borrowing their article titles from James Carville's now famous statement from the 1992 election, "It's the economy, stupid," George Melloan and Guy Molyneaux in the *Wall Street Journal* have surveyed the political and social climate and trumpet the stagnation doctrine in terms that help to illustrate just how much of a foregone conclusion it is for them. Melloan's piece rebuts President Clinton's observations about the economy in his 1996 State of the Union Address, and in it, Melloan flatly asserts, "Living standards for a large group of Americans are falling," predicting the 1996 presidential victor to be the one most successful in "analyzing why the American dream isn't working out for so many of the country's citizens." Molyneaux credits Buchanan's early successes in the 1996 Republican primaries with breaking "a conspiracy of silence about the issue of living standards" and making "a critical connection between declining living standards and high corporate profits."[10]

During this same period, Roger Lowenstein wrote a *Wall Street Journal* article entitled, "Intrinsic Value: Why Primary Voters Are So Angry," in which he states that real median family income has been stagnant for twenty years as confidently as he would state that Neil Armstrong walked on the moon in 1969.[11] The editorial staff of the *Atlanta Constitution* jumped in on these Buchanan results and, though disagreeing with his solutions, praised him because "his focus on job insecurity and declining living standards has awakened other politicians."[12] In the *Washington Post*, John Yang noted that congressional leaders were beginning to pick up on the idea of attracting votes among voters worried about their standard of living.[13]

Ronald Yates, in the *Chicago Tribune*, had earlier discussed this seeming conspiracy of the economic number crunchers to mislead the general public and how the public was not buying it. Besides other tidbits designed to show declining living standards, he quoted a partner of a New York human resources firm as saying, "People kept hearing how well the economy was doing. . . . But while they were hearing this, they knew they were not better off. . . . Most people will tell you they are worse off today than they were 20 years ago."[14]

In a 1996 *Los Angeles Times* column, Carolyn Bell Shaw matter-of-factly accepted the message of economic stagnation—"two decades of income stagnation"—and not only discussed the broad theme of stagnation but ventured into the evidence behind it. She noted "dimming hopes that two decades of American income stagnation might be coming to an end. . . . Most measures of real income have stagnated.

Average hourly and weekly earnings, median family income and other measures fit the same descriptions—they all show fewer dollars today than in 1979, after allowing for price change."[15] She restated many of the same ideas a few days later in a *Boston Globe* column.[16] By her estimation, the ripples of corporate downsizing and other anxieties felt by American households diminish the trustworthiness of what on the surface may appear to be excellent economic performance. She sees better worker education and training as the only sure ways out of the current dilemma of stagnation and income inequality.

The role played by a stagnant living standard in driving families to despair is another recurring subtheme of the despair message as it appears in print. The *New York Times* ran a series of articles that it eventually turned into a book chronicling these problems. In the series, Rick Bragg wrote, "For families whose chief bread-winner has lost a job, there are not only matters of doing without new cars, vacations, and trips to the mall, but the chance that their downsized existence may be permanent."[17] Charles Stein, in an unrelated *Boston Globe* piece, bemoaned the same kinds of difficulties for families—the necessity of compromising family and community involvement just to keep living standards constant.[18]

Of course, economic doomsday predictions in the press are not a new thing. Back during the "golden era of economic growth," the no-growth predictions were already being cast. *New York Times* columnist Anthony Lewis wrote in 1973, "Growth is self-defeating. . . . the planet cannot long sustain it. . . . To ignore the tendency to predict that growth can go on forever is like arguing that the earth is flat. Only the consequences are more serious."[19] His views were not novel; in fact, they merely echoed statements put in print by the no-growth academics discussed later in the chapter.

Moreover, the extent to which the print media have bought into the message is illustrated by the fact that it is not isolated to the editorial pages, where one could more easily insist that political axe-grinding lies behind the despair message. *Wall Street Journal* reporter David Wessel, in a front-page column about Clinton's 1997 budget proposals, demonstrates the blatant acceptance of the stagnation message. In the article's first sentence, Wessel states: "President Clinton's new budget gives him a chance to attack some underlying, long-run economic problems: a disproportionately slow rise of living standards and a widening gap between the well-off and the poor."[20] In another front-page article in the *Wall Street Journal*, this one concerning the

1997 United Parcel Service (UPS) strike, the reporters ask if the strike signals a conversion of a "docile American worker too cowed to demand a pay raise despite corporate profits" into a "newly emboldened and empowered workforce."[21] Although the writers acknowledge that this is a caricature of today's economy and workers, they continue as if the caricature were the real thing.

On the back-page political analysis section of the same paper, Gerald Seib had earlier evaluated President Clinton's 1996 election outlook. In playing the role of adviser, Seib wrote, "Clinton . . . must make the problem of Americans having to work harder to stay even the most important issue." We would emphasize that this was the "analysis" section of the paper—not the editorial page. Sue Schellenbarger, writing a regular column called "Work and Family," notes disputes about whether Americans work more or less but conveys the message in her title, "Either Way, We Feel Frazzled." Among other things, she attributes the problem to too much integration of leisure and work—too much work taken home or on vacation.[22]

But the newspaper journalists have not monopolized all of the print space devoted to the creed of economic decline. Wide-circulation magazines have added their pages to the mix, and this includes magazines of all stripes, whether oriented toward business, politics, family, culture, or whatever. A few titles such as "Preparing for Leaner Times" (*Fortune* 1992), "Downward Mobility" (*New Yorker* 1993), "The American Dream and Today's Reality" (*Money* 1992), "Has Our Living Standard Stalled?" (*Consumer Reports* 1992), "The Productivity Paradox: Rising Output, Stagnant Living Standards" (*Business Week* 1993), and "Standard of Living Probably Will Drop" (*USA Today Magazine* 1994) provide a glimpse of the proliferation of the stagnation theme.

During the fall of 1996, even the sober-minded *U.S. News and World Report* ran a feature article with the subtitle "The Economy Is Rosy, But People Aren't. So What Is Going On Here?"[23] The article mimics an *Atlantic* article also critical of the rosy picture painted by GDP growth.[24] Both articles emanated from a San Francisco–based think tank called Redefining Progress and stressed that the typical measure used to monitor economic health, gross domestic product, is not only a poor measure of well-being on a broader scale but also a poor measure of economic growth. The think tank substituted its own measure, dubbed "genuine progress indicator" (GPI), which showed much less progress than GDP. The *New York Times, USA*

Today, and the *ABC Nightly News* all followed the *Atlantic* story with similar commentaries on the misleading picture painted by GDP.[25]

The message, though, is not merely that GDP contains flaws but that it is biased toward showing growth where it does not exist. Because GDP includes increased spending on items such as phone solicitations, obtaining divorces, repairing crashed cars, increased payments for medical bills, and so on, the claim is that GDP vastly overstates even economic growth—at least economic growth truly related to items that raise people's happiness. The bottom line of these reports is that economists have mindlessly conspired to prop up the picture of a booming economy, when economic realities tell a very different story.

Television has also jumped in on the stagnation dog pile. It is likely that the most frequent occasion to exploit the economic-problems-all-around thesis is on the nightly features centering on the personal lives of people in the United States such as CBS's *Eye on America* or ABC's *American Agenda*.[26] One particular *American Agenda* reveals the degree to which reporters buy into economic stagnation. The piece related the work of two economists who, through careful and detailed analysis of data, had shown that job turnover rates had not increased as many people had expected and as the stagnation message would predict. Rather than accepting the study and asking what then might be wrong with the perception of economic stagnation, the reporter made unsubstantiated conjectures about how the turnover figures probably did not provide an accurate picture of the real underlying problems, speculating that turnover today is likely due to more involuntary turnover. As is usual in such reports, these conjectures were made without any input from the researchers themselves.

Popular Books

Economic despair has also been the cornerstone of several widely read books. Kevin Phillips's *Boiling Point: Democrats, Republicans, and the Decline in the Middle Class,* may be one of the most influential.[27] It continued a theme he began in 1990 with *The Politics of Rich and Poor: Wealth and the American Electorate in the Reagan Aftermath.*[28] *Boiling Point* asserts the stagnation-of-the-masses message, whereas the earlier book covered the stagnation subplot of class-driven gains. In Phillips's own words, "For many U.S. families in the 1980s and the early 1990s, a broad range of economic circumstances were worsening." Among the purported signs of the downward slide: the decline in the quality and availability of public services, less affordable health care, higher expenses for education and insurance, problems with employee benefits and retirement funds, reductions in family leisure time, and slippage in net worth. In his view, the expanding middle class of the 1960s and 1970s was no more: "Downward mobility was everywhere. . . . The potentially critical change by the 1980s and 1990s was that the middle class was no longer expanding but was declining even in intervals of economic recovery like the mid-eighties."

Phillips also threw in a healthy dose of related statistics to give his broad brushing a feel of legitimacy. We are told that workers put in almost 6 percent more time for over 3 percent less income in 1987 than in 1979. Leisure time fell off. The inflation-adjusted salaries of husbands fell. One of his favorite targets is the lack of affordable housing, and he claims that "57 percent of all households could not afford a median-priced home in their market."

In *The End of Affluence,* Jeffrey Madrick toned down the rhetoric compared to Phillips but displayed just as much pessimism about America's economic fortunes.[29] Relying on the kinds of statistics generally accepted by economists, he emphasized the decline in the long-term rate of growth of real GDP—from its historical 3.4 percent to 2.3 percent over the 1970s and 1980s as prima facie evidence of the stagnation. Because of the ever-accumulating nature of such long-term reductions in growth, the United States finds itself over $12 trillion in the hole, versus what would have been the case if productivity gains had continued at their previous, higher rates. Madrick's matter-of-fact style and use of mainstream statistics garnered supporting statements from well-respected economists such as Columbia University's Richard Nelson and Harvard University's Benjamin Friedman.[30]

In contrast to some other writers, Madrick identifies the culprit not as faulty social policy or the like but as a decline in productivity. Interestingly, although he compares the decline in living standards to the nearly "imperceptible loss of time by a clock" and predicts much of the impact is yet to be fully felt, he asserts that the economic losses are implicitly behind the negative feelings of Americans as measured in public opinion polls. Occasionally, some small bit of attention is paid to the high standard of living in the United States, but usually as a preface to more poor-mouthing of the real status. In a later editorial, Madrick added that "postwar living standards are artificially high and can't be maintained. Capital investment, research and development, and education are needed to improve living standards."[31]

The Winner-Take-All Society, coauthored by Cornell University professor Robert Frank and Duke University professor Phillip Cook, states: "The problem of our time is not depression but the multiple evils of rising inequality, budget deficits, and slow growth."[32] The book bases many of its conclusions on the "fact" that only a select few in our society are reaping significant economic rewards, while most people are stuck in an economic quagmire. The astronomical salaries of top athletes, performers, and executives provide the backup for the book's main premise.

This book extends Frank's academic contributions emphasizing the role of relative comparisons in determining people's economic station and level of satisfaction gained from their income. Frank and Cook lament that big differences in economic outcomes are often based on minimal differences between skills of the winners and losers and that Americans try to compensate for these large differences by working too much, emphasizing elite education too much, and engaging a number of other allegedly wasteful activities. In essence, Frank and Cook take the statistics of misery and their relationship to economic problems at face value and try to develop a framework that explains how it got so bad.

Based on the seven-part series appearing in the *New York Times* in March 1996, which we mentioned earlier, *The Downsizing of America* is one of the more inflammatory attempts to describe the lifeless economy, employing emotional buzzwords like "casualties," "body counts," "victims," and "real suffering."[33] The book claims that jobs are being destroyed by a technological monster and that the jobs that are being created are lousy ones. The authors arrive at their general claims mainly by pointing to the individual economic misfortunes of many different people who are without jobs, have lost better jobs, or are sick, but these authors also rely on the stagnation mantra of declining real wages to make their case.

The 1990s was not the first decade in which books lamenting current or impending economic decay rose to best-seller status. Even before anybody really claimed stagnation had come about, Paul Ehrlich's *Population Bomb*, written in 1968, made predictions concerning the inevitability not only of stagnation but of decline. His book shared in the zero-growth and limits-to-growth thinking that had become chic in some academic circles, and it was widely hailed as a harbinger of future economic realities and a source of anxiety in itself. Ehrlich extrapolated rapid rates of growth in world population unmatched by less rapid food growth and surmised the inevitability of a coming worldwide economic apocalypse unless policymakers adopted drastic measures to lower fertility rates. In his own words: "America's vast agricultural resources are gone. . . . The battle to feed humanity is over. In the 1970s, the world will undergo famines—hundreds of millions of people are going to starve to death, and nothing can prevent a substantial increase in the world death rate."[34] Repeating and updating his pessimism in a coauthored book a few years later, Ehrlich warned that "before 1985 mankind will enter a genuine age of scarcity," "the accessible supplies of many key minerals will be nearing depletion," and "nutritional disaster seems likely to overtake humanity in the 1970s (or, at the latest, the 1980s)."[35]

Although Erhlich's predictions might have been extreme even for the tastes of many current devotees to stagnation, his book was not the last to capture the public's interest in the stagnation message carried to the limit. Ravi Batra's best-seller, *The Coming Depression of 1990,* did not sell the idea of current economic stagnation as much as it trumpeted the inevitability of economic stagnation.[36] Even so, its popularity attests to the appeal of the message of economic despair. Batra followed it up with *Surviving the Great Depression of 1990.*[37]

The stagnation dogma even crept into books that have ostensibly criticized parts of it or its alleged ramifications. We have already alluded to Robert Samuelson's admission to the slowdown in the rate of growth in his book, which is largely critical of the economic despair message. In his 1984 book, *Losing Ground*, Charles Murray, the widely read conservative author, attempts to discard the stagnation notion as a basis for post-1950s growth in crime, poor education, family breakdowns, and persistent poverty. However, Murray, like Samuelson, refers to the high rates of growth in the 1950s and 1960s as unsustainable: "Thus we made our decisions about the poor and about social policy from what seemed at the time to be a position of impregnable economic strength. Not only were we enjoying an unprecedented boom, we now thought we had the tools to sustain it indefinitely. . . . At the time, almost everyone thought the economic pie would grow ever larger."[38] In Murray's defense, he was writing shortly after the recessionary period of 1980–1982 and at the very outset of an eight-year economic expansion.

The rest of this book could be filled with little more than a review of volume after volume published in the 1980s and 1990s devoted to the theme of economic decay in the United States.[39] The current hair pulling over the dismal state of the U.S. economy is an especially odd viewpoint when set against the fashionable idea of U.S. "overabundance," which arose during the late 1960s and early 1970s. This worldview took mainstream America to task for too great an emphasis on material well-being.

Politicians

Politicians, especially those running against an incumbent or railing against the majority party, have always been given to making the worst out of the current situation. Not wanting to lose out on opportunities to seize even the perception of bad economic news and use it to their advantage, many politicians have also cultivated pessimistic themes about the U.S. economy. Because the desire to win usually trumps ideological leanings, both Democrats and Republicans have utilized the strategy. As one would expect, though, the commitment of politicians and their entourages to the stagnation message has shifted as they have moved from challengers to incumbents and back to challengers. Politicians most consistently using the message are those who have been perennial challengers.

As political candidates hoping to win the presidency and vice presidency, Governor Bill Clinton and Senator Al Gore, along with their troops, pushed the stagnation message with unrelenting zeal during the 1992 campaign. Most people remember their campaign slogan—"It's the economy, stupid"—coined by their aide, James Carville. Their main points were summarized in the Clinton-Gore book, *Putting People First*.[40] A few excerpts make clear that they are not complaining about the results of the 1990–1991 recession but are instead trumpeting the stagnation premise of long-term, structural problems in the economy. Near the beginning of the book, they state that the prior twelve years of Ronald Reagan and George Bush were "the worst economic record in fifty years, slowest economic growth, slowest job growth, slowest income growth since the Great Depression." The barrage continues: "Record numbers of Americans are unemployed and millions more must settle for insecure, low-wage, no benefits, jobs." In his announcement speech, Clinton added, "Middle-class people are spending more hours on the job, spending less time with their children, and bringing home a smaller paycheck." In a later speech, Gore reemphasized the "second-only-to-the-Great-Depression" theme of the stagnation era.[41]

The complaints did not end with overall economic problems but focused in on the subplot of class-driven outcomes. Gore emphasized, "During the 1980s, the wealthiest 1 percent of Americans got 70 percent of the income gains, and the forgotten middle class worked harder for less money."[42] In addition, the contribution of economic despair to family problems surfaced, "forced parents to choose between the jobs they need and the families they love."[43] Much more could be quoted here, but the point is fairly obvious.

Clinton and Gore left some of the despair mongering to their underlings. Among this group, Labor Secretary Robert Reich most regularly harped on economic woes facing working Americans. In a 1995 criticism of the Republican "Contract with America" legislative agenda, Reich bluntly restated the central idea of the despair message, saying the contract "has little or nothing to do with the U.S.'s central problem, the stagnation of middle-class living standards."[44] Over his career, Reich has written two books that focus on the stagnation topic.[45] Another Clinton appointee, chairperson of the Council of Economic Advisers Laura Tyson, stated that "the U.S. is teetering on the abyss of economic decline."[46]

Although Bill Clinton waded around in the stagnation muck, Ross Perot was the 1992 candidate who belly flopped right into the middle of it. He bundled his stagnation message with oft-repeated concerns about federal deficits and trade agreements like NAFTA, going so far in pushing the message as to purchase prime-time network programming segments to present his "infomercials" concerning American economic woes and his proposed remedies. In the first of these segments, he used thirty minutes of time on CBS and flipped chart after chart presenting his critique of the economy. In his typical plain-talk fashion, he said, "We used to have the world's greatest economic engine. We let it slip away and with it went millions of jobs. . . . We got into trickle-down economics and it didn't trickle." For his efforts, he collected a whopping 19 percent of the vote as a third-party candidate, the highest third-party percentage since Theodore Roosevelt in 1912. Roosevelt, unlike Perot, had the extra help of having been president from 1901–1908.

Republicans did not miss out on their own opportunities to utilize the message of economic despair when it happened to be to their advantage. During the 1996 presidential primaries, Pat Buchanan took over leadership as the "we're-in-bad-economic-shape" candidate, using it to win a Louisiana beauty contest and the New Hampshire primary. As we have noted above, Buchanan's primary successes caused a frenzy among both politicians and the reporters covering the political scene. Both left- and right-leaning columnists fell over themselves to dissect the source of Buchanan's support and what it portended for other declared and undeclared candidates.

Buchanan himself, being well trained in the media arts, played the attention for all that it was worth. In a New Hampshire speech, he announced, "We're going to have a Republican Party that looks out for working men and women in middle-class families. . . . Look what's happened in New Hampshire in the last five years. Wages of the working people are down. . . . Medium [median] income is down." In his very first post-win speech, he reiterated his commitment to ending economic insecurity among average working families.[47]

At the Republican convention, although the economy was not the sole or even the most prominent issue, the undercurrent of economic problems continued to flow. In his acceptance speech for the presidential nomination, Bob Dole made reference to the diminished economic dream. Jack Kemp echoed this sentiment in the vice presidential debates by referring to America's stunted economic growth.

Academic Voices

Whether inciting or just reflecting the outcry about stagnant living standards in the United States, a significant amount of academically oriented work, in addition to statements by academics with lofty credentials, has accompanied the other sources. Some of these contributors with academic pedigrees such as Robert Frank and Ravi Batra have already been discussed above.

One strand of this academic support can trace an intellectual heritage all the way back to Thomas Malthus's eighteenth-century statements concerning cyclically stagnant and low standards of living. For example, Ehrlich's *Population Bomb* grew out of the 1960s and 1970s academic fascination with zero growth or growth with severe limits due to natural resource constraints. To them, stagnation was not so much a matter of currency as it was one of inevitability. Although some of the people pushing the zero- or limited-growth ideas would have been viewed as outside the mainstream of their academic disciplines, these views received at least passing support from highly respected academics.

In particular, three economists devoted considerable scholarly effort to supporting the zero-growth or limited-growth agenda. Kenneth Boulding, a respected economist of his day, said that we have moved from a "cowboy economy," where great open spaces were endless, to a "spaceman economy."[48] The concepts of "spaceman economy" and "spaceship earth" became widely used metaphors implying a limit to possibilities for economic growth because of the fixed and exhaustible resources of our planet. MIT-trained economist Nicholas Georgescu-Roegen made the unique and not widely accepted twist of linking the inevitability of growth limits to the law of entropy, the tendency for systems with a fixed amount of initial energy to move to states of less order.[49] In two books, the 1977 *Steady State Economics* and the 1996 *Beyond Growth: The Economics of Sustainable Development,* University of Maryland and World Bank economist Herman Daly probably pushed the limited-growth agenda with as much vigor as anyone. Daly views limits to economic growth as undeniable, in view of the ultimate decline in the ecological and resource base necessary to sustain the growth, and he supports policy initiatives that would limit the use of nonrenewable resources so that their depletion would match the discovery of renewable substitutes.[50] The Arab oil embargo and attending gasoline shortages in the United States during the winter of 1973–1974 simply added fuel to the fire and added many adherents to this general thesis as well.

Although none of these ideas have been embraced by the majority of academic economists, they were not left packed away in a remote corner, either. For example, an economics textbook authored during that period by Robert Heilbroner includes several citations to the "spaceship earth" mantra. Heilbroner and Lester Thurow also published a 1981 book called *Five Economic Challenges,* which includes fairly bold statements about the inevitability of economies having to face up to stagnant living standards in the face of limited and many nonreplenishable resources. For example, one snippet they use that draws on Boulding's "spaceship economy" theme adds, "What is certain is that all industrial systems, socialist as well as capitalist, will have to change their attitude toward growth in the coming decades."[51] Herman Daly has received front-page coverage in the *Wall Street Journal* for his latest book. Some economists with the highest of academic credentials and achievements such as Nobel Prize–winner Paul

Samuelson and growth theorist Nicholas Kaldor, though stopping short of espousing zero-growth views, have taken the view that resources are a practical brake on economic growth.[52] The weaknesses of the various limits-to-growth views have been eloquently discussed at length by Julian Simon in several places.[53]

Not all of the academic support for the stagnation idea has surfaced from the zero-growth circle. Some support has been provided by stand-alone pieces purporting to make dispassionate observations of trends in living standards, working conditions, and the like. One of the early contributions—on the borderline between a scholarly study and a popular book—was Lester Thurow's *The Zero-Sum Society,* first published in 1973 and updated in 1980.[54] With his MIT economics doctorate and as dean of the MIT Business School, Thurow carries some substantial credentials. In both editions, he paints a bleak picture of economic realities in America. In part, he focuses on a very important development of twentieth-century society—the push for redistribution and its growing grip on political debate.

In Thurow's way of thinking, the underlying reason for all of the zero-sum political positioning is the slowing rate of economic growth and living standards. In his words, "Economically, Americans face a relative decline in their standard of living." He adds: "Whatever our precise ranking at the moment, the rest of the world is catching up, and if they have not already passed us, they soon will."[55] In particular, he mentions countries such as Sweden, Denmark, West Germany, and Switzerland as having passed the United States in terms of per capita GDP to back such statements up. The assertion that Sweden had bypassed the United States in terms of economic prosperity became a sort of cocktail party factoid of the 1970s.

An eminent MIT economist, Paul Krugman, made the poor state of the U.S. economy the basis for his 1990 book, *The Age of Diminished Expectations: U.S. Economic Policy in the 1990s.* To Krugman, the poor performance of the economy in the 1980s is an established fact: "The performance of the U.S. economy in the 1980s was disappointing by past standards" and "for the median American worker, there has been no increase in real take-home pay since the first inauguration of Richard Nixon." For people with lower incomes, his statements are even stronger. He calls the 1980s "little short of nightmarish" for people at the lowest fifth of income levels. For them, he portrays a nearly Third World existence of "real incomes dropping, the fraction of the population in poverty rising, and homelessness soaring." Krugman views the main culprits as lagging productivity and lack of attention to the distribution of income.[56]

In the 1990s, Juliet Schor, a Harvard economist, has supplied additional academic-based support for the economic decay idea, and she is regularly cited in the work of such writers as Kevin Phillips. In *The Overworked American: The Unexpected Decline of Leisure*, Schor surveys a lot of historical data, from which she makes the conclusions obvious from her title. We find out that the average hours worked per week increased from 39.8 in 1969 to 40.7 in 1987 and that the number of weeks worked per year went from 43.9 in 1969 to 47.1 in 1987. And although Americans work less than they did during the 1800s, she claims that "if present trends continue, by the end of the century, Americans will be spending as much time at their jobs as they did back in the 1920s." This would leave work efforts above what she calls the "pre-capitalist" levels of the 1300s and 1400s, when the medieval feudal system granted more holidays. The changes for women that she cites are even bigger, and surprisingly even to Schor, innovations in household appliances have not shown up as fewer hours worked by housewives.[57]

She also offers some explanations for the apparent trends. One is a seeming conspiracy among firms in the 1930s and 1940s to ensure that nobody adopted a thirty-hour workweek. However, one of the biggest culprits in preventing more leisure has been the work-spend addiction—"consumerism." In comparing the outcomes today to those in medieval times, Schor says, "[In those societies there was] the absence of consumption and accumulation. There was far less interest in and opportunity for earning or saving money. Material success was not yet invested with the overriding significance it would assume. And consumerism was limited."[58] As modern examples of people who have not succumbed to the consumerists' addiction, she cites primitives like the Kapaku and the Bushmen. She has extended the themes of preoccupation with consumption in her latest book, *The Overspent American*.[59] In that book, she emphasizes that Americans spend dollars that they do not have just to keep up with the Joneses.

The liberal think tank that funded Schor's work, the Economic Policy Institute in Washington, D.C., has served as a regular source of reports touting economic decline. A 1994 report entitled "The State of Working America 1994–95" purports to present a broad assessment of American economic problems and received national media attention. The report candidly states: "The majority of Americans remain worse off in the early 1990s than they were at the end of the 1970s." The authors, Lawrence Mishel and Jared Bernstein, rely most heavily on evidence that tracks inflation-adjusted wages, showing their deterioration in the 1980s and 1990. According to the authors, real wages of even college-educated men declined about 3 percent from 1979 to 1994, falling 5 percent since 1989.[60]

A study prepared by Northeastern University's Center for Labor Market Studies and entitled "The State of the American Dream in New England" paints a bleak economic picture, particularly for poorer, low-trained people. Even for families able to sustain their standard of living, the achievement has resulted only from working longer hours and the greater participation of women in the labor force. As one contributor put it, "They are doing better by working like crazy." The study notes that men's earnings are flat from 1990–1995 and up only 7 percent from 1975.[61]

The Competitiveness Policy Council issued a report in September 1995 that also backs up the message of economic decline. Not really an academic-based group, the council is an advisory group for Congress and the president, made up of politicians and business leaders. Their report acknowledges continued steady economic growth but points to living standards that continue to stagnate and decline. According to the report, American workers average about $50 per week less in real wages than they did in the mid-1970s. The council not only perceives economic decline but blames the living-standards rut on Americans: Americans are overinvesting in their houses and underinvesting in the kind of new products and technologies that lead to higher wages.[62]

Beyond these books, reports, and scholarly articles, the stagnation premise has received less formal support from some very lofty academics. One of the best examples is the December 1992 conference that president-elect Bill Clinton held in Little Rock, Arkansas, concerning the economy. At the meeting, Robert Solow, an MIT professor and 1987 Nobel Laureate in economics, made a detailed presentation showing that the recovery from the 1990–1992 recession had been slower than earlier recoveries and that problems had been mounting over the previous two decades. He relied on statistics showing poor employment figures, slow productivity growth, slow family-income growth, and increasing disparity between rich and poor. He added, "This is not just a short-term glitch."

At the same conference, Alan Blinder, a Princeton economist who would later be appointed vice chairman of the Federal Reserve Board of Governors, backed up Solow's views. Blinder had already offered a more complete statement of his negative views about the economy in his 1987 *Hard Heads, Soft Hearts.*[63] The *New York Times* editorial page called these presentations "insightful" the next day, citing the double-edged whammy of an "economy operating well below capacity and recovering slowly," and "a two-decade drop in productivity growth."[64]

Prominent economists with ties to the Clinton administration, though, were not the only ones to keep the stagnation message alive. A highly respected Stanford University–based economist, John Taylor, serving as an adviser to Bob Dole, stumped for it in a *Wall Street Journal* editorial entitled "The Path to Growth." The main "facts" presented in the piece are that productivity gains in the economy have been at post-1953 lows during the Clinton presidency. The source of his data is the Center for Economic Policy Research at Stanford. Tied to the slow growth of productivity is slow growth in income and living standards. As Taylor puts it, "Since the end of 1992, productivity growth has been only 0.3 percent per year, close to the zero growth of the pre-Industrial Revolution days. At that rate it would take 10 generations to double a person's income."[65]

The Threads of the Message

The preceding sections have presented just of few of the many possible examples indicating the kind of pessimism and downright despair concerning U.S. living standards. For a person who has closely monitored leading newspapers or who regularly checks out the titles of new books at the local bookstore, the citations above cover familiar territory; for others not as tuned in to the stagnation message, these quotations and summaries outline several salient features of the despair message.

First, they illustrate the far-reaching acceptance of the message among people who are taken very seriously in public circles. We have not built a straw man about economic stagnation beliefs out of the statements of just one or two cranks who were lucky enough to get their letters to the editor or even a couple of feature editorials published. With regularity, editorialists, staff reporters, and editorial-page editors at the most widely circulated papers in the country have bought into the idea. Writers have climbed onto best-seller lists by pushing the message, and politicians have attracted devoted followings by building their platforms around it. Even academic economists with the most respectable credentials have stated the message and have tried to back it up with technical reports.

Second, beyond merely illustrating the wide circulation and acceptance of the message, the cited passages given here make plain the despair message's focus on long-term, deep-seated problems within the economy. These writers and speakers are not just reflecting on short-term dips brought about by the recessions in 1979, 1981, or 1990. Instead, they use such phrases as "not better than twenty years ago," "worse off in the 1990s than they were at the end of the 1970s," "not a short-term glitch," and similar descriptions. The message is clearly about living standards in the 1990s, as opposed to those in 1969, 1979, and 1985.

Third, the message about flat or declining living standards encompasses much more than a small percentage of Americans. Yes, the rhetoric of inequality rears up frequently within the stagnation club, but even these statements about wealth and income inequality are not just about the very poor versus everybody else. Instead, the messengers of economic despair make no bones about the fact that at its core, the message is about millions of Americans at or near middle-income levels and below. The phrases "downward mobility was everywhere," "the middle class is no longer expanding but declining," "living standards for a large group of Americans," "forgotten middle class worked harder for less money," "what most people know from their household budgets," and the like bear witness to the very inclusive nature of the stagnation doctrine.

Fourth, the message is one of genuinely bad economic times and prospects. It does not just talk of little inconveniences for families but claims outright hardships are either the order of the day or just in the offing. For example, "not only doing without new cars . . . chance that their downsized existence was permanent," "U.S. teetering on the abyss of economic decline," "spending as much time on their jobs as in the 1920s," "second only to the Great Depression," and "real suffering" are nearly apocalyptic in their verbiage.

Last, the stagnation mantra crosses political lines. Both liberal and conservative commentators and politicians have gone on and on about these kinds of problems. Bill Clinton, Bob Dole, Ross Perot, Robert Reich, Pat Buchanan, Robert Kuttner, David Wessel, Lester

Thurow, John Taylor, and the others mentioned above represent people ranging from one side of the political spectrum to the other. The stagnation message and our criticisms of it later in the book are not about taking political sides.

In the next two chapters, we use data and argumentation to consider these aspects of the stagnation message: (1) its widespread acceptance, (2) its emphasis on long-term trends, (3) its broad inclusiveness, (4) its claims of severity, and (5) its nonpartisan political appeal.

THREE

THE MYTH OF STAGNATION

*And these were the common people of America ... Waitresses drove
sleek leather-lined automobiles to work. Dock laborers went home at
night to swim in their heated backyard pools. Charwomen and
plumbers changed at the end of the day into exquisitely cut manu-
factured clothes.*

—Lestat, in Anne Rice, *The Vampire Lestat*

It is hard to imagine that a novelist speaking through the voice of an
eighteenth-century vampire observing life around New Orleans in
1984 would convey a clearer understanding of the tremendous affluence of American households than authors of widely read books or
editorialists for major newspapers, but this is exactly the state of affairs. Anne Rice's prose detailing Lestat's awe and amazement at the
affluence of the common people in America spans several pages at the
opening of the book.[1] Rather than relying on a small set of government statistics and misinterpretations based on those statistics as most
pundits do, Lestat's assessment of living standards is based on a large
swath of information about expenditure patterns, asset ownership,
and product availability in comparison to bygone eras.

To bring these experiences into the 1990s, imagine Lestat stepping
into a room with a basketball team and observing players wearing expensive court shoes, sporting the latest "team-wear" jackets, and an-
ticipating an upcoming cross-country trip to play in a tournament.

Then, he realizes that this is not a professional team made up of million-dollar athletes, not a college team propped up by megabuck contributors, and not even a team from an affluent suburban school; instead, he is observing a high-school team made up of kids from semirural households in a Kentucky county with few management-level jobs and a population of less than 20,000.[2] Would he conclude that his original 1984 assessment of American affluence had been wrong or that some of the economic ground gained had been given back?

Although these snapshots of American lifestyles seem grossly out of sync with the stagnation view, its staunch supporters will not even remotely entertain the notion that the stagnation premise might be wrong, avowing its truth to be undeniable regardless of the evidence. To those truly devoted to peddling the message of declining living standards, attempts to reject the premise of a decaying economy amount to cooking the data or furthering the naysayers' agenda. For them, the anxieties of Americans about economic conditions settle the matter; no further evidence is really needed.

For those whose minds have not yet elevated the stagnation message to such a pedestal, we simply ask: Could the accusations of economic stagnation as described in Chapter 2 be wrong? Does the pervasive existence of negative attitudes about American economic fortunes accurately reflect the direction of standards of living in this country? Might these anxieties stem from misplaced perceptions or other kinds of problems? Could the stagnation critics have wandered so deeply into the trees of misleading and even bogus statistics that they ignore the obvious growth of the economic forest?

If a person is firmly entrenched in the message of declining living standards, this chapter will make tough if not altogether repulsive reading, because we not only raise a few questions about the accuracy of the stagnation gospel but attempt to bury the premise. We begin by exposing the errors in the evidence put forward to support the stagnation theme. Although a few points may grow a little technical for noneconomists, we attempt to keep the discussion focused on the key issues and not bog down too much in minutiae. Then, we move on to the evidence concerning the path of U.S. living standards. This evidence is so straightforward that it shows how the pessimism about economic fortunes is not only incorrect but also far-fetched.

Not-So-Subtle Errors in the Stagnation Message

Maybe to a public thoroughly indoctrinated in the information about declining living standards, the more relevant question might be: How could the doctrine of stagnation be wrong? After all, public opinion and other data support the economic-decay thesis. Before proceeding with the more subtle errors, we deal with the statements made by the stagnation promoters that contain errors very easily exposed.

Take, for example, the broad numbers concerning performance of the U.S. economy over the past fifteen years. Since 1982, the U.S. economy as a whole has experienced one quarter of growth after another, with the exception of the short and shallow recession of 1990–1991. Total expenditure on goods and services for final uses as measured by gross domestic product (GDP)—unadjusted for purchasing power changes—jumped from about $3 trillion in 1982 to approximately $8.5 trillion in 1998. In other words, Americans spend $5.5 trillion more now than they spent sixteen years earlier—nearly three times the 1982 amount. These figures for GDP provide a rough equivalent to income received by all U.S. households.

Even the ardent defenders of economic decay often recognize that some kind of economic growth has occurred over the past fifteen years, given the $5.5 trillion more in income that is floating around, and this growth must translate into higher living standards for somebody. The extra $5.5 trillion in expenditures winds up as income in somebody's pocket. Even accounting for the share grabbed by the multimillionaires and billionaires, $5.5 trillion leaves a lot to go around. One would think that this enormous amount would at least cause a stagnation advocate to stop and ponder whether the doctrine contains serious flaws.

To typical people who normally encounter figures in the thousands or millions at home or at work, $8 trillion is so unimaginably large that it is like the "gazillion" dollars bantered about by kids trying to come up with ever-larger sums of fantasy dollars. Figure 3.1 helps to put $8 trillion more in line with everyday experience by presenting per capita GDP both in actual dollars and in purchasing-power-adjusted 1992 dollars. To add further perspective to the kind of income growth represented over the period, the difference in 1998 income and expenditure versus 1982 expenditure and income tops $20,000 more per person per year, even when spread over all 260 million

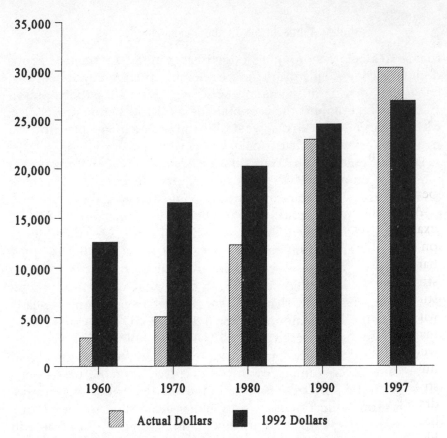

FIGURE 3.1   Per Capita Income, 1960–1997 (in actual and 1992 dollars)

NOTE: Per capita income is gross domestic product divided by population.
SOURCE: *Economic Report of the President, 1997* (Washington, D.C.: USGPO, 1997),
pp. 300, 337.

Americans. On a per household basis, the growth amounts to more
than $55,000 more per year. Over the same time period, the econ-
omy added more than 30 million net jobs. Clearly, massive economic
growth of some kind has taken place.

What about inflationary reductions in purchasing power or the
skewing of rewards toward the well-to-do? This would be a common
comeback in response to the figures just cited. A little mental exercise
illustrates that neither inflation nor a skewing of rewards toward the
wealthy can change the fact that the bulk of Americans have seen
their material well-being grow. Even if the top 10 percent of house-

holds had received more than three times the amount received by an average household—which they did not—the growth left over for the remaining 90 percent of households still tops $4.5 trillion. Even if the cost of living had doubled—which it did not—the income left over for households below the upper 10 percent still exceeds $2.2 billion, or about $24,000 per household—that is, $24,000 more per household per year than in 1982. When such figures are summed over several years, the additions to spending power for households below the top 10 percent are tremendous. Is it really so far-fetched to at least entertain the notion that the message of economic stagnation might be wrong?

As for particular segments of society, we previously mentioned the example of college campus discussions about the economic pressures on college students today to perform academically while struggling so hard to maintain living standards. What about the living standards of students in the 1990s versus those of the 1950s and 1960s? The stuck-in-the-economic-mud students of the 1990s not only drive cars with stereo equipment, maintenance records, and gas mileage performance that are vastly superior—these are the icing on the economic well-being cake—but they drive cars, of any kind, in much larger numbers than their 1950s and 1960s counterparts. For recreation, students of the 1950s might have hung out at the local malt shop or drive-in. The most economically advantaged or most frugal might have been able to wring out of their budgets a spring-break trip to Florida.

Today, one can find college students of average economic backgrounds hanging out on municipal golf courses in large numbers in their spare time; the CDs and tapes they purchase do not just prop up a few well-known stars such as Elvis Presley or Buddy Holly; instead, they provide lavish lifestyles for performers with names completely unrecognizable not only to many parents but to many younger music fans. They own color televisions connected to a variety of stations that 1950s and 1960s students could only have barely imagined. Today's students not only overrun Daytona Beach but they swamp South Padre Island, Colorado ski resorts, and other spring-break destinations. Of course it is true that some students live much more meager lifestyles, but these statements are about large numbers of students and not just a privileged few.

It is not only that the anecdotes about students and their economic pressures do not ring true upon deeper reflection—they fly in the face of sensibility. Yes, students work in greater numbers than before, but these employment decisions reflect an expansion of job and income opportunities available to contemporary students relative to their predecessors rather than forced marches to an economic gulag. Yes, a bachelor's degree is not the leg up it may once have been, but this reflects increases in the number of people with such degrees as well as the number of people pursuing advanced degrees. Other questions might pop up, but the lifestyles of college students begin to provoke, at a minimum, the following question: Is it economic well-being or perceptions about it that are out of focus?

A few sentences about the seemingly affluent lifestyles of U.S. college students do not prove the error of the stagnation premise, but they are intended to spur thinking about the inconsistencies between perceptions about living standards and the reality. The remainder of this chapter develops these insights in more systematic ways and presents a broad spectrum of evidence illustrating the economic gains that have been made in the United States since the 1960s.

As for some, though certainly not all, of the statistics used to back up the stagnation claim, their advocates are either overlooking the most obvious kinds of facts or are using distorted figures. In particular, the evidence concerning real wages has been subjected to such treatment. The reports of flat or declining real wages over any sizable time period since the early 1970s use wages defined in the most narrow sense—as take-home pay excluding noncash compensation to employees. Although higher take-home pay is certainly desired by just about everyone, employees and their employers have very prudently chosen to steer much of their compensation toward noncash benefits over the past twenty years because fringe benefits are nontaxable.

For simplicity's sake, assume an individual can either receive a $1,000 pay increase out of which that person either pays for insurance or receives an insurance policy for which the firm pays $800. All else being equal, the $800 firm-financed policy is a better choice for the worker. If the worker pays for the policy out of income received, the worker would need a raise of $1,111 to stay equal. This is so because the income paid to the worker is taxable (assuming a 28 percent rate), whereas the policy purchased by the firm is nontaxable. Workers have been making this kind of choice in ever-growing numbers. The percentage of total worker compensation distributed in the form of noncash benefits has skyrocketed, jumping from only 8 percent in 1960 and 11 percent in 1970 to 19 percent in 1995.[3]

Seen graphically, as in Figure 3.2, the distortion from using only take-home income in figuring earnings becomes even more apparent. The figure shows the movements of cash earnings per hour in the economy versus the total of all compensation per hour to employees since 1970. The earnings data are expressed as fractions of the amount paid out in 1970 and are based on real earnings. Cash earnings—the data used to allege deteriorating conditions for U.S. workers—do decrease over the time frame. Earnings per hour in 1995 were only about 93 percent of their 1970 values. However, the more accurate measure of worker pay—total employee compensation per hour—has shown significant increases. Since 1970, this figure has grown about 15 percent, which is large, considering that estimates of price inflation have overadjusted the wage gains. The relevant figure to evaluate changes in compensation to U.S. workers is total compensation. A quick way to boost these cash payments to employees would be to wipe out all of the tax-sheltering provisions for retirement

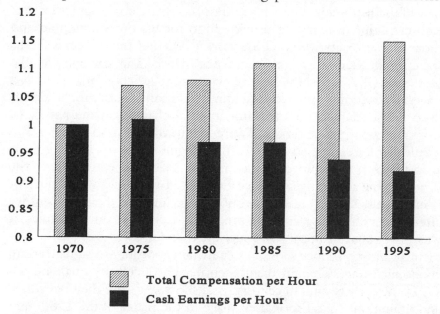

FIGURE 3.2   Cash Earnings Versus Total Compensation per Hour, 1970–1995

NOTE: Figures are expressed as fractions of their 1970 value and are for nonfarm businesses. Ratios for total compensation include all cash and noncash benefits and are computed from 1992 constant-dollar amounts. Ratios for cash earnings are computed from 1982 constant-dollar amounts.

SOURCE: *Economic Report of the President, 1996* (Washington, D.C.: USGPO, 1996), pp. 330 and 332.

contributions, medical insurance, automobile use, and so on. The pros and cons of changing these tax policies is a different issue, but the point here is to expose the completely erroneous conclusion concerning employee compensation.

Another example of evidence offered up by the stagnation supporters that affronts good sense is Juliet Schor's focus on workers in her *The Overworked American*.[4] Schor finds working time during feudal periods roughly equivalent to late-twentieth-century working time. She interprets the lack of improvement in spite of technological developments, which would be expected to reduce the workweek, as evidence of the greater devotion of modern households to materialism. The fact that these feudal societies granted fewer economic and civil liberties, so the incentive to work was reduced, or that the work and working conditions faced by these feudal citizens could hardly be imposed on animals in today's society garners no mention. She also ignores the incredible effort expended in nonconsumerist societies like that of the Bushmen, where a working Bushman labors approximately eighteen-hour days just to provide food for his own household and those in the society who do little work.[5] Whether the subject is feudal societies, housewives in this century, or workers in general over the past twenty-five years, the kind of evidence that Schor and others put forward concerning the lack of improvement in leisure time misinterprets and underaccounts for fundamental changes in the nature of work and working conditions. We return to this point in Chapter 5.

Another egregious error concerning living standards that seems to crop up every generation or two is the "spaceship earth" idea—the idea that the economy's reliance on limited resources will sooner or later (usually sooner) lead to economic decline and disaster. Century after century, doomsayers have predicted decline. In ancient times, it was a shortage in bronze production that set them off. In the sixteenth century, timber shortages in Britain appeared to signal certain economic doom. The nineteenth century produced the whale-oil crisis. In the early twentieth century, coal shortages were the bogeyman, and limitations on oil took their place in the scares of the 1960s and 1970s. In each case, technological progress—figuring ways of using existing resources more efficiently or the discovery and innovation of productive uses of new resources—quickly pushed the seeming crisis to the forgotten annals of history.[6]

The errors made by these limited-growth doomsayers have been well documented, both in the past and recently. In *Doomsday Myth:*

10,000 Years of Economic Crisis, Charles Maurice and Charles Smithson show that every ten or fifteen years since the late 1800s, experts have assumed oil reserves would last only ten more years.[7] As someone once said, these experts have predicted the last nine out of zero oil-reserve exhaustions. A recent article in the *Economist*, devoted to exposing the flawed doomsday predictions, noted that since 1961, world food production has increased by almost 25 percent and food prices have dropped by 50 percent.[8] Even as world population has increased dramatically, world food supplies have outstripped this growth. The only cases of widespread starvation such as in Somalia or Rwanda can be nearly exclusively attributed to political corruption and instability disrupting the distribution of available food rather than the lack of food. Probably the most thorough exposé on the folly of the latter-day Malthusian doomsayers is provided in a volume edited by Julian Simon, entitled *The State of Humanity*.[9]

Still, the notion that the economy will inevitably melt down because of limited resources has a strong appeal for many. No doubt, we do not know with certainty that technological advances will always pull economies out of the fire even though they have in the past. However, the economic decline due to limits on important raw materials has been shown to be no sure bet.

In a rather odd twist, another seemingly obvious contributor to the current confusion about living standards is the failure to distinguish social problems from problems of material well-being. Indeed, U.S. society is plagued by a number of important problems such as divorce, teen pregnancy, general malaise, anxiety, violence, and others that may arise even where standards of material well-being are rising. In themselves, these are simply not evidence of economic stagnation. Many of the stagnation writers have often protested that economic statistics are not always accurate guides to overall happiness and welfare in a society, yet they are the very ones to use general societal problems as evidence of economic problems.

Since the inception of GDP calculations, economists have recognized that GDP merely measures material output and income—not "well-being," broadly defined. The writers of articles in *U.S. News and World Report* and the *Atlantic*, discussed in Chapter 2, act as if they had dropped a bombshell when they inform readers of the difference between GDP and social well-being and the GDP's inconsistencies.[10] The economics profession is scolded for turning a blind eye to the GDP measurement problem, although nearly every

introductory textbook in economics contains a straightforward discussion of these facts, and this has been so for decades.[11] Thus, when
U.S. News and the *Atlantic* publish articles that contemptuously
chide economics textbooks because the texts ignore practical kinds of
problems with GDP, the authors of these articles, along with these
magazine editors, are demonstrating their own ignorance about what
even the elementary economics textbooks have to say.

The reliance on public opinion polls as a guide to economic trends
falls prey to the failure to distinguish material well-being from general
happiness and overall well-being. Public opinion polls that show pervasive disgruntlement among Americans with regard to their incomes, jobs, living standards, future prospects, and the like are just
not an accurate guide to what is happening to standards of material
well-being. Responses to such polls, on the one hand, can be subject
to biases introduced by the set of questions and the framing of those
questions. On the other hand, even where these kinds of question-
based biases are not present, the sour outlook on life reflected in
these polls really indicates lack of contentment and satisfaction with
the personal situation, not a genuine lack of material well-being. General contentment may be influenced by material well-being, but it
also responds to a host of factors other than material well-being.

Further, the linkage between levels of contentment and economic
well-being becomes more tenuous as economic fortunes grow higher
and higher. An example illustrates our point: If a man can bring home
five potatoes for dinner for his family instead of four, he may enjoy
and express a great deal of satisfaction at this increase because it helps
lift his family from the brink of starvation. In contrast, the father
whose income rises by 20 percent—and this extra income allows his
children to buy twice as many CDs and video games—may not feel
the same sense of satisfaction from this increase in economic well-
being or respond as favorably to a questionnaire about economic
well-being. In other words, increases in well-being at low incomes
may frequently register a greater benefit with the beneficiary than the
same increase in benefit to a richer person.

Subtle Errors in the Stagnation Message

Although the errors discussed above amount to outright misrepresentation, incompetent handling of data, or blatant disregard for facts,
other bases for the stagnation view arise from much more subtle er-

rors. One can hardly levy harsh criticisms against authors such as Jeffrey Madrick *(The End of Affluence)* with dishonest analysis for using changes in purchasing-power-adjusted GDP—a.k.a. real GDP—since it is the most commonly accepted means of tracking economic performance. If an economist such as Stanford's John Taylor bases his criticisms of the long-term performance of the economy on poor productivity numbers, he is merely using a standard measure of economy-wide performance.

Figure 3.3 presents the kind of evidence typically presented by reasonably well-informed stagnation advocates to back up the stagnation

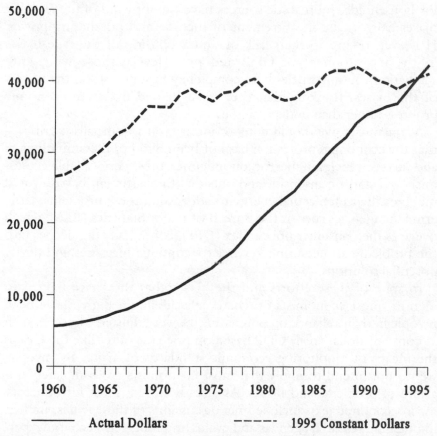

FIGURE 3.3   Median Family Income, 1960–1995 (in actual and 1995 dollars)

SOURCE: U.S. Bureau of the Census Web Site, *Historical Income Tables—Families,* Table F-6, available: www.census.gov.

clusive use of real GDP and other closely related purchasing-power-adjusted measures as the exclusive gauges for standards of living that guides down misleading paths. These biases, in sum, help to understate the true gains in living standards rather than to overstate them.

The shortcomings and myopia regarding GDP and average price indexes extend to other economy-wide performance measures that are, in part, derivatives of GDP or prices. For example, the rate of inflation is just measured as the percentage change in an average price index like the CPI. Nationwide productivity is measured as the adjusted value of goods and services (real GDP) at the average price level divided by the total number of hours worked in the economy—in other words, productivity is merely real GDP per hour worked. Likewise, real wages are nothing more than nominal wages divided by a measure of average prices such as the CPI. Therefore, if real GDP is underestimated, then, by definition, these other measures must also be underestimated.

GDP Biases

Even before adjustments are made for changes in the purchasing power of each dollar (price-level changes), the measurement of GDP itself introduces biases, though none are likely as severe as the purchasing power measurement. A one-sided picture of the direction of these biases has been offered by the journalistic trumpeters of stagnation, creating the impression that GDP overestimates material gains. In reality, it underestimates them.

Those who created GDP in the 1940s invented a measure of the dollar value spent on goods and services across the U.S. economy—essentially, a total sales figure for the whole country.[12] With only slight modification, GDP also provided a measure of total income received from these sales—that is, national income. By and large, the GDP creators avoided subjective evaluations of the legitimacy of one kind of expenditure versus another or evaluations of weights to put on income by who received it, choosing instead to simply add up the totals.

Although the efforts of these inventors are creditable, their methods sidestepped a few thorny issues and emphasized the items that were most easily measured, given 1940s technology. These decisions ultimately contribute to mismeasurement in GDP, price indexes, and derivative measures. A few of these measurement problems, such as how to establish the weights for products and services that make up the price indexes or how frequently to adjust these weights, involve relatively technical problems and have been or continue to be addressed by government statisticians in efforts to improve average price, inflation, and real GDP estimates.[13]

Other sources of GDP mismeasurement, although understood, have not been addressed because of the complexities of the problems involved. For example, one well-known source of error in GDP estimates arises because GDP accounting leaves out certain items that directly bear on material income and wealth. Although basic college economics textbooks mention these exclusions, this recognition does little to improve GDP estimates. Their exclusion from GDP estimates raises legitimate concerns because GDP would be lower if they were included. The stagnation advocates have pounced on these concerns for obvious reasons.

For instance, GDP accounting methods do not take into account items where people or businesses impose costs on society as a whole but do not have to pay anyone for these costs—"externalities," in the language of economists. The classic examples involve activities like polluting or commercial fishing. If a company pumps toxic effluents into the air without restriction or penalty, then a valuable resource— the air—is used, but the company treats its cost as zero and overuses it. Likewise, if a fishing trawler can load up fish without having to pay anyone for the fish or at least for the right to catch them, then the valuable fish are treated as if they had no value and are depleted too rapidly. As originally established, the GDP framework did not incorporate estimates of these kinds of real economic costs.

Similarly, the value of illegal economic activity is left out of GDP, leading some critics to believe that this is another source of overvaluation; but crime's effect on GDP is hard to evaluate as it is not clear whether it would lead to downward or upward revision. On the one hand, many criminal activities increase true GDP in spite of their illegality. If someone grows marijuana and sells it to a user, this transaction differs little from other transactions that are included, such as the selling of tobacco products. On the other hand, if someone pays a hit man to kill someone, one would hardly view this transaction as a gain to society even in purely material terms.

In contrast, other items excluded from GDP would unambiguously increase GDP if included. For instance, GDP does not include any estimate of the value created by members of households doing work for their own households. If a family hires a company to mow the lawn, take care of the children, place new plants in the flower beds, or add a room to the house, the expenditures made would be included in GDP—if the payments are reported. In contrast, if the husband, wife, or children in this family provide the labor themselves to mow the lawn, oversee the children, install plants, or build the new room, the value of these services will not be included. The explosion of warehouses such as Home Depot and Lowe's, which provide materials for do-it-yourselfers, as well as the child-care industry highlights the magnitude of undercounting of GDP because of excluded household production. In terms of the GDP accounting methods, the exclusion of household production is possibly the most inconsistent, since the labor services excluded are often identical to other labor services that are included. Historically, these labor services were excluded because of difficulty in accurately assessing their amount and value.

Besides illegal activity, other kinds of economic activity go unreported that involve trades that are legal except for the failure to report them. These kinds of exchanges in the cash or barter economy include exchange of services such as those between two physicians or the cash payments to domestic workers or nannies in which neither party reports them to the Internal Revenue Service (IRS). Such legal but unreported economic activity would unambiguously increase GDP if included. Estimates of these kinds of trade vary widely, but 10 percent of reported activity is a relatively conservative estimate.[14]

What is the net effect upon GDP of the excluded items and therefore upon GDP as a measure of material living standards? If we listened to the *Atlantic* and *U.S. News* articles on the subject, we would be led to believe GDP vastly overstates true economic activity. Of course, these stagnation-leaning articles focus solely on the excluded items that would decrease GDP estimates. Once we include the GDP-increasing items that are excluded, GDP estimates would likely go up rather than down. Does the exclusion of unpenalized pollution costs and some kinds of criminal activity outweigh the GDP-enhancing activities such as legal underground economic activity and household production? If the underground economy by itself accounts for more than $800 billion per year, the case of GDP overstating economic activity becomes difficult to sustain.

A few additional aspects of exclusions from GDP crop up in the press. For example, certain writers have complained about including expenditures on telemarketing in GDP because these are not genuinely

valuable expenditures. These complaints take the paternalistic posture
of determining what is really valuable—the "anti-consumerist" philosophy. More crippling to this GDP-overstates-economic-welfare
mantra, though, is the exclusion of leisure as a component of GDP.[15]
Expenditures made to go skiing on a Saturday afternoon—the skis, lift
tickets, gas—would be counted as part of GDP, but if the same people
decided to enjoy themselves playing basketball, their activity would not
be counted. Without a doubt, people value leisure time, but GDP ex-
cludes any estimate of its value. Further, as affluence has grown and
people can more easily afford leisure-augmenting goodies, the value of
an hour of leisure may have increased over what it was in bygone days.
For example, radios may have increased the value of leisure time to
families in the 1930s and 1940s, television for families from the 1950s
onward, and PCs and the World Wide Web for 1990s households. If
underground economic activity is just 10 percent of reported activity,
then GDP is understated by about $850 billion per year. Adding in the
omission of leisure would bump the understatement of GDP due to
these two factors alone into the $1 to $2 trillion per year range.

Purchasing Power Adjustments and Quality

Even if the GDP-reducing items were somehow large enough to
counterbalance the GDP-increasing items that are excluded from its
measurement, the biggest contributor to the downward bias in the
typical evaluations of standards of living stems from the conversion of
actual dollar amounts into purchasing-power-adjusted (a.k.a. constant-dollar, or real) amounts. In spite of significant efforts, this
"mother-of-all" macroeconomic-measurement problem persists relatively unabated. The problem originates, in large part, from the complexity of taking account of quality changes in the goods and services
traded in the economy. Adequately solving the quality measurement
problem has proven to be the search for the holy grail in macroeconomic statistics. The ultimate effect has been a tremendous underval-
uation of long-term growth in living standards.

Although the technical details are complex, at a general level, the
problems of adjusting for purchasing power are relatively simple to
understand. With the recognition that no real gain in purchasing
power occurs if households and businesses spend 10 percent more on
goods and services (nominal GDP) but prices on those goods and
services rise on average by 10 percent, average price indexes were in-

troduced to keep track of price changes. The most recognizable average price index is the consumer price index (CPI), collected and computed by the Bureau of Labor Statistics. The CPI and alternative average price measures pursue the same goal—to provide a basis for comparing, say, wages in 1965 to wages in 1995 in terms of the purchasing power of those wages.[16] Because of the role that these price indexes play in adjusting for purchasing power, the press and many economists popularly refer to them as "cost-of-living" measures. Figure 3.4 shows cost-of-living increases as measured by the CPI. According to these estimates, the cost of living in 1995 exceeded the

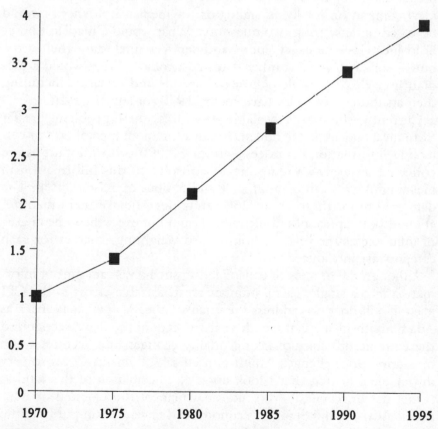

FIGURE 3.4   Cost-of-Living Increases, 1970–1995

NOTE: Consumer price index as multiple of 1970 CPI.
SOURCE: *Economic Report of the President, 1997* (Washington, D.C.: USGPO, 1997), p. 365.

1970 level by more than three and one-half times. In other words, each 1995 dollar would purchase only about $0.25 as much as a 1970 dollar. With these kinds of purchasing-power adjustments, we can easily see how conversion of nominal GDP or nominal median family income into constant-dollar figures leads to huge downward assessments of living standards.

As with comparisons of just about any kind, including GDP and wages, a fixed measuring rod is necessary to ensure the validity of those comparisons. The objective of the CPI is to measure changes in prices, given a fixed basket of market goods and services. The conversion of nominal values into real values is intended to make the adjustments necessary to allow for just such a fixed measuring tool. The ideal comparison for living standards for median households would be based on answering two questions: What would a median household lifestyle—the exact goods and services, including their attributes—of 1970 (or any other date) cost today? What would a median household lifestyle—the exact goods and services, including their attributes—of today have cost in 1970 (or any other date)?

Currently, the means available to address these problems are far from ideal and are error-ridden. Besides the monumental task of collecting information on prices—about 80,000 price quotations are collected monthly—attempting to consolidate this information in meaningful ways can be a difficult and tedious exercise in itself. The data are grouped into about 200 categories to make them manageable. Also, the price of bubble gum should not exert the same degree of influence as the price of housing, so weighting schemes for each category are introduced.

Although the process of consolidating such a vast amount of information into a single, useful number creates sizable errors in the CPI itself, it still does not address the quality issue. At least as far back as Adam Smith in the eighteenth century, economists have recognized the extreme difficulty of taking quality changes into account when measuring price changes. Smith himself said, "Quality . . . is so very disputable a matter, that I look upon all information of this kind as somewhat uncertain."[17] Former chairman of the Council of Economic Advisers and Stanford economist Michael Boskin put it a little differently: "The biggest problem in the system itself is measuring the concepts people care about."[18]

Certainly, most consumers know that price differentials often reflect quality differentials, although the two may not maintain an exact relationship to each other. An owner of a Lexus would hardly feel fully compensated if a Geo were substituted for the Lexus with the explanation that the Geo is a "car." The two may share some attributes and differ in comfort, size, resale value, and so on, but the price differential reflects the differential in value supplied to consumers by the two cars.

An innovation like the VCR provides a very common illustration of the problems that quality poses for price indexes. VCRs improve the quality of life in several ways: (1) by allowing consumers to watch (and rewatch) programs at their own convenience, (2) by allowing viewers to eliminate or speed through commercials if they wish, and (3) by allowing consumers to view personal videos. The first problem for computing price indexes and converting nominal into real GDP cropped up when VCRs were first introduced and became commonly purchased. How should a completely new product be included in average price measures and comparisons? Then, as VCRs began to improve in terms of their capabilities—picture quality, sound quality, programmability—the question changed. How much are quality attributes worth to consumers so that nominal VCR prices can be adjusted downward to reflect these improvements? In terms of VCRs, living standards have increased. However, measuring the cost of living and adjusting nominal measures by an average price index becomes difficult precisely because one should now compare prices for what are essentially different living conditions relative to VCRs and, in general, relative to all new products or products with quality changes.

The magnitude of the quality problem is staggering. Because of improved growing, transport, and storage technology, supermarkets carry a much wider and healthier array of fruits and vegetables than ever before. Automobiles now travel farther on a gallon of gas, require much less maintenance, contain many more amenities and safety devices, and emit only a fraction of the pollutants compared to their counterparts of the 1960s. There were no personal computers in 1980 households. Now not only are they present in a large percentage of homes but their speed, storage capabilities, and multimedia attributes continue to skyrocket as their prices plummet. With little effort, most readers can think of similar examples in their own lives.

Currently, the Bureau of Labor Statistics uses several procedures to attempt to adjust price level measures for quality changes. First, when a new product is introduced, they assess whether it is comparable or noncomparable to an older item that it replaced. If deemed comparable, the old price is used as a benchmark for the new item. Second, if a product is deemed noncomparable, the bureau may use one of a variety of methods. These include direct estimates of the quality change by means of sophisticated statistical models that account both for characteristics of the good and for estimates of production costs. They sometimes look at average price changes for other items in the same general category as the item under consideration.

In spite of all these methods devised by ingenious economists and statisticians, a survey conducted by price-measurement experts drives home the fact that the uncertainty about quality that Adam Smith spoke of 200 years ago still hounds price-level measurement today. More than fifteen studies of the quality bias in the CPI have been conducted since 1994, with all of them finding an understatement of quality change and, therefore, an overstatement of the true price change in the CPI. The middle ground for most of these estimates of the bias is about 1 percent per year and may range as high as 2 percent. Even with these estimates, many of the experts in this field still view the exact amount of bias as very uncertain.[19]

Although biases of 1 or 2 percent per year may seem small, the effects of biases of this size on evaluations of living standards are large. Basing his work on some of the existing bias estimates, University of Maryland economist Charles Hulten computes that when the CPI bias is taken into account, a person earning $50,000 would have gained almost $1,000 more in purchasing power in 1995 than in 1994.[20] As these biases compound from year to year and decade to decade, the understatement of quality change, overstatement of price changes, and understatement of living standards grow.

The prices for services demonstrate the magnitude of the problem as well as the reasons the understatement of quality changes may be even more severe than indicated by the experts. Goods that have tangible characteristics, such as automobiles, at least provide price-level statisticians with hard data with which to compare different products. We can compare horsepower, power versus manual windows, antilock brakes versus standard brakes, and so on down the line in the pursuit of accurate assessments of the effects of quality on prices. However, many services, by contrast, do not so readily present identifiable characteristics.

Medical care services conspicuously illustrate how cost-of-living increases can be overstated for a service and living standards understated because average price measures do not incorporate quality very well. Typical price indexes report that medical care prices have risen by more than 700 percent since 1970,[21] leading to the belief that medical prices have made the cost of living shoot through the roof. If open-heart, triple-arterial-bypass surgery carried a total price tag of $5,000 in 1966 and now carries a $50,000 price tag, has the price of this service multiplied by a factor of ten in the past thirty years? We would arrive at such a conclusion only if we ignore improvements in the attributes of the surgical procedure that consumers value—survival rates, reductions in discomfort, fewer complications, shorter recovery periods, and so on. The relevant but unanswered question in terms of price is how much would a surgical procedure of 1998 quality have cost in 1966 had it been obtainable? Would it have cost $10,000, $20,000, or $100,000? Heart transplants were merely experimental in the early 1970s, with survival measured in days. Today, that mortality rate of transplant patients has fallen dramatically, so how should price comparisons be made?

With the correct questions identified, vast quality changes pose tremendous if not insurmountable challenges to answering them. All of the methods, including the most sophisticated statistical methods, are much more accurate in assessing small variations in quality than large jumps in quality.[22] Yet in areas such as medicine, the gains can hardly be viewed as incremental. Modern medical imaging technology—ultrasounds, magnetic resonance imaging (MRIs), CAT scans, nuclear imaging, and other methods—is another example of this problem. Not only do such imaging techniques allow many invasive procedures to be avoided and provide more accurate targeting of problems but they also reduce the physical, emotional, and financial hardships imposed by mis- and undiagnosed medical problems. How much should the 700-percent increase in medical care prices be reduced in order to adequately take into account these kinds of improvements? In medical care alone, the list of improved services is long, including such procedures as endoscopic techniques for diagnosis and surgery, new drugs, and improved prosthetic devices.

Maybe the easiest way to accent how little our measures of economic performance account for the tremendous repercussions of quality is to ask—putting nostalgia and sentiment for older things aside—what goods and services have not increased in quality in the past thirty years? That list is very short. Nearly every good and service purchased is either an improvement upon a previously existing item or is an altogether new way of meeting an existing desire of consumers, and yet our price level measures do not make widespread quality adjustments.

The ultimate problem with the commonly employed cost-of-living measures is that they give the false impression of a fixed measuring rod. The CPI and similar measures are supposed to be making the appropriate cost-of-living adjustments in order to make purchasing-power comparisons of real GDP or real wages. In reality, these kinds of cost-of-living measures are biased against showing improvements in living standards because they do not take account of quality improvements. For the purposes of ongoing studies, most academic economists use the data without adjustment in part because they do not have a desire or incentive to place a moratorium on their work until better numbers are devised. Once we jump from academic to popular media outlets, the appreciation for the quality-and-price problem erodes even further. When complex ideas are discussed in newspapers or on television, whether the subject is medical research, physics, or economics, the "ifs, ands, or buts" that are needed for precision are normally excluded in favor of concise, unequivocal statements that translate into newspaper-length articles, good copy, or snappy sound bites.

After making comparisons of living standards over several years or decades, we can hardly overstate the significance of mismeasurement. To draw out this point, if the CPI overstates actual economy-wide price increases by 1 percent per year, then after thirty years, the CPI will be more than 30 percent higher than an accurate measure of average prices. Using some specific numbers in the relevant range of U.S. inflation, if prices had been estimated to have increased by 4 percent per year but in reality increased by only 3 percent per year, then the error in the data at the end of thirty years is about 34 percent.

These figures can also be cast in the perspective of a working person. For a person who began the thirty-year stretch with an annual income of $30,000 and received a steady 4 percent increase every year, annual wages without any inflation adjustment would have reached $97,200 by the end of the thirty years. However, using the overestimated CPI figure of 4 percent would lead one to compute a real wage still stuck at $30,000—or stagnant real wages. By contrast, the accurate measure of CPI growth of 3 percent results in a wage at the end of the thirty-year period in excess of $40,000. For an entire economy with total incomes of more than $8 trillion per year, the mistake would underestimate inflation-adjusted incomes by nearly $2.5 trillion after the thirty-year period.

In sum, comparisons of real GDP and incomes in 1970 and 1998 may be widely accepted but are nonetheless grossly misleading. The seemingly fixed and consistent measuring rod of average price measures and real values like real GDP are not nearly as fixed as they might at first seem. In fact, they lend a false sense of security that the appropriate adjustments have been made, leading even sincere analysts into making strong statements based on comparisons of the real values.

The Reality of American Living Standards

In the two preceding sections, we explained how the data typically used to buttress the stagnation viewpoint distort accurate evaluation of economic performance either through blatantly using wrong-headed methods or by failing to adjust fully for the more subtle problem of an ever-changing standard such as real GDP-based measures. If data concerning living standards propagated by serious-minded and capable thinkers within the stagnation camp are wrong or misleading, how can we or anyone get a handle on changes in economic well-being over time?

The most important principles to keep in mind in trying to make valid assessments of living standards over time are these:

- The best kinds of comparisons over time keep the benchmarks across time as constant as possible.
- Because of measurement difficulties, a portfolio of economic measures related to living standards is more useful than any single measure used in isolation.

We hardly think it necessary to defend the idea of making standard-of-living comparisons using fixed benchmarks. To make valid comparisons of economic living standards in 1970 to those in 1999, it is absolutely essential to try to find measuring rods that are more or less the same. Although average price indexes and related "real" measures of economic activity are ostensibly providing fixed benchmarks, we just discussed the reasons they fall far short of this goal. We hinted at the importance of using a portfolio of measures rather than a single, comprehensive measure in the preceding section's discussion of the items excluded from GDP and will devote a more full-blown discussion to it here. Below, we utilize a collection of comprehensive aggregate measures such as real GDP, measures of expenditures on and access to necessities and nonnecessities, and ownership of assets. We now discuss the reason for these alternative measures.

In Chapter 1, we broadly defined the level of affluence as the ability to consume over some indefinite period of time and briefly discussed how income data alone may not be an accurate guide to material well-being. Now, it will be useful to be a little more precise in describing the way income, consumption, and wealth measures relate to economic affluence. Although most people have an idea of the meaning of income, consumption, and wealth, the precise meanings and linkages of these terms are not always well understood. Income is measured as a stream of payments received between two points in time—wages, profits, rents, and interest per month, year, decade, and so forth. As arbitrarily measured in national accounts, consumption is the stream of expenditures on perishable items (average life of less than one year) plus all expenditures on services. Wealth is measured as a value of an asset at a specific point in time—the value of an "intangible" asset, in the case of a stock portfolio, at the end of a year or the value of a "tangible" asset, in the case of a house.

Obviously, the income a person receives, purchases of consumption goods and services, and purchases of long-lasting assets can all have bearing on and be used as indicators of material living standards. Additionally, the three are interrelated: Income equals the value of consumption plus changes in wealth.[23] If information on income, consumption, and wealth were accurately measured and disclosed, then income could be computed by adding changes in wealth over the time frame to any consumption over the given time period. Or changes in wealth could be computed by subtracting consumption from income over a given time period. In general, with accurate and full information, a person can infer one of the items from information on the other two items. However, as the preceding section details, the GDP and national income data do not come to government statisticians out of this kind of pristine world.

All sorts of examples from actual to fictional criminal investigations and civil suits illustrate the problem of relying solely on reported income or wealth in isolation from data on consumption. Drug lords may report little income but purchase million-dollar homes and expensive sports cars. These purchases indicate that something is amiss with the income data. A party to a divorce settlement may direct income and assets through a maze of individuals, organizations, and offshore accounts, but past purchases provide insight into the true level of affluence. The future income lost to a worker losing arm function in an on-the-job accident normally exceeds the weekly income and benefits paid to the worker when healthy. If hard work or home projects formerly performed by the worker must now be farmed out or left undone, the value of the projects represents additional income losses that would be missed by looking at paycheck stubs alone.

In addition to those problems, the distinction between purchases of consumption items and purchases of assets that are included in wealth is often fuzzy. For example, because heart-bypass surgeries are a service, they are lumped into consumption expenditures even though consumers pay for heart bypasses in order to receive a healthier heart that they intend to use for a number of years. In fact, the expected life span of the effects of this kind of medical service may be much longer than an item lumped into purchases that count as increased wealth, such as an automobile.

As a result, relying solely on income, expenditure, or wealth data is inadvisable if a person is seeking to establish a broad-based understanding of affluence across time. Certainly, focusing on any single measure within any of these three categories is bound to lead to erroneous conclusions. Therefore, in the next section, we use income data, expenditure data, and wealth data to allow for a comprehensive look at living standards.

A historical perspective on approaches to measuring living standards lends further credibility to our strategy of using a portfolio of measures on income, expenditures, and assets. Back when many people in this country lived closer to the edge of economic failure, the topic of living standards was of keen interest to many writers. A number of detailed studies are available concerning living conditions of the latter half of the nineteenth century and the early part of the twentieth century. These studies took place before large summary measures like GDP were invented, and they rely instead on data that most contemporary economists pass over. They described and evaluated very detailed aspects of daily life such as how much family income went toward food, rent, clothing, whether the family owned property, what their housing conditions were, and what kinds of foods they ate.

As crude as they were, these studies gave a picture of the entire economic landscape faced by families instead of relying on a single aggregated figure of total expenditures for the economy or expenditure per capita. Because many families still struggled to put sufficient food on the table, the average percentage of family budgets devoted to food was a commonly cited statistic. These food expenditures amounted to 45 to 50 percent of total expenditures for poorer families immediately before and after the turn of the century. According to these studies, minimum food costs ranged from $0.18 to $0.33 per day for an adult male in 1885, about $0.23 to $0.25 in the mid-1890s, and around $0.22 in 1907.[24]

Even after economic analysis began to become more formalized and theory oriented during the twentieth century, the lack of overall summary measures of economic activity continued to prompt analysis of basic household expenditures. In 1945, George Stigler, who would go on to win the Nobel Prize in economics in 1982, published a study that estimated the minimum food expenditures that would achieve fixed nutritional requirements.[25] As late as 1959, another respected economist from Michigan State University named Victor Smith updated Stigler's earlier methods and results for basic food expenditures in the 1930s and 1950s.[26]

By the 1960s, though, interest in these kinds of studies had waned among most mainstream economists. Not only had measures such as real GDP (or gross national product [GNP], at the time) become widespread in their use but advances in the economic conditions of even very poor households had made the whole issue of subsistence living and minimum food expenditures a matter more suited for economic historians than for economists interested in contemporary issues. In their classes and writings, economists became reluctant to use the word "needs." Economic affluence had become widespread, leading most Americans to refer to "needs" merely as items or services they wanted rather than as something necessary for survival. In fact, many students in elementary economics classes have been chided for using the word "needs" when they were referring to matters that did not pertain to survival. The whole issue of economic survival became moot for nearly all American households. In response, economists' interests turned more heavily toward taking people's wants and desires as givens and explaining their decisions rather than defining minimal needs and basing any comparisons or analyses on these basic needs.

With a few notable exceptions, detailed studies of expenditure patterns for households and, certainly, most discussions of minimal food budgets faded from the attention of influential economists and became a topic relegated to "home economics" or "family economics"—a topic outside the interest of the mainstream economics profession or at least outside the domain of graduate training for nearly all economists.[27] Modern doctoral-level economists would hardly esteem these kinds of studies as worthy of the interest of people as capable as George Stigler. Also, the discipline has become more specialized as it has grown, meaning that fewer professional economists know much at all about household-level economics.

The ramifications of this relative disinterest in the details of household expenditures and in minimal expenditures extended far beyond academia, however. As economists paid less and less attention to a wide array of household facts relating to living standards and more attention to GDP and aggregate "cost-of-living" measures like the CPI, popular reporting of economic conditions followed suit. Whatever movements in the CPI, real GDP, or real wages allegedly told us about living standards became every person's dose of economics packaged on the nightly news or in newspaper headlines. In this setting, household "needs" were continually redefined to reflect rising expectations. Various economic studies occasionally paid attention to more detailed facts, but such studies mainly just circled within academia; Americans and their reporters already had the facts they needed.

What we try to accomplish below by using a portfolio of measures related to living standards really goes back in time. We have already reported the typical output and income results using the typical GDP and median income data, so we now turn to the data on expenditures and assets.

Expenditures: Necessities and Beyond

One of the most basic ways to try to make living-standard comparisons with a fixed benchmark is by defining a very basic or even subsistence existence level of existence. Although in everyday conversation we talk about "needs" very loosely, in the most narrow sense, a need is something absolutely required for survival. By looking at the incomes of families existing at or near the very cusp of subsistence, a benchmark can be established that reflects true needs with all of the distortions introduced by affluence and growing expectations swept aside.

If, for example, a family in 1900 had to earn $500 in income to sustain its most basic food requirements without outside support, we have a fixed mark with which to compare past and present generations.

In anticipation of criticism, we stress that using such a benchmark does not mean that public policy should attempt to ensure that some citizens are living at this subsistence level. Whether anyone is or should be living at subsistence, our point is that the bare minimum provides a fixed standard for comparison across time periods. It allows an assessment of how far above the minimum any specific household income is. Also, the difference between subsistence and a given level of income allows insight as to what is left over after the absolute necessities of life are met. How much do Americans today in comparison to their predecessors have to spend on the indulgence of their wealth?

This approach is especially valuable because it overcomes the problem of a seemingly rising "cost of living," which in reality is rising because people are spending more money on new and higher-quality items. If a person in 1900 had 50 percent of income left over after subsistence, a person in 1970 had 80 percent left over, and today a person has 90 percent left over, we can conclude that the American standard of living has improved, but we can also produce a meaningful measure of the degree to which it has improved. Data of this kind provide insight into discretionary expenditures whereby "discretionary" has a fixed meaning.

Our application is an offshoot of what economists call "Engel's Law"—the observed regularity of the proportion of income spent on food declining as real income per person increases. Hendrik Houthakker, a Harvard economist and former editor of a prestigious journal in economics, said, "Of all empirical regularities observed in economic data, Engel's Law is probably the best-established; indeed it holds not only in the cross-section data where it was first observed, but has often been confirmed in time-series analysis as well."[28]

Table 3.1 provides comparisons of minimum food expenditures, median family income, and income left over after minimum food expenditure for 1970 and 1994, using basic diets from detailed economic studies of subsistence-level diets.[29] These basic diets provide for caloric and nutritional minimums plus just a little extra to be conservative. One basic fact arising from the evidence is just how little income devoted to food is absolutely necessary for survival—only about $500 for each adult per year as recently as 1994. The required expen-

TABLE 3.1 Minimum Food Expenditures and Median Family Income (MFI), 1970 Versus 1994

	1970	1994
Family (3) food expenditure (most restricted diet)[a]	$ 822	$1,437
Family (3) food expenditure (broader diet)	$ 890	$1,587
Median family income	$9,867	$38,782
Income left over (most restricted diet)	$9,045	$37,345
Income left over (broader diet)	$8,977	$37,195
Food expenditure as % of MFI (most restricted diet)	8.3%	3.7%
Food expenditure as % of MFI (broader diet)	9.0%	4.1%

[a]The most restrictive diet includes milk, margarine, carrots, potatoes, pork, and flour. The broader diet includes milk, margarine, oranges, carrots, potatoes, pork, eggs, cereal, flour, sugar, coffee, and several cooking aids/spices. Computations are explained in the text.

SOURCE: Victor Smith, "Linear Programming Models for the Determination of Palatable Human Diets," *Journal of Farm Economics* (May 1959): 272–283. Data for 1970 and 1994 are authors' calculations (see note 29, Chap. 3).

diture is slightly more or a little or slightly less than $500, depending on the details of the diet chosen. Median family income exceeded both of the food-subsistence expenditure levels by more than $37,000 in 1994, whereas it exceeded food-expenditure levels by only one-fourth of that amount (about $9,000) in 1970. For families near the median, truly discretionary income had rocketed over the quarter century. For a family with only one-half the 1994 median income ($19,000), more than $17,000 remains after meeting the subsistence-level food expenditures. This evidence—reflecting a genuinely fixed benchmark—hardly leaves room for doubt about the direction and magnitude of improvements in strictly defined discretionary income since 1970.

The next piece of evidence related to food expenditures chronicles the decline of food-at-home expenditures. Growing affluence empowers families to purchase more meals where someone else cooks the food and cleans up afterward. It is an expenditure of convenience, not necessity. As a result, a decline in total expenditures on food is not as accurate an indicator of growing affluence as is the decline in expenditures on food at home. Figure 3.5 shows the percentages of median family income spent on food at home in 1960, 1970, and 1995. In 1960, households spent about 25 percent of their incomes on food and almost all of that at home. By 1970, both figures had fallen to around 20 percent, but the proportion of the total spent at

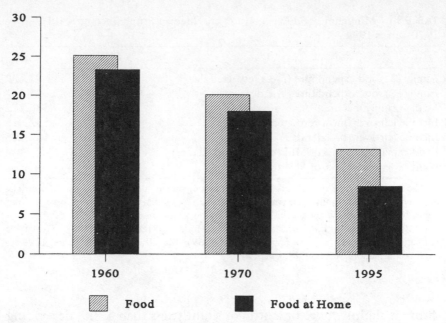

FIGURE 3.5   Food Versus Food-at-Home Expenditures, 1960–1995

NOTE: Expressed as percentage of median household income.
SOURCES: U.S. Bureau of the Census, *Historical Statistics of the U.S.* (Washington, D.C.: USGPO, 1975), Series G 416-49; Bureau of Labor Statistics Web Site, *1995 Consumer Expenditure Survey,* Table 1, available: stats.bls.gov.

home was about the same as in 1960. By 1995, the situation had changed dramatically. Total food expenditures were around 15 percent of income, but at-home food expenditures accounted for only about one-half of total spending.

In addition to data on food expenditures, broader expenditure patterns of families over time are useful in gauging relative affluence. Both economic data on the responsiveness of people in terms of consumption changes due to income changes—income elasticities, in economics terms—and common sense tell us that expenditure on certain kinds of goods grows at a slower pace than income and wealth when income and wealth are increasing, whereas other kinds of goods such as cell phones and luxurious automobiles will grow at a faster pace than income and wealth. Expenditures for food at home are an example. Thus, when we observe increases in the higher income and wealth goods relative to the lower income and wealth goods, we know material progress is occurring. Table 3.2 lists data on shares of claim. The figure shows median family income in both actual (nominal) and purchasing-power-adjusted (1995) dollars. The nominal figures show a tremendous increase, whereas the 1995 constant-dollar figures appear relatively flat since the mid-1970s. This lack of growth in purchasing-power-adjusted measure of household income and similar numbers provides the statistical backbone of the stagnation case.

Yet this common practice of using constant-dollar (real) median incomes, real GDP, or other purchasing-power-adjusted measures to assess changes in living standards creates subtly false impressions concerning long-term trends in living standards and their "stagnation." Biases introduced in the measurement of purchasing power that make overadjustments create the illusion of flat income growth for households. Journalistic sources have caught wind of the fact that biases exist in the measurement of income and purchasing power. However, owing to their lack of understanding of the true biases in the measurement of GDP and price levels, those who write stagnation-touting articles have completely misunderstood the impact of the biases, thinking that they have helped overstate economic progress rather than understating it.

At the outset, we should note—contrary to the journalistic critics—that the economics profession has not been blind to the limitations of and inconsistencies in macroeconomic measures. Very capable economists and statisticians inside and outside of government have devoted much of their intellectual energy to addressing these problems. Government agencies such as the Bureau of Labor Statistics (BLS), which oversees the consumer price index (CPI), continually dig deeper into the problems of measuring key macroeconomic measures and devise potential solutions.

In spite of these efforts and the biases that they have helped to identify, most economists of whatever academic pedigree have been myopic in their reliance on purchasing-power-adjusted measures such as constant-dollar (real) GDP based on price measures like the CPI as the means of monitoring economic standards of living. By myopic, we do not intend to imply that most economists are completely unaware of problems and biases. As already noted, most introductory macroeconomic texts include brief discussions of these issues. Rather, in pursuing research agendas and evaluating long-term economic performance, the effects of the biases are brushed aside with little thought. The problem is not that real GDP and the CPI are occasionally used to monitor economic performance, rather it is the nearly ex-

TABLE 3.2 Attendance and Participation in Sports and Recreation as Percentage of
U.S. Population, 1960–1994

	1960	1970	1980	1990	1994
Air travel	34	82	120	187	200
Overseas travel	1	2	4	6	7
Major League baseball attendance	11	14	21	22	27
Softball participation	4	8	13	16	16

SOURCE: U.S. Bureau of the Census, *Statistical Abstract of the U.S.* (Washington, D.C.:
USGPO), various volumes.

total spending directed toward several "affluence-sensitive" categories
for 1960, 1970, 1980, 1990, and 1994.[30] These include specific measures of air travel, overseas travel, Major League baseball attendance,
and softball participation. Consumer use of or participation in each of
these activities as a percent of U.S. population doubled from 1970 to
1994. One might quibble with any particular expenditures, claiming
that it only reflects a shifting of consumer expenditures rather than the
growth of affluence. However, many other categories could have
been included such as recreational expenditures in general, expenditures on personal computers and computer software, expenditures on
vacations and holidays in general, and so on.[31] The point is a simple
one: When we observe people flying rather than driving or spending
more money on ball games and green fees, we can infer that material
abundance has improved.

Some stagnation advocates might complain that these figures
merely reflect technological advances. Although it is obviously true
that technological advances can be credited with making flying affordable for the masses, this explanation merely dissects the mechanism through which living standards have risen rather than providing
a cause to reject the premise of rising living standards. Presumably,
even the staunchest stagnation supporter would recognize that advances in locomotive and track technology, which first allowed people
to travel from New York to San Francisco in a few days rather than
ten months and now allows people to travel in hours instead of days,
are indicative of advances in the standard of living. We would doubt
that any of the families driving a wagon and mule team for a year
would dismiss the advances in locomotive technology as "only technology." Why should twentieth-century technological improvements
count for less?

As a final means of gauging the growth in consumption by middle- and low-income families in the United States, we can perform a couple of simple "what if" illustrations. These "what ifs" relate to families that choose to live well within their means, forgoing some consumption in order to build up wealth. What if a family earned the median income from 1970 to 1996 and salted away 20 percent of its income per year in an account earning 5 percent annually. How much money would that family accumulate? By 1996, the family would have accumulated more than $230,000 in this account. Of course, a saving rate of 20 percent of gross income may seem like a lot, but our point is about a family that chooses to live frugally. A family earning median income over these years could have spent 30 to 35 percent on taxes, 10 to 15 percent on food, 15 percent on housing, and still have 15 to 25 percent left for other expenses—certainly a modest existence by American standards, but not a bare-bones existence, either.

Or what if a family earned only one-half of median income, and yet lived thriftily enough to save 10 percent at an annual rate of 5 percent? Over the 1970 to 1996 period, this family would have accumulated a nest egg of $58,000—not exactly a fortune to rival the Rockefellers or Kennedys but, nonetheless, a sizable amount for a family that would barely stay above the official designation of poverty in the United States. But at 1996 income levels, this family earning about $21,000 per year could spend 15 to 20 percent of income on food, which is well above subsistence; 25 to 30 percent on housing, which amounts to more than $500 a month; 20 percent on taxes; and 20 percent on other items, while still leaving room for the 10 percent going to savings. By American standards, such an existence would be bare bones, but by worldwide standards, this family would still be consuming at a substantial level.

Assets: Ownership and Quality

Beyond measuring incomes and expenditures, one way to assess the standard of living within a society is to look at the things people possess—their assets. If people in the 1960s owned substantially fewer and lower quality items than the people of the 1990s, a strong case can be made that substantial economic progress has occurred regardless of the data about GDP and wages. One advantage of peering into people's lives to see what they own is that it provides a broad picture of wealth in a society. As we mentioned earlier, gaining a view of the

wealth of a society is of special importance when income may be un-
derreported due to household production or underground economic
activity or may be mismeasured because of the biases inherent in
price-level measurement discussed earlier. If a person (or economic
analyst) is reporting no change in income for several years but the
person is accumulating ever-greater wealth in the form of various assets—houses, cars, mutual fund accounts, and so forth—then the
usual presumption is that income is being inaccurately measured.

Inconsistencies between reported incomes and observed levels of
wealth are not without precedent. For example, one means that has
been used to assess the level of unreported drug trafficking and income in various cities is to compare bank assets in cities to reported
income in cities. After adjusting for other differences among cities,
when reported incomes are very low relative to assets held by banks,
the presumption is that people—often drug dealers and distribu-
tors—are engaging in lucrative transactions but are not reporting
such transactions for fairly obvious reasons. Likewise, owners of baseball and other sports franchises often report small and even dismal net
incomes for several years. However, the value of the franchise may increase by many times even while such poor annual profitability is reported. As an example, the average price of a National Football
League franchise between 1975 and 1996 has risen approximately 20
percent per year, yet many owners complain that it is hard to make
ends meet.[32] Two explanations can be forwarded for this. Either the
very wealthy businesspeople and firms paying the tremendously high
franchise prices have suspended their interest in making money—an
unlikely proposition—or the divergence in reported net income versus asset values indicates some imaginative accounting procedures
that help to hide the true annual profitability from the prying eyes of
the media, players' unions, and fans.

The standard measure of household wealth—net worth—shows the
tremendous growth that has occurred after making the typical
(over)adjustment for purchasing-power changes. Figure 3.6 shows
changes in household net worth from 1960 to 1995, using 1992
constant dollars. Even with the overadjustment for inflation introduced by using 1992 constant dollars, net worth grew by more than
250 percent, edging above the imposing sum of $25 trillion—about
$250,000 if spread over every household. The enormous holdings of
the very wealthy do account for a large share of these assets. Still, net
worth for the median family rose to more than $50,000.

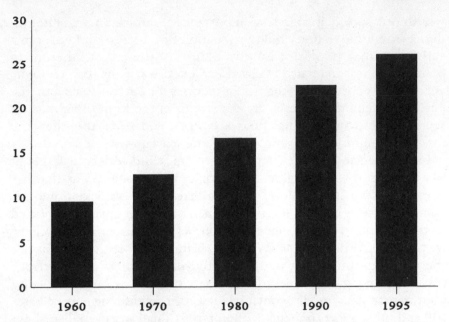

FIGURE 3.6   U.S. Household Net Worth, 1960–1995 (in trillions of 1992 dollars)

SOURCE: John Weicher, "Wealth and Its Distribution, 1983–1992: Secular Growth, Cyclical Stability," *Federal Reserve Bank of St. Louis Review* (January–February 1997):3–23.

As huge as the gains appear, these most frequently cited wealth statistics are biased downward even without the inflation adjustment problem.[33] For one thing, they do not include valuations of future social security benefits. For typical middle- and lower-class families, these expected benefits function much like stock or mutual fund accounts do for wealthier families: They will provide a source of future income. In spite of scares about the disappearance of social security benefits, the likelihood that future beneficiaries will continue to draw substantial amounts from the system is very high. Additionally, the wealth figures typically reported include valuations only for houses and vehicles, ignoring the large amounts of wealth represented by consumer durables—furniture, various appliances, stereos, computers, and the like. Many of these goods, such as furniture, may have useful lives exceeding those of automobiles and are widely distributed throughout U.S. households.

For example, the economic doomsayers make much ado about the difficulties facing families, especially younger families, in purchasing homes. They cite figures on home prices to back this up. In sharp contrast to these worries, scrutinizing widely owned assets bolsters the reality of economic prosperity over the past three decades. Although new home prices have increased dramatically in nominal terms and even in constant-dollar terms, the definition of a "median" home and what it includes has also changed dramatically. Table 3.3 compares characteristics of new homes in 1970 with those in 1996. The improvement in homes is obvious: The median new home is 39 percent larger; the percentage containing two or more bathrooms has doubled—now including most houses in America; the percentage containing central air-conditioning has more than doubled, as has the number of multilevel homes.

The picture is the same when all occupied units are analyzed rather than just new single-family homes. This comparison also appears in Table 3.3. If one were to look only at monthly expense in nominal terms, the increase would seem alarming. Yet, in constant-dollar

TABLE 3.3   Characteristics of American Housing, 1970 Versus 1996

	1970	1996
New single-family homes:		
Median selling price[a]	$23,000	$140,000
Median selling price[b]	$91,000	$140,000
Median sq. ft.	1,385	1,940
% under 1,200 sq. ft.	36	7
% 2 bathrooms or more	48	94
% central air-conditioned	34	84
All occupied units:		
Median monthly cost[a]	$143	$545
Median monthly cost[b]	$572	$545
Median sq. ft.	1,288	1,732
% over 1,000 sq. ft.	NA	87
% 2 bathrooms or more	15	60
% central air conditioned	10	47

[a] In current dollars.
[b] In 1992 dollars.

NOTE: Median monthly cost for 1970 is a weighted average of median costs for renters and owners. Median square footage for all units in 1970 was estimated by taking 93% of the new single-family home figure. This percentage was derived by using 1980 figures.

SOURCES: U.S. Department of Commerce, *Current Construction Reports* (Washington, D.C.: USGPO, June 1997); *American Housing Survey for the U.S. in 1995* (Washington, D.C.: USGPO, 1995); *American Housing Survey, 1975* (Washington, D.C.: USGPO, 1975); and *Statistical Abstract of the U.S.* (Washington, D.C.: USGPO), various volumes.

terms, the monthly expense has remained about the same. Even more important for demonstrating economic progress, the characteristics of the housing have improved significantly. Median square footage has grown by 400 to 500 square feet. Nearly all units are more than 1,000 square feet in size. The majority of units now contain two or more bathrooms, in contrast to a mere 15 percent in 1970. Nearly one-half now utilize central air-conditioning systems, whereas only 10 percent did so in 1970. The information about median size is especially important since it dismisses the notion that it is just the mammoth size of the homes of the wealthiest Americans that is skewing the "average" size of homes in the data.

To those thoroughly indoctrinated in the stagnation message, these data may be meaningless—just numbers cooked up by political apologists. But it is hard to see how these figures demonstrate anything other than increasing living standards for typical American families. It is a peculiar definition of living standards to say that having more space in one's home, cooler air in it during the summer, or better access to bathroom facilities in the morning is not an improvement. In fact, writers who look past such improvements are indicating their own affluence-adjusted biases. Although many 1996 families may have trouble affording a median-priced home, a median-priced home in 1996 is a much different creature than it was in 1970. A home containing the features of a 1970s median home would be affordable for families earning far below 1996 median incomes. As always, apples must be compared to apples in order to make valid comparisons, and in their home ownership and buying rhetoric, the stagnation thinkers make their points by comparing apples to brussels sprouts.

Figure 3.7 and Table 3.4 show ownership rates and utilization rates for a variety of assets such as vehicles and services such as cable TV. The TV ownership data may be the most astounding. America has almost reached the level where there is one TV for every person, with vehicle ownership not far behind. Although significant growth of ownership/usage has occurred in every category in Table 3.4, items such as VCRs, air-conditioning, and cable TV stand out. Again, the increased ownership of valuable assets could include many more items than listed here. Taken as a whole, the asset ownership and utilization data reemphasize not merely growth in living standards, but explosive growth.

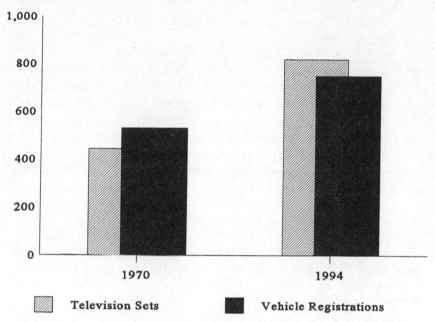

FIGURE 3.7   TV and Vehicle Ownership per 1,000 People, 1970 Versus 1994

SOURCE: U.S. Bureau of the Census, *Statistical Abstract of the U.S.* (Washington, D.C.: USGPO), various volumes.

TABLE 3.4   Ownership/Usage Rates on Selected Household Items, 1971 Versus 1993

	1971	*1993*
Clothes washer	71.3	77.1
Clothes dryer	44.5	68.6
Dishwasher	18.8	43.7
Microwave	0.0	81.3
Refrigerator	83.3	96.5
VCR	0.0	59.7
Air-conditioner	31.8	68.4
Cable TV service[a]	6.7	63.4

[a] CATV service is for 1977 and 1994.

SOURCES: W. Michael Cox and Richard Alm, "These Are the Good Old Days," *Federal Reserve Bank of Dallas Annual Report, 1994*; and U.S. Bureau of the Census, *Census of Housing and Population, 1990* (Washington, D.C.: USGPO, 1990).

Dark-Tinted Glasses

Increased asset ownership and usage supplies evidence that even some among the stagnation advocates find difficult to ignore, since microwave ovens, CD players, and the like are tangible items and are found in so many homes. In an effort to downplay such undeniable evidence of economic progress, the true believers of economic decline usually resort to poor-mouthing the contribution of such items to living standards, viewing them contemptuously as just so much modern gadgetry and consumerism. For instance, in *Boiling Point*, Kevin Phillips writes:

> Pollyannas could bubble about the enjoyment and benefits of new technology and products ranging from PCs to videocassettes and microwavable "gourmet" meals, but for households below the top tier, these were often overshadowed by more basic situations like unaffordable housing, escalating taxes, deteriorating services, undereducated children, declining leisure, and eroding purchasing power.[34]

Ironically, such rebuttals show either flawed logic, bias, or stuffy elitism. In effect, the rebuttals say, "If you show me something that advances living standards, then it doesn't really count" or "Those things don't count for much because although people like to spend their money on them, they are not the kinds of things I think are important." An approach that denies concrete evidence to the contrary is hardly scientific, and one that attempts to define for others what kinds of items they should be buying is pompous and paternalistic. These retorts introduce a real "catch-22": The tremendous affluence of Americans allows them to purchase items that the stagnation critics view as superfluous, and superfluous items do not demonstrate affluence in the stagnation circles.[35]

Yes, Americans spend their money on lots of stuff, some of which may be fanciful or even silly, but do these expenditures express the desperate cries of huddled economic masses, or do they vividly illustrate the kind of affluence these critics are so intent on ignoring? Critics treat consumer expenditures on items like PCs or fancy athletic shoes as a sort of second-place substitute for the items that supposedly really matter—such as housing. If these criticisms stem mainly from moral philosophy, then we have little to say about that in this book, but if these criticisms are forwarded as primarily economic arguments, they will not stand. From an economic perspective, the critics do not come to grips with the idea that in a society where people are more or less free to spend their money on items of their own choosing, purchases of items like PCs, microwaves, and athletic shoes are expressions of affluence. They cannot get or will not accept the point that if people are spending money on "goodies," this spending in and of itself is evidence that the basics are covered. When the same people who complain about unaffordable housing are stocking up on the latest electronic equipment, it is not their living standards that are declining but their "complaining factor" that is increasing. If decent living space were really a primary concern, then these people have the option to do what our ancestors did—scrimp and save in order to purchase a better living space.

Our main goal in this chapter has been to present a readable overview of the evidence concerning U.S. living standards, with the aid of some simple figures and tables. We have presented technical information here, but only enough to make the point without obscuring the big picture. Our task here is akin to demonstrating that a clear sky is blue: The biggest problem is not in surmounting the evidence but in persuading people to take off their tinted sunglasses. Although the evidence considered in this chapter might seem to leave little defense for the stagnation argument, its supporters do not give up easily. The next chapter turns to the last-ditch tools of the stagnation messengers.

FOUR

STAGNATION'S LAST DEFENSE

Men do not desire merely to be rich, but to be richer than other men.
—John Stuart Mill, *Essay on Social Freedom*

In the face of the sort of evidence presented in Chapter 3, even the most entrenched of the stagnation devotees might begrudgingly admit that some kinds of economic gains have occurred since 1970. Yet experience has shown that any admissions ultimately prompt the true believers supporting the stagnation message to roll out their big guns—income inequality, corporate downsizing, health care, emotion, and accompanying objections. Their focus turns away from grand statements about decaying living standards among America's middle class to more narrow attacks that seek either particular victories or the moral high ground. In this chapter, we discuss these commonly raised issues of last resort. In addition to the topics just listed, we resurrect two of the arguments that have served as the heavy artillery of the past: comparisons to economic growth in countries such as Sweden and Japan as well as the stagflation of the 1970s.

What About Class Dominance?

As indicators of economic gains of the 1980s and beyond—color TVs, VCRs, microwaves, athletic shoes, and the like—became harder to deny, those skeptical of economic progress nurtured the class disparity subtheme of the stagnation message probably more routinely than any other comeback. The inequality card is the "ace in the hole" of the stagnation messengers. Its dogma can be briefly stated: Whatever economic gains have been made, lower-income families have not shared in these rising living standards. In challenging George Bush in the 1992 election, Ross Perot and Bill Clinton relied heavily on the class rhetoric. In 1996, Pat Buchanan joined in the melee, disparaging the plight of the working-class man and woman.

Politicians and their political allies, though, are not the only ones playing the class card. Alan Blinder, a widely respected Ivy League economist and vice chairman of the Federal Reserve Board during Clinton's first term, stated the disparity hypothesis at one of the economic roundtables held by president-elect Clinton just prior to his inauguration. Robert Frank and Phillip Cook, the Cornell and Duke economists responsible for *The Winner-Take-All Society*, bluntly stated, "Despite a flurry of denials from Bush administration officials when burgeoning income inequality first made headlines in the late 1980s, there is now little doubt that the top U.S. earners have pulled sharply away from all others."[1] Such bold statements made by reputable Ivy League economists certainly carry with them an air of respectability, but are they right?

Those who push this class-inequality variant of the stagnation message usually back it up with numbers. Often, they appeal to the percent of total income received by households in the lowest fifth or lowest tenth percentile in comparison to the highest group, or the highest group versus everybody else is used. For example, Frank and Cook use the doubling of incomes in the top 1 percent from 1979 to 1989 versus flat median incomes and declining incomes among the lowest 20 percent as an open-and-shut case of the "winner-take-all society" theme.[2] In fairness to Frank and Cook as well as the other writers, such data do give the superficial appearance of rising inequality. Comparisons in the 1990s also show the lowest fifth of households with only about a 4-percent share of total incomes in the United States and the second to lowest with less than 10 percent, whereas the highest fifth accounted for almost 50 percent of income. Further, those alleging a class-driven story attempt to make their case stronger by displaying evidence showing that the incomes of the highest fifth have grown dramatically since the 1960s, while those of lower groups have risen only very little.[3]

The conclusion seems cut-and-dried: All of the apparent growth in living standards has landed in the hands of the relatively wealthy—or has it? Although the numbers cited above may be accurate as far as they go, the conclusions drawn from them distort the economic progress across income classes by disguising both the absolute gains in living standards made by all income classes and movements of households between income classes.

A few of the critics appear to miss a simple but important fact about income distributions, which is that 50 percent of households will always be below the median and 50 percent above. Twenty percent of people will be in the top income quintile, and 20 percent will be in the bottom quintile. Garrison Keillor's suggestion that Lake Woebegone is a place where "all the children are above average" is not possible for obvious reasons. As an example of this kind of reasoning among stagnation writers, we can use the quotation from *Boiling Point*, in which Kevin Phillips states that "57 percent of all households could not afford a median-priced home in their market."[4] For Phillips, this is strong evidence of troubled economic waters. Yet we would always expect 50 percent of households to struggle to afford a median-priced home since the median is at the fiftieth percentile. Once an allowance is made for people living in apartments, a figure such as 57 percent is hardly shocking. The important issues are not whether income differentials exist but whether families, regardless of income class, have made gains in living standards and whether substantial mobility between classes exists.

The fact of absolute gains for all income classes can hardly be disputed. As we showed in Chapter 3, going beyond the limited information supplied by income statistics can be enlightening.[5] For example, expenditure patterns for low-income families indicate the same kind of improvement experienced by wealthier families. For households making up the lowest fifth of income, spending on food, shelter, and clothing amounted to 45 percent of income in 1996, down from 52 percent in the early 1970s, 57 percent in 1950, and 75 percent in 1920.[6] In other words, even without any adjustments for the amount of eating away from home taking place or the improvements in the quality of the items available to poor people today, their discretionary income has improved.

Asset-ownership patterns for the poor may demonstrate the gains of the poor better than any other measure. Table 4.1 shows ownership

TABLE 4.1 Rising Affluence of U.S. Poor, 1994 Versus 1970

Percent of Households with	Households Below Poverty Line 1994	All Households 1970	Households Below 1/3 of Median Income 1970
Refrigerator	97.9	83.3	75.5
Color TV	92.5	43.3	13.1
Car(s)	71.8	79.5	42.5
Washing machine	71.7	71.3	50.0
Microwave	60.0	<1.0	0.0
VCR	59.7	0.0	0.0
Clothes dryer	50.2	44.5	11.8
Air-conditioner	49.6	31.8	4.3
Dishwasher	19.6	18.8	3.0
Personal computer	7.6	0.0	0.0

SOURCE: W. Michael Cox and Richard Alm, "By Our Own Bootstraps," *Federal Reserve Bank of Dallas Annual Report, 1995*, p. 22.

rates for various items for households below the official poverty line in 1994 versus those for all households in 1970 and for households below one-third of median family income in 1970. (We chose one-third of median family income because it is close, although not identical, to the poverty-line definition of the poor.)[7] Whatever the current status of the poor versus the rich, these figures debunk the notion of the poor as mired in stagnant or declining living conditions. Whether the items are cars, TVs, air-conditioners, or anything else listed in the table, the "poor" of 1994 own a much greater percentage of them than did the "poor" of 1970. Even more revealing, the "poor" of 1994 possessed all of the items in greater percentages than the average household of 1970, with the exception of cars. Even in that case, the difference is not large. Additionally, items that did not exist in 1970—VCRs and microwaves—are now in 60 percent of the households below the poverty line. Illustrating the differences, a 1994 poor household would very likely own a color TV, a car, a washing machine, a microwave oven, and a VCR and might enjoy central air-conditioning and a clothes dryer, whereas the poor household counterpart from 1970 might own a car and a washing machine but probably none of the other items.

To be sure, we do not claim that the poor households of 1994 use the highest-quality televisions or have the most reliable refrigerators, but such was also the case in 1970 as far as the quality of these household items goes. For any of the items on our list, they are now more reliable, of higher quality, and cheaper (in inflation-adjusted terms) than in 1970 or 1984.[8] Even though not listed in the table, comparisons between 1994 and 1984 data also show improvements have occurred in every category, so the comparisons provided in Table 4.1 are not just stacked in our favor because of the twenty-plus year frame.

The slippery nature of the term "poverty" along with the lack of reporting about basics of economic life has left many Americans without any feel for just how much things have improved for all income classes. When asked to guess about the percentage of Americans living near subsistence, one graduate-level business administration student responded with an estimate of 40 percent. It was not that this student was dumb—in fact, the student was very bright; instead, the absurdly high estimate stemmed from confusions in the student's mind between the terms "subsistence" and "poverty," along with lack of acquaintance with data concerning income and expenditure patterns of poor households in the United States versus other countries.

For example, the same income level that could place a U.S. family at the poverty line—say, $4,000 per person, or $16,000 for a family of four and without any valuation of assistance programs—would exceed per capita incomes for about one-half of the countries in the world. It would place the family far above the $500 to $1,000 per capita incomes found in places such as Chad, Rwanda, and other poverty-stricken nations. Typical households in well over one hundred countries receive less income than the amount that defines a U.S. family as in poverty.[9] In fact, a family of four could be defined as being in poverty in the United States in 1996 with a preassistance income more than seven times larger than the food subsistence levels that we calculated in Chapter 3. In 1970, the dividing line of poverty would have placed the family about three times above subsistence food expenditures.

The changing nature of family relationships can also obscure gains. Households are defined as related or unrelated individuals living under one roof, whereas families are related individuals living under one roof. As divorce, single-parent families, and teenage motherhood have skyrocketed and made the Ozzie and Harriet family—father, mother, two kids, and a dog—much more scarce, the family or household income and expenditure data have become more difficult to make comparisons with over time. For example, if four families earn $50,000 each, then average income is $50,000. If two of these families divorce—and to simplify, we assume each parent makes $25,000—then we will observe six families with an average income of $33,333. A seeming reduction in family income has occurred, although incomes have actually remained the same.

Beyond the absolute gains of lower-income households and changing definitions, the data that show the share of income accruing to lower-income households as flat or falling since 1970 suffer from comparing apples to oranges—or, more literally, from Joneses to Smiths, Gonzalezes, and Kims. If all or most of the households making up each income class had remained the same over the past twenty-five years, then this kind of data would be meaningful. If, in contrast, a great deal of movement has taken place between groups, and especially if the bottom groups are moving up and being replaced by households that were not even in the picture in 1970, then the data about income shares to various classes are meaningless because they do not provide any information about true income changes for households over time, even though they give the appearance of doing so.

If we ask what has happened to the poor households of 1970 and 1980, we are asking a very different and more useful question than if we ask what has happened to an income "class." By considering data that tracks individual households over time, we can see that a tremendous amount of movement by households between groups has taken place since the early 1970s. A U.S. Treasury Department study found a high degree of income mobility between 1979 and 1988. Tracking more than 14,000 taxpayers over the ten years, these researchers observed 86 percent of the tax filers who began 1979 in the lowest-quintile income group had moved to a higher quintile by 1988. Astonishingly, those in the lowest quintile of income in 1979 were more likely to be in the highest quintile by 1988 than to have remained in the lowest quintile.[10] Isabel Sawhill and Daniel McMurrer of the Urban Institute in Washington, D.C., collected data showing that between the late 1960s and the early 1990s, up to 40 percent of the individuals moved into a higher income quintile in a given year. Over different five-year periods of these years, about 45 percent moved to higher income quintiles, and over longer periods, 60 percent made these jumps.[11]

Data collected by Michael Cox and Richard Alm of the Federal Reserve Bank of Dallas lend further credence to the idea of income mobility, showing the most common movement has been from the bottom upward, although some move from the top down has also occurred.[12] The first set of data, depicted in Table 4.2, shows what

TABLE 4.2   Rising Incomes of the Poor, 1975 Versus 1991 (in 1993 dollars)

Income Quintile in 1975	Average Income in 1975	Average Income in 1991	Absolute Gain
5th (highest)	$45,704	$49,678	$ 3,974
4th	22,423	31,292	8,869
3rd (middle)	13,030	22,304	9,274
2nd	6,291	28,373	22,082
1st (lowest)	1,153	26,475	25,322

SOURCE: W. Michael Cox and Richard Alm, "By Our Own Bootstraps," *Federal Reserve Bank of Dallas Annual Report, 1995,* p. 8.

has happened to the incomes of specific households that were in each of these quintiles since the early 1970s. The table illustrates a class-driven outcome, but just the opposite of the one usually trumpeted by the stagnation critics—a person starting in 1975 in one of the lowest two quintiles experienced real income increases ($25,322 and $22,082) by 1991, more than five times greater than the typical person starting in the highest quintile ($3,974) and two and one-half times greater than the typical person in the next-to-highest quintile ($8,869).

Table 4.3 makes the same point, using income shares rather than income. It lists the percent of people in each quintile in 1991 based on where they started in 1975. For example, only 5.1 percent of the people in the lowest fifth in 1975 were still in the lowest fifth in 1991. Fourteen percent had moved into the second fifth, 21 percent had moved into the third fifth, 30.3 percent had moved into the

TABLE 4.3   Rising Relative Positions of the Poor, 1975 Versus 1991 (in 1993 dollars)

Income Quintile in 1975	Percent in Quintile in 1991				
	1st	2nd	3rd	4th	5th
5th (highest)	0.9	2.8	10.2	22.6	62.5
4th	1.9	9.3	18.8	32.6	37.4
3rd (middle)	3.3	19.3	28.3	30.1	19.0
2nd	4.2	23.5	20.3	25.2	26.8
1st (lowest)	5.1	14.6	21.0	30.3	29.0

SOURCE: W. Michael Cox and Richard Alm, "By Our Own Bootstraps," *Federal Reserve Bank of Dallas Annual Report, 1995,* p. 8.

next-to-highest fifth, and 29 percent had moved into the highest fifth. On the other end of the spectrum, only 62.5 percent of the people starting out in the highest fifth were still there by 1991.

The same kinds of results are apparent in other studies that track people and households over time rather than just using group-level data. One study compared the income and wealth of people today with their parents at similar ages. Those currently in their thirties and forties receive approximately two-thirds more income than their parents and had accrued twice the net wealth—in real terms.[13] The casual experiences of most families from 1970 to 1990 confirm the systematic data, especially for those families that have not experienced breakups of spouses. If people were asked to compare consumer durables that they own to those their parents owned, along with the goods and services that they now purchase in comparison to what their parents purchased, most would recognize that the improvements are apparent. These kinds of comparisons are much more tangible than overly broad questions such as "Are you better off than your parents?" which seem to stand behind many of the public opinion polls.

In a rough analogy, the data used to show stagnation can be compared to the changing level of water in a bathtub that is filling with water colder than the water already in the tub. The colder water sinks.[14] Those skeptical of progress for the poor look into the tub and see that some cold water (the number of poor) is always at the bottom. However, they fail to notice both that the overall water level is rising and that the water molecules that were at the bottom of the tub have heated up and have also risen, being replaced with the water flowing into the tub.

If the poor of the 1970s have moved into the ranks of the middle and upper incomes of the 1990s, who then is filling the ranks at the bottom of the U.S. economy? The previous tables show that, by and large, these spots are not being filled with people who were part of the economy in 1975. Instead, they are being filled mainly by new entrants into the economy—immigrants and the young.

Even though U.S. immigration policy has attracted a lot of attention, immigration stands out as probably the most overlooked influence on the income-share statistics for the poor. The very reason for much of the immigration to the United States is to escape poverty. Most immigrants enter the United States without much wealth and without jobs. The jobs that many of them take are among the lowest paying in the economy, involving work that native-born Americans apparently do not want, for example, as farm laborers or roofers or in other such physically demanding jobs. As a result, any great influx of immigrants supplies a constant source of people with low incomes. Our point is not that these immigrants actually damage the economy; rather, the mere ability of an economy to attract large numbers of foreigners says something about the economy's health. Absorbing poverty-stricken immigrants, most of whom are poor when they arrive, distorts aggregate-level income-distribution data that do not track specific people or households, even if those foreigners are productive members of society. If every time a person moves out of a lower income bracket and into a higher one that person is replaced by a new, lower-income person—say, an immigrant—then aggregate snapshots of the income distribution will miss the economic improvement that has occurred. In our bathtub example, dropping a group of poor people who are seeking economic opportunity into an economy will always keep the ranks at the bottom of the economic tub filled up, even as the tub overflows with gains.

The tidal wave of immigration to the United States in the 1980s and 1990s provides just such a distortion. Figure 4.1 displays both immigration statistics in total numbers of people as well as the number as a percentage of the population of the lowest fifth of households by income. By official estimates, almost 40 million people immigrated to the United States between 1971 and 1996, as compared with about 20 million between 1951 and 1970. This immigrant wave amounts to nearly 20 percent of the population in the lowest fifth of income. This is not to say that all immigrants entered or stayed in the lowest fifth, but it lends perspective to the capacity of immigration to influence income statistics for the poor.

Aside from these flaws in the class rhetoric evidence, we would also comment specifically on the matter of the incomes of the very top wage earners. According to the stagnation writers concerned about income disparity, the fact that Steven Spielberg earned $283 million in 1997, that Oprah Winfrey earned $104 million, and that there are similar figures for the income elite of the country[15] present an open-and-shut case regarding income inequity. To these writers, our whole economic system is just a big testosterone-laden competitive jungle, rewarding very minor ability differences or the sheer luck of a precious few with incredible sums, while doling out peanuts to everyone else.

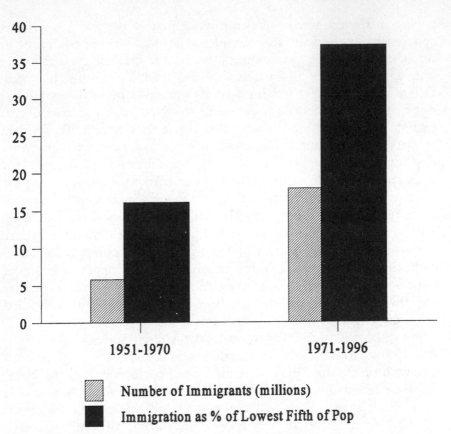

FIGURE 4.1   Immigration Statistics, 1951–1970 Versus 1971–1996

SOURCE: U.S. Immigration and Naturalization Service, *Annual Report of the Immigration and Naturalization Service* (Washington, D.C.: USGPO), various issues.

Even though it is appealing to use data on the top percentages of income earners or asset owners to show economic inequality, this evidence could hardly be more misleading. In a dynamic and growing market economy that allows people to retain a decent portion of their gross income, it is possible that invention, innovation, skillful imitation, hard work, genetics, or just dumb luck will occasionally put enormous sums in the pockets of the people responsible for them. But Bill Gates's fantastic income and wealth in the 1990s do not reflect an economy that rewards only aristocrats and shuns middle- and lower-income individuals. Rather, it demonstrates just the opposite: the opportunities available to a twenty-two-year-old who works hard and takes risks in projects that ultimately tap into people's desires. In these circumstances, rewards, sometimes of unimaginable size, come to people who hit the right circuit. It is strange that the stories of people such as Bill Gates and Oprah Winfrey, which demonstrate tremendous success despite a modest background, could ever be turned into ammunition in the effort to show how unfair the U.S. economy is to middle- or lower-income people.

Moreover, the literature so critical of top incomes in the United States teeters on the edge of viewing the country like a medieval fiefdom where the nobility and aristocrats hover over masses of peasants living in daily squalor. Although the United States certainly hosts its share of aristocratic elites—film and television celebrities, sports figures, leaders of industry and commerce, some politicians, "old money" families—in terms of incomes and assets, the "peasant" masses enjoy fancy lifestyles themselves. The data that track specific families and the data regarding expenditures and assets of households flatly refute any kind of claim that the top income earners extract their gains out of the hides of the masses. A suburban, working-class family with a three-bedroom house, two cars, two televisions, a VCR, a microwave oven, a refrigerator with freezer, clothes-stuffed closets, and money for additional entertainment is hardly pressed down by the aristocrats.

Sure, Bill Gates makes incredible sums, but midlevel computer programmers across the country enjoy lifestyles far above most of the world's citizens. Very few who set out to be entertainers will pull down Oprah Winfrey's $104-million income, but Los Angeles, New York, and Nashville support thousands of actors, singers, songwriters, and musicians, not to mention thousands of others in ancillary entertainment-world employment, all with enormous incomes when assessed against world standards. Anyone who visits a music store and witnesses the wide diversity of artists would hardly see a market captured by two or three performers with the rest in utter poverty. Just as in the case of looking at income statistics for the poor, if an analyst of income distributions lumps Bill Gates into an amorphous class called the "highest fifth" and does not track the path of his success, the billions of dollars he has earned just appear as just so much more gravy to the rich and wealthy.

Finally, even the data that some think are incontrovertible—rising income inequality between classes without regard to the households making up the classes—depend on the way in which the data are interpreted. Economist Robert Haveman found that income inequality held steady between 1973 and 1988 as well as from 1988 to 1991, when holding the amount of working constant.[16] Interestingly, much of the inequality that exists stems from workers choosing leisure over work. Another Urban Institute study found that between 1987 and 1994, overall wage inequality fell in the United States, and, more to the point, the gap between the top 10 percent and the lowest 10 percent of wage earners fell by 7 percent.[17] Taken together, the evidence about the absolute gains for the poor, the relative gains when tracking specific households, and the source of elite incomes depicts a nation full of people across all income classes who have made substantial improvements in their material well-being over the past twenty-five years.

What About Downsizing?

In recent years, among the most frequent targets of those who poor-mouth the economy are the reductions in the workforces of many large corporations. The *New York Times* ran a seven-part series on "downsizing" in March 1996. In a journalistic tactic often used so that readers or viewers are not left with only stale statistics, the evidence about downsizing normally includes case studies of individuals and families directly impacted by the downsizing—the human, emotional side of economic suffering. What about an unfortunate man who lost his job to a corporate buyout, a man with young mouths to feed, limited employment skills, and a tragic illness? Do the downsizing and the hardships caused by this prove the case of economic stagnation? This question really strikes at two separate issues, and we address them both in this section because they are so often linked. One pertains to the data on corporate downsizing, the other to the use of "case study" evidence.

First, on the issue of downsizing itself, the reports of job loss by the economic doomsayers are true but so myopic in their interpretation as to be ridiculous. The error is as gross and simplistic as fretting because a consumer paid out $2,000 last month in bills while failing to mention that the same person received $3,000 in income over the month. Yes, from 1979 to 1995, about 43 million jobs were lost. In 1996, the top ten corporate downsizers of 1996 alone cast off 103,000 workers—AT&T dropped 49,000; Wells Fargo, 15,000; Apple, 6,900—but this considers only one side of the ledger.[18] On the other side of the ledger, the economy added over 19 million net jobs from 1979 to 1995.[19] Any innovative and dynamic economy will experience downsizing and upsizing. Jobs will disappear in declining industries and in industries where technology and consolidation allow them to perform with fewer employees, but jobs will sprout up in other current or new industries. The movement of jobs and workers is not instantaneous, but it is the path by which economies grow over time.

The U.S. agricultural sector provides a clear example of misplaced worries about downsizing. In 1800, agricultural workers made up about 80 percent of the U.S. workforce. By 1870, the percentage had fallen to 46 percent; by 1950, it was merely 12 percent; and now it is less than 3 percent of the labor force.[20] Innovations in farm technology—tractors, combines, seeds, fertilizers, pesticides—made these reductions in the agricultural labor force possible while dramatically raising the production of foodstuffs for consumption in the United States and sales to foreigners. These developments in agriculture have often brought on complaints about "dying farms," "technological unemployment," and losses of farm families, but these worries miss the big picture: More production with fewer workers "frees" these workers to go out and help produce other items that are now affordable because of the productivity gains in agriculture. To a displaced worker, the outcome may hardly seem like an improvement, but for society as a whole and even for the displaced worker over time, this is the only path to greater consumption. What kind of economy would we have if zero "downsizing" of the agricultural sector had occurred? When 80 percent of the workforce must commit itself to producing enough food for the economy to survive, not many TVs, VCRs, and PCs will be produced.

Moreover, at the same time that AT&T, Wells Fargo, Apple, and other companies experienced significant downsizing, many other companies enjoyed upsizing. The Federal Express workforce increased from zero in 1975 to 34,000 in 1985 and went to more than 100,000 by 1995.[21] MCI jumped from only 500 employees in 1975 to 50,000 in 1995.[22] Many other recognizable names such as Staples, Compaq, United Parcel Service, Circuit City, Microsoft, Oracle, and others have added thousands to their payrolls. Again, the ebb and flow of employment across firms and industries goes hand in hand with a dynamic, growing economy. Highlighting the fate of the straggling and dying companies hardly represents the whole picture or even the major trends.

Second, the evidence used to show the effects of downsizing—as well as other stagnation claims—is equally myopic. What about men in midlevel managerial positions losing their jobs? What about single mothers torn between welfare, a low-paying job, facing unaffordable day care, living in a bad neighborhood to raise these children? The kinds of newspaper articles we cited in Chapter 2 are replete with references to specific individuals—giving "a face" to the dismal economic realities. For example, a *New York Times* piece, "Big Holes Where Dignity Used to Be," chronicled the economic hardships imposed on a plant manager for Eastman Kodak who lost his job when the plant was closed and on a former aircraft machinist now making half the pay he did in his former Northrop job.[23] A 1998 PBS series hosted by Hedrick Smith, *Surviving the Bottom Line*, used similar techniques of employing anecdotes as evidence to describe the heartache of downsizing. In one episode, Smith talked with the Hague family of San Diego. Three generations of the Hagues worked for General Dynamics—a total of ninety-nine years of employment— only to lose employment to the economic vagaries of our times. Such stories, carrying out the theme of general economic decline, are geared toward infusing broad and impersonal economic statistics with humanity.

To be sure, these stories are about real people and significant cutbacks in their standards of living. In supporting the premise of declining standards of living for a large percentage of Americans, though, they hinge precipitously on the validity of more general figures. Stories about a family under hardship here and a worker making a lot less money there do not necessarily provide evidence of much of anything for the bulk of society, with its millions of employed workers. Someone summarized this point by saying, "The plural of anecdote is not data."[24]

We would be foolish to defend the premise that any society, no matter how wealthy, can achieve a level of material well-being to alleviate all anxiety, all suffering, or all of the disturbing outcomes that life can present. If this is the standard above which the U.S. economy must rise in order for living standards to be proclaimed healthy and growing, then the United States will never make it. Serious illness, permanent injury, and death have not been eliminated. Loss of employment, sometimes under very surprising, impersonal, or unjust circumstances, has not been eradicated. Honest and capable people sometimes find themselves unable to provide nearly as much for their

families as they would like or as much as most other people are able
to, through little or no fault of their own. Yet most of these undesirable outcomes address basic facts of life that may be reduced by advances in living standards, though never eliminated.

To discern what is happening to living standards even for these unfortunate families, it is not enough merely to point to their existence;
rather, demonstrating stagnating or declining living standards requires evidence showing these families are in worse shape now than if
life's cruel shocks had hammered them twenty, fifty, or one hundred
years ago. As little comfort as it may be to these families suffering the
misfortune of lost employment and income, even they almost certainly enjoy a less precarious state than their predecessors of bygone
decades. To lose one's job in the Great Depression of the 1930s
might have meant near subsistence living rather than trading a big
house for a smaller one, reducing trips to the mall, or limiting meals
eaten in restaurants.

Attempting to turn the hardships imposed on a small subset of families into a story about American living standards in general is as an
expression of the "fallacy of composition." For almost any topic under consideration, no matter how far removed it may be from the experience of most citizens, reporters from tabloid news programs like
Hard Copy, from talk shows like *Oprah,* and from mainstream "news"
programs like *Dateline* habitually troll the countryside looking for a
story and without a great deal of difficulty can supply individual stories that will confirm almost any premise that makes good copy. If the
premise is economic hardship, then it is a near certainty that out of
100 million households, several specific examples can be found to
substantiate the premise.

The breakdown in logic occurs when reporters and politicians gen-
eralize the experience of these few into a national problem. A problem for 0.001 percent of all households does not mean a problem exists for the rest of households. Many of the subjects covered on the
innumerable daily talk shows, TV news "magazines," and the like testify more to the ability of reporters and TV producers to dredge up
real, but very isolated, stories than to the state of the bulk of American households. Whether tragic, humorous, repulsive, or whatever,
most of these stories lie way out on the very fringes of everyday life
for most Americans. No matter how small the percentage of households that actually face these problems, their impact is compounded
in a society that is heavily influenced by television and possesses few

skills for separating anecdotal evidence from methodical and careful analysis of data. The impact of the reports relies more on the number of people tuned in to the show than on the number of people truly experiencing the same problems.

If anecdotes are to be the basis for judging the economy, a person could easily counter the downsizing examples with upsizing examples. In these, individuals work up from meager economic beginnings and now enjoy living standards far above those beginnings—and there are literally thousands of such stories. The 1995 Federal Reserve Bank of Dallas publication "By Their Own Bootstraps" chronicles a number of such rags-to-riches stories.[25]

Again, these rejoinders to the question of hardships imposed on specific families are not intended to make people living under difficult or tragic conditions really feel any better about those conditions. They are a legitimate response, though, to the people setting themselves up as economic analysts who think that pointing to a specific example of economic troubles is devastating to a premise about rising living standards for the overwhelming majority of families.

What About International Comparisons?

One of the favored digs of the stagnation thinkers in the 1970s and 1980s was to ask "What about the United States versus country X?" Lester Thurow wrote in 1980, "Where the U.S. had once generated the world's highest standard of living, it was now well down the list and slipping farther each year."[26] The countries that have filled the blank have changed over time. In the 1970s, countries such as Sweden and Germany filled the role. In 1981, Heilbroner and Thurow wrote, "We are no longer the nation with the world's highest standard of living but the nation with the fifth-highest standard, outranked by Switzerland, Denmark, West Germany, and Sweden with Japan only 7 percent behind. . . . The basic fact that American living standards are now shared or bettered abroad is indisputable."[27] More recently, Japan became the country of choice, demonstrating the flaws in the U.S. economic system. In 1990, MIT professor Paul Krugman explained the dominant view: "With Japan now overtaking the United States in one field after another, the previous murmur of complaint has become a loud clatter."[28]

As each of these rival economic powers has experienced significant slowdowns during some part of the past twenty years, the critics of

U.S. living standards have either backed off a bit or jumped to a new country. Still, these critics have missed the main point: Living standards in these other wealthy countries were never really very close to American living standards. Like the comparisons of living standards within the United States over time, the comparisons of the United States to other countries have suffered from an overemphasis on summary measures of national output such as GDP and its derivatives, whether the objective is to jump on the foreign bandwagon or get off it.

Broader examination of expenditures, assets, and utilization of services exposes the continued dominance of the United States in terms of living standards, indicating that the other relatively wealthy countries have gained little ground over the past few decades. The attributes of housing for typical families in the United States and Japan help to illustrate our point. In 1987, the square footage per capita was 670 for the average U.S. citizen and 405 for a poor U.S. citizen. The square footage per average Japanese citizen was less than 200 square feet.[29] Whether Japan's GDP-measured growth rate was outpacing America's in the 1980s and is now straggling behind it is irrelevant to our discussion; the characteristics of U.S. and Japanese housing demonstrate that a considerable chasm in affluence existed in the 1980s, before Japan's current economic problems started.

Moreover, comparisons between the United States and middle-income or poor nations—comparisons not written about in the stagnation literature—go even further, highlighting the affluence of average Americans and even the poor in America.[30] These comparisons reinforce the points discussed in the prior section, showing the affluence of lower-income families in the United States relative to a worldwide standard.

Figure 4.2 shows at-home food and nonalcoholic beverage expenditures as a percent of total expenditures for a cross-section of some of the wealthier nations. Even with the U.S. appetite for relatively expensive foods and the volume of food consumed, the U.S. percentages fall well below these other wealthy nations. Using Japan as a particular example, the average U.S. family would have to spend more than $5,000 per year more on food in order to equal the food expenditure of a typical Japanese family. The comparison with middle- and lower-income countries is much more stark. In middle-income kinds of countries like Greece, consumers spend about one-third of their incomes on food. In poor but somewhat developed nations like India and the Philippines, average consumers retain less than one-half their

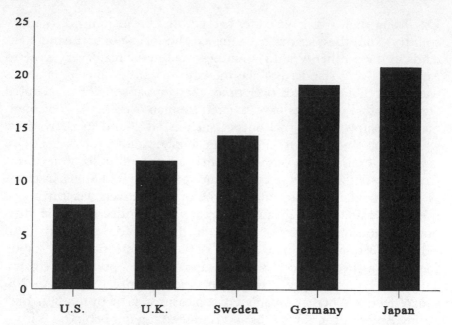

FIGURE 4.2   At-Home Food and Nonalcoholic Beverage Expenditures, 1992
(as % of total expenditures)

SOURCE: U.S. Bureau of the Census, *Statistical Abstract of the U.S., 1997* (Washington,
D.C.: USGPO, 1997), p. 841.

income for nonfood items. By contrast, a family of four with an income around the official U.S. poverty line, that is, around $16,000,
could triple the subsistence food-expenditure level used in Chapter 3
and still retain more than 70 percent of family income for nonfood
expenditures.

A different angle on affluence comes across in Figure 4.3, which
lists TV ownership rates per 1,000 people for several countries of varied living standards. In the United States, there are more than 800
TV sets (nearly all color) for every 1,000 people. This number is truly
staggering, amounting to almost one set per person and almost double the ownership rate in economically advanced nations such as the
United Kingdom and Sweden. Japan ranks a distant second place,
with just more than 600 sets per thousand. Whatever such a number
may say about U.S. citizens from a sociological perspective, it indicates substantial economic muscle in comparison with rival economic
powers. In countries still mired in the depths of poverty like Pakistan
and the Philippines, ownership rates are less than 50 sets per 1,000

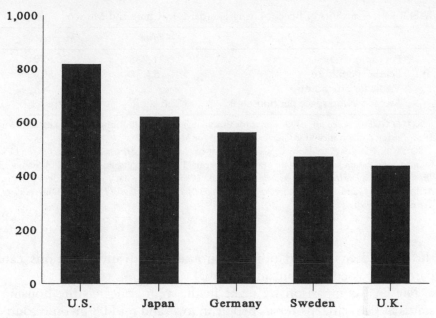

FIGURE 4.3   Televisions per 1,000 People, 1993

SOURCE: U.S. Bureau of the Census, *Statistical Abstract of the U.S., 1997* (Washington, D.C.: USGPO, 1997), p. 842.

people. Thailand, a country with a modest degree of economic development, has just over 100 sets per 1,000 people. In a telling contrast, the data presented in the preceding section show ownership rates for color televisions among those U.S. households listed as officially "in poverty"—at more than 92 percent. Even if this represents just one set for every four people (250 sets per 1,000 people), the rate places these U.S. "poor" on about the same level as an average citizen of Israel or Argentina.

A few additional items are also enlightening. Among the highest-income nations in the world (the G-7 countries), Belgium has the highest ownership rate for automatic clothes dryers—39 percent. In the United States, nearly 70 percent of households contain automatic clothes dryers. More than 80 percent of U.S. households contain a microwave oven, whereas Sweden tops the other G-7 nations at 37 percent. Ownership rates for VCRs in nearly all European countries fall at or below ownership rates among U.S. "poor."[31] Naturally, ownership and use of particular goods and services depend upon cultural differences to some extent. Still, the massive differences between

TABLE 4.4   Snapshots of Recent Living Standards in China and Mexico

	China	Mexico
Per capita GDP	$1,738	$3,679
Food expenditure	53.5%	50%
Medicine expenditure	1.3%	NA
Average living space per household	266 sq. ft.	819 sq. ft.

NOTE: GDP data are for 1993. Other Mexican data are for 1990. Other Chinese data are for 1985. Living space is mean for China and median for Mexico.

SOURCE: GDP data are from U.S. Department of Commerce, *Statistical Abstract of the U.S.* Other Chinese data are from State Statistical Bureau, People's Republic of China, *A Survey of Income and Expenditure in Households in China, 1985*. Mexican data are from Henry Selby, Arthur Murphy, and Stephen Lorenzen, *The Mexican Urban Household* (Austin: University of Texas Press, 1990).

the United States and other economically advanced nations can hardly be passed off as inconsequential.

The final comparison we make in this vein concerns the housing status of U.S. citizens versus people in low- and middle-income countries such as China and Mexico in recent years, as shown in Table 4.4. Median household income and per capita income in Mexico was only about 15 percent of U.S. levels. In China, per capita income amounted to only 7 percent of the U.S. level. To put these in perspective, a U.S. family could be included in the official "poor" stratum and still have an income of about 35 to 40 percent of the median. The bottom fifth of family income in the United States for 1993 ran from $16,000 downward; less than 10 percent of all U.S. families received incomes in 1993 of less than $10,000. Food expenditures alone chewed up more than 50 percent of the incomes of the average Chinese and Mexican citizen. As we noted earlier, food, shelter, and clothing together account for only about 45 percent of expenditures for U.S. households in the lowest fifth of incomes.

What About Stagflation?

Periods of slow or negative economic growth—recessions—have turned the typical stagnation rumble into a roar. Since 1970, the United States has experienced relatively minor economic downturns in 1970 and 1990–1991, with more substantial dips in 1973–1975 and 1979–1982. At a minimum, perhaps the existence of relatively severe recessions over the past thirty years indicates that not everything has been rosy for American living standards. Surely the double-digit inflation coupled with double-digit unemployment in the late 1970s and early 1980s—the era of stagflation (that is, high inflation coupled with anemic economic growth)—is not evidence of a buoyant economy.

In the previous chapter, we discussed trends in living standards over the past twenty-five to thirty years. These were not just statements about the direction of economic well-being in any given year, or for that matter, several years. Standard measures of economic performance show economic growth was about half of its long-term average over the years from 1973 through 1982. In large part, the slow growth can be attributed to the recessions occurring in 1973–1974 and 1979–1982, in which large increases in the price of oil contributed to economic problems. The factors behind this slow era of growth have garnered considerable attention from macroeconomists.

We can use this lackluster economic performance in these years to help illustrate our point about long-term trends in living standards. For one thing, these years vividly illustrate what economic stagnation really is. Economic stagnation does not cause a husband and father to settle for the Ram pickup without the CD player or four-wheel drive; economic stagnation causes him to sell his big pickup and $10,000 bass rig to put food on the table and pay the electric bill. We must ask, then, why it is that 1974 or 1981 are viewed as such bad years. Why are years of obvious and measurable economic turmoil with 11 percent unemployment the exception rather than the norm?

Furthermore, the fact that asset ownership and 1990s expenditures reflect so much affluence in spite of a few truly stagnant years in the past twenty-five is a testament to the tremendous economic performance in many of the years outside of the recession years. If families were routinely pinched the way they were in those years or even half as much as in those bad years, would a median home have increased in size by over one-third and come with all kinds of added amenities, to boot?

What About Health Care Costs?

Undeniably, the share of income devoted to health care expenditures has grown by leaps and bounds in the United States. As late as 1970, the expenditures accounted for only about 7 percent of national income. Currently, they account for 14 to 15 percent. Per-person expenditures have risen from only $350 per year in 1970 to about $4,000 per year in the late 1990s.[32] These developments are usually depicted as a sign of a broken health care system and, more generally, of an economy in crisis, especially if we do not "fix" the health care system. Even many highly trained economists occasionally deplore the magnitude of these figures.

Outcry about the necessity for health care reform, especially for radical reforms, illustrates how "we've never had it so good" can be turned around and actually used to argue that "we've never had it so bad." The main message of the massive medical expenditures is not about a faulty health care system or an economy in trouble but about the enormous affluence of a society that can afford to pursue the highest-quality health care in the world. Without a doubt, medical markets can be improved—largely by releasing markets rather than restricting them more. Yet whatever reform agenda we might want to pursue, we should be clear on the main factor behind growing medical expenditures—rising affluence.

Because medical expenditures sometimes boil down to life-or-death decisions, we do not usually think of medical care as a luxury. Yet in societies where survival means scraping from day to day for almost all citizens, households must face the unenviable choice of letting nature take its course with a sick loved one. The rest of the household or even the whole society cannot afford to give up much or risk the demise of everyone. When contrasted with these bare-bones societies and eras, Americans today possess the economic wherewithal to afford all kinds of expensive treatments and diagnostic measures that extend life—organ transplants, arterial bypasses, MRIs, CAT scans. The means of financing the expenditures may be directly out-of-pocket, through insurance premiums, or through public-sector programs like Medicare, but nonetheless, all of these financing schemes illustrate the power of American affluence.

In addition to these life-extending treatments, the huge medical care expenditures in the United States also reflect treatments that improve the quality of life without necessarily extending life—a definite luxury in very poor societies. Procedures such as joint replacements, prosthetic devices, corrective eye surgery, and the like would fall into this category, and that does not even count the billions spent to ease the pain of sore throats and headaches and on more mundane medical treatments.

Those who think that rising shares for medical expenditures express something fundamentally wrong with the economic system often point to lower shares of income spent in other wealthy nations. For instance, in 1996, German consumers spent only 10.5 percent on medical care and United Kingdom consumers, 6.9 percent.[33] As many have pointed out, these figures hide important differences in the quality of care that usually lean in the direction of U.S. consumers. Even with these quality differences notwithstanding, these critics do not look far enough into the medical expenditure share data to grasp their true indications of affluence for the United States. The data reveal a pattern of affluence: Countries with higher levels of affluence spend greater shares on medical care. Of course, socialization of medical care and quality variation make the picture a little fuzzy for countries with nearly the same income, but still, if we look at countries with major income differences, the pattern is obvious. For example, Greece, which has a per capita income of only about one-third of the wealthiest European nations, spends less than 6 percent on medical care. In a slightly poorer country such as Mexico, the figure is just less than 5 percent. Turkey, whose per capita income is only one-tenth of the wealthiest European nations, spends less than 3 percent of its income on medical care. In China in 1985, when per capita annual income was an abysmal $1,700, average medical expenditures were only 1.3 percent of total expenditures.[34]

The data here and in the previous section on comparing U.S. affluence to the other wealthy nations show how one wrongheaded idea about affluence can contribute to another. First, observers err when they do not recognize that U.S. affluence is well above the level of the other major economic powers. Then, thinking that affluence is about the same in the United States as in these other nations, they misinterpret the data on medical expenditures as indicating severe problems in the U.S. system. Instead, the difference between U.S. and European nation shares spent on medical care can be explained, in large part, the same way anyone would explain the difference between shares spent by German citizens and Greek citizens, especially once adjustments are made for quality of care: Wealthier people spend more on health care.

Vilifying the growth of health care expenditures because of its growth in the share of total consumer spending uses an upside-down standard. For example, what happens if we used this same standard when looking at spending on personal computers? In 1980, the share spent on personal computers was infinitesimal. By the late 1990s, the share had started to approach 1 percent of national income: Is this evidence of decay or affluence?[35]

The same general trend holds if we broaden the category under discussion to include all consumer electronic equipment. We are quick to see consumer electronic equipment as a luxury of an affluent society, however, and do not worry about growing income shares flowing its way. The fundamental flaw in thinking about medical care this way is that because such expenditures relate to our health, we cannot as readily see these expenditures as "luxuries," but they are. Even the practice of insuring oneself against large medical expenditures—a contributor to growing medical care prices because of diminished incentives to monitor cost—reflects rising wealth in a society. Cross-sectionally, the people without insurance in America are the poor—not the rich. The same effect has occurred over time. In 1960, nearly 70 percent of medical expenditures were made directly by households. By the early 1990s, this percentage had fallen to just over 30 percent.[36] In sum, claiming that the economic system is broken by pointing to medical care expenditures turns affluence into decay by fiat and ignores reality.

Decay or Deception?

One of the most sensitive questions concerns the motives behind the stagnation message. How can intelligent people draw conclusions that upon deeper inspection are so far off-base? When it comes to politicians, the answer would appear obvious; this is self-serving behavior by people trying to win office or motivate a legislative agenda. The flip-flop of the Clintonites back and forth on the stagnation message as they moved from challengers to incumbents with a congressional majority to incumbents with a congressional minority illustrates this kind of activity. Pat Buchanan's love affair with stagnation would fall into the same category. The media's cooperation is also not hard to figure. Whether in the "news" or "entertainment" division, TV producers simply want attention. Reports about economic troubles stir interest, regardless of how unrepresentative they may be.

The most unsettling group among the stagnation messengers is composed of the academic economists who have buttressed it. Their support is particularly unsettling because it provides legitimacy for the editorialists and politicians. Even academics with preeminent credentials can be wrong—grossly wrong. The almost complete reliance on real GDP as an indicator of economic success and the movement away from subsistence-level benchmarks deserves some of the blame enticing some academic economists to sign onto the stagnation theme.

Also, economists are people and are not above allowing their political views to bias their professional judgment. It is difficult to explain the statements made by some economists concerning income inequality without suspecting that political biases are creeping into the picture. Many are expertly trained economists of the highest order who are aware of the data tracking household performance and the like or, at least, are around colleagues who know this data. There is a kind of intellectual dishonesty at work here that should be exposed much more frequently than it is.

The next chapter begins the second section of this book, using the basic premise developed so far as the starting point, which is that Americans can afford a lot more material possessions and services than they could even twenty years ago. The previous two chapters have detailed in part a number of the beneficial ends to which this increased purchasing power has been directed. The following chapters explore the darker side of wealth's rampage in America: the increased affordability of activities that have directly or indirectly created many of the problems that plague Americans today.

FIVE

AFFLUENCE, EMPLOYMENT, AND EDUCATION

If all the year were playing holidays, to sport would be as tedious as to work.

—William Shakespeare, *Henry IV*

Up to this point, our main thrust has been that post-1970 improvements in incomes and living standards now allow all classes of Americans to afford many more objects of desire than they could even twenty-five years ago. These tremendous economic gains have directly and indirectly produced a variety of consequences. Many of these consequences would be universally hailed as beneficial, for example, the lower infant mortality rates reported in Figure 5.1. Others, such as increases in leisure time, which we discuss below, would be viewed mainly as beneficial but with potential negative offshoots. In other cases, severe social problems can, in part, be attributed to the rising affluence. In this and the next two chapters, we explore the varied consequences of improving material wealth, paying special attention to the many social problems that can be attributed to it.

Among all of the claims and dire predictions, the most commonly accepted adage among the stagnation writers may be the sad state of American workers. The stagnation camp receives considerable support on this front from academic sources. It is often asserted that

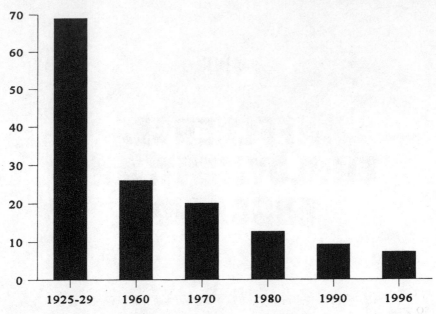

FIGURE 5.1   Infant Mortality per 1,000 Births, 1925–1996

SOURCE: Ronald Alsop, ed., *Wall Street Journal Almanac, 1998* (New York: Ballantine Books, 1998), p. 695; National Center for Health Statistics, *Vital Statistics of the U.S.* (Washington, D.C.: USGPO), various volumes.

frequently cited employment statistics such as the unemployment rate understate the true employment weaknesses in the economy. From this viewpoint, much of the anxiety and discontent in America can be attributed directly to these work- and wage-related issues. As with the rest of the stagnation message, the poor-mouthing of labor-sector data is another example of a mixture of partial truths, misinterpreted facts, and outright distortions. In obscuring the facts about U.S. labor markets, the stagnation message also misinterprets some of the important consequences for personal and household decisionmaking that the robust labor conditions have fostered.

We should note at the outset that many of the labor-related consequences of rising affluence are by no means negative. Even among the outcomes where a downside can be identified, the labor-related effects may not be as dangerous as the effects considered in the next chapter. Still, starting out by analyzing the effects of affluence trends on labor markets allows us to make a few easy-to-understand points about growing affluence and decisionmaking. We first address the basic labor-leisure choice faced by people. Then we discuss the effects that rising affluence has on leisure as well as problems created in measuring it. Then, as part of this labor story, we also propose a link between job-related statistics and educational outcomes in the United States.

Affluence and Leisure Choices

All individuals and households face fundamental choices about the mix of how much to work versus how much leisure to enjoy. This "labor-leisure" tradeoff is basic economics. More time devoted to labor—whether working overtime, working a second job, working at home, operating a business on the side, or whatever—means greater compensation and, as a result, greater consumption possibilities and higher material living standards for the person or household. More time devoted to leisure produces its own rewards—time with the family, time with a hobby, recreational pursuits, and so forth—which are also highly valued by many people. In the simplest terms, a decision to pursue more leisure time implies a reduction in labor, consumption, and living standards, at least as they are measured by ability to buy goods and services.

Leisure Choices and Labor Statistics

As a basic fact, people pursue more leisure as their material well-being increases—at least on average. The reduction in the average work week per laborer in the United States over the first half of the twentieth century reflects just this kind of decisionmaking. Occasionally, analysts may think that unions or other institutions and groups that have fought for shorter work weeks are the underlying reason for more leisure; however, these groups merely express the collective wishes of individuals and families who desired more leisure as their material living standards began to increase. In a subsistence culture, leisure time is hardly more than a residual—brief moments left over after minimum needs have been met.

This tendency for leisure to rise as affluence increases is one reason Juliet Schor's *Overworked American* received so much attention among the stagnation proponents. In that book, she claims that leisure time has actually diminished in recent years—a sure sign of economic problems.[1] Indeed, using Schor's data—economy-wide, employer-reported data on the average hours worked per week—the amount of leisure time chosen by individuals appears to have stabilized since midcentury. Gains from the first half of this century in this kind of easy-to-measure leisure dwarf more recent fluctuations in work weeks, at least in absolute terms. Seemingly, this places the anxiety about American workers on a solid foundation.

This way of measuring trends in leisure time—although not common—is by no means the final word, because it overlooks changes in household work. University of Maryland professor John Robinson and Penn State professor Geoffrey Godbey, in a rebuttal to Juliet Schor's data on leisure in the *Overworked American*, closely studied leisure time for Americans in a way that takes account of on-the-job work as well as household chores.[2] Whereas Schor relied on survey questions, Robinson and Godbey used time diaries. In another key departure from Schor, they defined leisure as free hours not devoted to sleeping, working, personal care, child care, or keeping house, which is a broader definition more in keeping with a typical person's view of leisure. Their results, appearing in Table 5.1, show leisure time increasing substantially since the mid-1960s. For all Americans, leisure time jumped by 14 percent, whereas the growth for employed women was a whopping 25 percent. The average working woman in 1985 enjoyed seven more hours per week of leisure time—almost an entire workday—than her 1965 counterpart.

Even the employment-based definition of leisure demonstrates gains for the "common" working person when inspected more closely. As Figure 5.2 displays, the average number of working hours per week for production and nonsupervisory workers has decreased

TABLE 5.1   Americans and Leisure Time, 1965–1985 (in hours per week)

	1965	1975	1985	1965–1985 % change
All Americans	34.6	38.6	39.5	14.2
All men	35.3	38.8	40.1	13.6
Employed men	32.6	35.0	36.1	10.7
All women	33.9	38.3	38.9	14.7
Employed women	27.2	29.9	34.0	25.0

NOTE: Leisure time is defined as duty-free hours not devoted to sleeping, working, personal care, child care, or keeping house.

SOURCE: John Robinson and Geoffrey Godbey, *American Enterprise* (September–October 1995):43. Reprinted by permission.

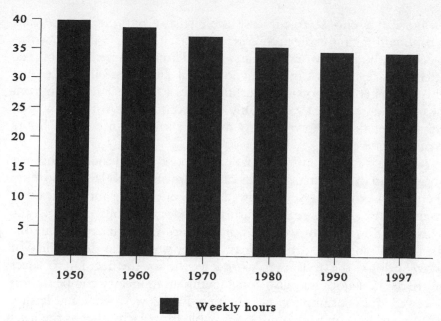

FIGURE 5.2   Decreasing Work Hours of Hourly Workers, 1950–1997

NOTES: Weekly hours worked for production or nonsupervisory, nonfarm workers on private payrolls. Data for 1997 are for January through March.

SOURCE: U.S. Department of Labor, *Employment and Earnings* (Washington, D.C.: USGPO), various issues.

steadily since 1950. Although the gains are smaller than those from earlier in the century in absolute terms, in relative terms, they are not trivial, representing a 15-percent decline since 1950. For the average worker, the reduction amounts to almost another full day off per week.

Whatever these various statistics imply about leisure, they miss a critical aspect of the enjoyment of leisure in the United States in recent decades. Using only marketplace employment as the basis for measuring work and leisure totally discounts any gains made in household work. If gains in affluence have reduced household chores, an accurate picture of work and leisure must take such a reduction into account. Leisure can encompass many more subtle dimensions and decisions than are captured by the simplistic more-versus-fewer-hours-worked view. For one thing, aggregate cross-sectional studies collected over time mask gains in leisure time that reflect affluence-driven changes in decisionmaking over the long run. For example, workers may choose to increase their leisure by building up their wealth and taking earlier retirements rather than by reducing work-week length during working years. For millions of American workers, such decisions are not merely hypothetical. Figure 5.3 illustrates just this kind of effect, showing a decline in labor force participation from nearly 87 percent in 1950 to only 67 percent in 1996 for men aged 55–64. Yet these improvements do not show up in data on hours worked per week.

Another way that an individual can choose more leisure without it showing up in the usual statistics on employment and leisure is by selecting an occupation or job viewed as less onerous or more enjoyable than another. In this regard, leisure includes decisions that not only reduce the quantity of work but also reduce the negative or onerous aspects of work—in other words, by improving the desirability of work. Just like the decision to work fewer hours, the decision to select more desirable jobs may also entail giving up monetary compensation received and consumption possibilities. In this way, work and leisure become more and more indistinguishable from each other as the level

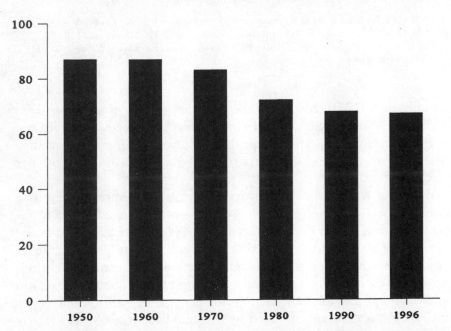

FIGURE 5.3   Labor-Force Participation for Men Age 55–64, 1950–1996 (in percent)

SOURCE: U.S. Bureau of the Census, *Statistical Abstract of the U.S.* (Washington, D.C.: USGPO), various volumes.

of affluence grows. Work becomes leisure, and leisure becomes work. The tendency to intertwine leisure and work is the basis for the quotation from Shakespeare in the epigraph at the beginning of the chapter. As Robert Browning put it in his poem "The Glove,"

> *When a man's busy, why leisure*
> *Strikes him as a wonderful pleasure;*
> *'Faith, and at leisure once is he?*
> *Straightway he wants to be busy.*[3]

Within the literature on labor economics, the theory of "compensating differentials" explicitly studies the importance of job characteristics to wages and employment decisions.[4] This literature developed to account for the premiums that employers pay to entice workers into relatively more disagreeable job situations such as hazardous settings or night shifts. However, the premiums they must pay are reduced to some extent by self-selection on the part of workers: Individuals who are not as averse to hazards or who do not mind working at night as much opt for those jobs, whereas workers who are highly averse to physical hazards move into safer jobs or those who dislike night shifts a lot move into day jobs.

Our interest centers not only on the importance of job characteristics but on their link with affluence. The degree to which workers will allow their likes and dislikes about a job's characteristics to grow in importance versus the job's wage rate is likely to be sensitive to living standards. As an example, subsistence-level farmers or hunter-gatherers may find aspects of their jobs very unpleasant but can hardly afford the luxury of producing less in order to reduce the unpleasantness. Over the past twenty-five years, rising living standards have increased the degree to which people search for "enjoyable" jobs and avoid jobs with "unpleasant" aspects—physically demanding jobs, jobs requiring moving to new locations, and the like. The increased use of immigrant workers to fill many of the most physically demanding jobs in agriculture and construction reflects the decisions of native-born citizens to bypass these jobs. Just like reducing the number of hours worked, seeking out more enjoyable jobs reflects the wealth of a society and the affordability of leisure.

The premium wages that certain employers must pay to attract their workforce indicate how widespread are the pursuit of enjoyable jobs and the avoidance of unpleasant ones. UPS, for example, pays high wages and benefits to drivers who deliver packages and even to part-time workers on loading docks. Most of these jobs are not demanding in terms of the education required but are very demanding in terms of the commitment to physically difficult work, often over long hours. The supply of workers available to UPS is not restricted in the way it is for National Basketball Association teams because few people possess the physical attributes needed or for architectural firms because few people possess the mental attributes required; instead, the supply of capable workers to UPS is restricted because few people want to work as hard as the UPS jobs demand. As a result, UPS pays healthy wages—up to the $50,000 range—and gives excellent benefits to its drivers.[5]

Moreover, the effects of rising living standards on the pursuit of leisure—including the pursuit of on-the-job leisure—point toward a couple of important implications. First, merely looking at average hours worked understates gains in leisure. Second, and in lockstep with the preceding point, assessments that dwell on the time people spend searching for jobs overstate the difficulty of finding well-paying jobs; once job selection is seen as an extension of taking more leisure time, then students and unemployed people who spend more time in their job search may well be pursuing leisure to a greater extent rather than having difficulty finding a less-desirable job.

Job Security and Unemployment

Within the general category of the American worker, another favored topic of the economic doomsayers is the angst felt by American workers over the threats to their jobs from import-enhancing trade agreements like the North American Free Trade Agreement, from corporate greed and downsizing, from technological advances, and other bogeymen. Ross Perot, Pat Buchanan, Richard Gephardt, and several other populist figures have paved an endless road poor-mouthing the lack of job security for American workers. Populist or not, no one can deny that specific workers have lost jobs that had been protected by U.S. trade restrictions. In an instance close to home for us, Fruit of the Loom has let go hundreds of workers in and around Bowling Green, Kentucky, moving most of these jobs to foreign plants with cheaper labor.

The question of downsizing raised in Chapter 4 is still relevant: Do these job losses for some show that job insecurity is an increasing problem across the entire economy? At the most basic level, the data will not bear out these worries for typical American workers. U.S. Department of Labor figures on job tenure, retention rates, turnover, and part-time work show almost no change in job stability.[6] Another study found that the percentage of people holding jobs for ten years or more held constant between 1973 and 1993.[7] Still other studies indicate that between 1971 and 1990, the number of workers with at least ten years of tenure has actually increased; the number of workers with at least twenty years of tenure has remained about constant.[8] Even where job losses to trade agreements such as NAFTA have been felt, the impacts on U.S. plants and workers have been magnified by the import restrictions that had artificially kept these jobs in the United States for many years. When the restrictions were lifted, decades' worth of job transitions waiting to occur came to pass over a few years.

Going beyond the basic figures, once we comprehend the links among wealth, leisure, job desirability, and job selection, the big political push in the United States for greater job security also takes on a whole different cast. Job selection and the ability to indulge preferences concerning the desirability of jobs not only pertain to initial jobs selected by young people but also to the desire of employed people to stay in particular jobs or, at least, to maintain employment in a particular location. We do not have to go all the way back to the time of utter subsistence to view the issue of job security as an extension of the wealth-leisure connection. The idea that a person has a right to expect employment in a specific kind of job for life was an idea largely available only to relatively wealthier people of bygone generations. Through the midpart of this century, primary wage earners for many families of moderate incomes might have jumped between occupations like farming, manufacturing, operating small businesses, and the like. Even for workers who maintained employment within a particular sector—say, manufacturing—the specific job might have moved around between different kinds of industries or companies.

Further, the idea of migrating to find employment was a much more common notion among earlier and poorer generations. If jobs were abundant in California, then a lot of people struggling for income moved to California. If jobs were abundant in Detroit, then a lot of people migrated there. In fact, the level to which wealth and living standards have risen in the United States is in part demonstrated by the willingness of large numbers of unemployed people to just stay where they are. A 1990s version of *The Grapes of Wrath* would not be about migrant workers stumbling around looking for greener employment pastures. Rather, it would more likely focus on unemployed workers sitting in front of their TV sets complaining to a network reporter about NAFTA.

Our claims about the increased desire for stability and the increased enjoyment of stability are borne out in mobility statistics. Figure 5.4 compares people's movements between counties and states in 1969–1970 and 1992–1993, showing a decline in such movements. We chose these years because they are near the endpoints of the time frame of interest and because they are nonrecession years. However, the same point could be made with other nonrecession years. Movements to new counties have remained flat. Although the county data may seem to, at best, show no deterioration in location stability, we would suggest that it shows improvement. The large metropolitan areas in the United States now sprawl over wider areas than in 1970 and include more counties. As a result, a person may move from Dallas County to Colin County, Texas, from Fulton County to DeKalb

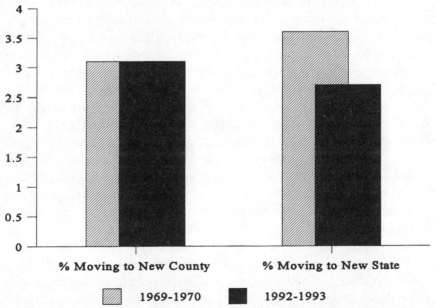

FIGURE 5.4   Increasing Location Stability, 1969–1970 Versus 1992–1993

SOURCE: U.S. Bureau of the Census, *Current Population Reports Series P-20, Geographic Mobility* (Washington, D.C.: USGPO), various volumes.

County, Georgia (metro Atlanta), from Los Angeles County to Orange County, California, or make many other such moves without making a true change in location in the wider sense. This is borne out by looking at movements across state lines, which dropped by nearly 1 percent, even though such movements were already infrequent by the late 1960s.

Beyond just the attention given to job changes and relocations, the employment naysayers also focus on unemployment numbers. According to these critics, unemployment rates—calculated as the number of unemployed persons divided by the labor force—supposedly understate true levels of unemployment. The reason for the understatement is that once a worker is out of work for several months, that person is labeled a "discouraged worker" and drops from the ranks of the official labor force. To bolster the claim, the critics point to statistics on the duration of unemployment. Among those officially listed as unemployed, the median duration of unemployment has risen from four to five weeks in the late 1960s to around eight weeks in the late 1990s. Moreover, the job-loser rate—the percent of the workforce losing (not leaving) their jobs—jumped during the recessions of the 1970s and early 1980s from only about 2 percent to nearly 6 percent. This supplies further fuel to claims of a poor job environment.

No one can deny that the "discouraged-worker" math can, in principle, lead to undercounting the unemployment rate. However, the existence of the "discouraged-worker" category itself is a testament to affluence. First, some people are listed by employment surveys as actively looking for work and therefore in the labor force but unemployed, when in reality they are quite content with their status and do not really desire employment, at least not immediately. If, in fact, these "discouraged workers" actually faced the options of an identical person in a far less affluent society—find a job or starve—most, if not all, would locate jobs, and quickly.

A second factor overstating the "unemployment rate" and the duration of that unemployment is that many of these people could be employed but have chosen to remain unemployed because of their unwillingness to accept jobs for wages they consider to be too low. Again, this kind of behavior is well understood, reflecting rational decisions by people balancing the desire for employment, the costs of job searches, and anticipated wage rates. In the context of rising affluence, it takes on even more importance because we would expect the duration of unemployment to increase as living standards permit unemployed people to pursue new jobs more leisurely.

Last, labor markets reacted to the oil-shock-driven recessions of the 1970s and the early 1980s with much more job turnover than in the 1950s and 1960s. A variety of reasons for the greater response are possible, not least of which is the size of the recessions during the 1970s. Still, the big jumps in the job-loser rate and overall unemployment rate must be understood primarily as being linked to short-term economic problems—significant recessions—rather than long-term trends in labor markets, since the figures have, more or less, come back into line with the figures from the late 1960s.[9]

All of this is not to say that other kinds of figures related to employment and unemployment—job separations, involuntary separations, duration of unemployment, and so on—cannot ever describe an economy with declining employment prospects. Rather, it just means that the use of real wage statistics and complaints about downward-biased unemployment rates as a basis to prop up the stagnation thesis are a shaky foundation.

Female Employment

If economic times are so great for American families, then why have so many families chosen the two-wage-earner route? Isn't the move to more two-wage-earner families a vivid demonstration of the exasperation felt by working-class families? This is a classic comeback of the stagnation message. The claim here is that the presence of more two-wage families provides concrete proof that households are supplying greater work "effort." The percentage of women in the workforce does tie into the overall health of the economy—in concert with many of the other influences on American families—but indicates its strength rather than its decay. Figure 5.5 displays the growth of female participation in the workforce since 1950. In 1950, only 33 percent participated, up to 43 percent did so by 1970, and in the neighborhood of 75 percent did by 1996.

Why do these numbers indicate economic progress rather than decline? The usual reasoning used by those who support the decline theory is that "it takes two wage earners to allow a family to make ends meet." However, the data do not support this conclusion. First, the two-wage-earner vocabulary and statistics are misleading. Women of the 1920s, 1940s, or 1960s may not have been wage earners in

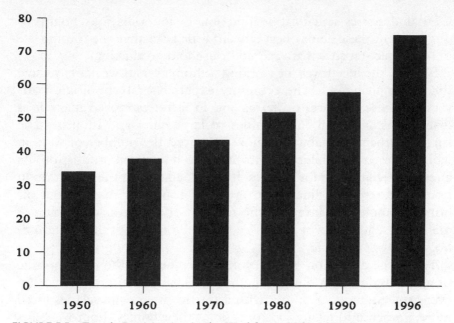

FIGURE 5.5   Female Participation in the Workforce, 1950–1996 (in percent)

SOURCE: *Economic Report of the President, 1997* (Washington, D.C.: USGPO, 1997), p. 346.

large numbers, but they were certainly contributing to family welfare. Viewing the contribution of women to a household only by the amount of outside income earned relies on arbitrary distinctions between valuable work performed within the home but not involving monetary exchange and valuable work performed outside of the home involving monetary remuneration. When economists developed measures of national income and output, they excluded household production because of the difficulty of obtaining accurate estimates of the market value of such work. This exclusion, based on practicalities, does not change household work into playtime.

These "out-of-necessity" omissions of household work soon became treated as completely irrelevant omissions. Just as in the case of quality and GDP, subsequent generations of economists and reporters used economic data on wages, income, and output that tossed aside work contributed by women for their own households as if the household contributions mattered little. Yes, economists continued to slip in qualifications in textbooks about how measured

GDP understates actual national income by ignoring household production, but these kinds of caveats did little to change the routine use of economic statistics that ignored household production.

Second, the incentives for working at home versus working outside the home changed as the economy experienced technological advances. These advances on farms and in factories moved many jobs from farms and rural communities to large cities and suburbs. The rural to urban and suburban moves reduced the number of ways in which women and children contributed to household production. As a result, fertility rates for families declined, adding to the reduction in household responsibilities for women. In concert with these out-of-home technological advances, the automation and semiautomation of many household chores further reduced the implicit value to households of work at home.

Third, the expansion of the economy influenced the relative value of work inside versus outside the home through another avenue. An ever-growing number of jobs with attractive wages and salaries lured more women into taking jobs outside of their homes. Improvements in working conditions and increases in the number of jobs with desirable characteristics since the 1960s have amplified these effects.

Taking all of these points together paints an entirely different picture of the move toward two-wage-earning families. It reflects job selection—a substitution of one kind of work outside of homes for another kind of work within homes. The choice has been driven by the financial value to the households themselves of working within versus outside the home. These are not just assertions. They are backed by solid evidence. For example, Chinhui Juhn of the University of Houston found that in families with the husband's income in the lowest 10 percent, there was an increase in the employment of the wife by 15 percent between 1969 and 1989.[10] This is a sizable increase, which might indicate the "economic pressure" interpretation of the two-worker family if it were not for the data on the other end of the spectrum. For families whose husbands were in the top 10 percent, wives who worked increased by a robust 35 percent between 1969 and 1989. What we see is therefore just the opposite of the "economic pressure" interpretation of more women working, since wife participation increased more among the rich than the poor.

Further, the move toward more outside-the-home work may also reflect selection of more "enjoyable" jobs for some. For a person who finds household work and child rearing tedious, boring, or unrewarding, selecting an occupation outside the home and paying someone else to take care of some of the household chores and child rearing may not only raise consumption possibilities for the household but may also increase personal levels of satisfaction—at least for the adults making the decisions. For some reason, even the stagnation messengers seem to understand these points when explaining the growth of females in the workforce between 1950 and 1970. Yet they want to attribute the growth from 1970 onward primarily to a reaction to economic hardships on families rather than to economic opportunities.

Affluence and Education

One of the most frequently cited sources of consternation is the supposed downward trend in U.S. education, which roughly corresponds to the time frame on which we have centered most of our attention—1970 to the mid-1990s. In part, the flurry of anxiety over U.S. education is caused by methods parallel to those used in establishing the economic stagnation spin—the highlighting of certain data that are either suspect or blown well out of proportion. Still, whether disturbing or perfectly reasonable, some education-related statistics do show changes in education-related outcomes. One might not typically think of the affluence-employment link supplying a basis for understanding these trends in education, but the same basic work-leisure trade-off discussed above also provides an overarching explanation for educational outcomes. We discuss this connection more below, but first we note some of the trends in the education statistics.

Education in Decline?

Most of the discouraging statistics concerning the educational performances of U.S. students have received considerable attention. Statistics commonly cited to show problems are scores on the Scholastic Aptitude Test (SAT). Figure 5.6 shows trends in U.S. SAT scores since 1970. Without a doubt, verbal scores declined from 1970 to 1980 and have remained flat since then. The decline between 1970 and 1980 might be partly attributed to larger percentages of students taking the test, which would tend to pull the scores down as less academically inclined students took the test. Even with this caveat, the flat performance in verbal and math scores since 1980 are not encouraging.

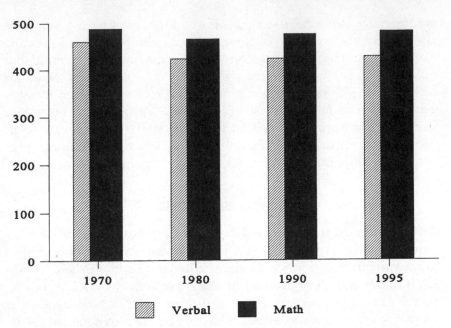

FIGURE 5.6   Scholastic Aptitude Test Scores, 1970–1995

SOURCE: U.S. Department of Education, National Center for Education Statistics, *Digest of Education Statistics, 1996* (Washington, D.C.: USGPO, 1996), p. 127.

Table 5.2 shows international comparisons of scores on reading, math, and science proficiency (achievement) tests for three age groups. The story here differs in some respects from the SAT results. In each subject area, the 1990s scores are higher than the scores for the 1970s. Reading achievement dropped slightly for nine-year-olds from 1980 to 1992 and flattened out for thirteen-year-olds. Because these figures do not show large decreases in proficiency, they raise questions as to whether the alleged precipitous decline is reality or scare tactics; still, they hardly demonstrate great success. International comparisons are also available concerning achievement test scores for these age groups. Again, this evidence is frequently cited as showing problems in U.S. education, but the data do not bear out dire interpretations. The United States ranks second in the world behind Finland in reading achievement and is fifth in math achievement.[11] These figures confirm those cited above that show, at worst, U.S. educational attainment has flattened out.

Other kinds of less-standardized comparisons do tend to bear out problems in U.S. education. For instance, an October 1996 NBC

TABLE 5.2 Proficiency Test Scores for Elementary and Secondary School Students

	Age		
	9 Years	*13 Years*	*17 Years*
Reading			
1970–1971	207	255	285
1979–1980	215	259	286
1991–1992	210	259	290
Math			
1977–1978	219	264	300
1991–1992	230	273	307
Science			
1977–1978	220	247	290
1991–1992	231	258	294

SOURCE: U.S. Department of Education, National Center for Education Statistics, *Digest of Education Statistics, 1996* (Washington, D.C.: USGPO, 1996), pp. 113–126.

Dateline report on a study entitled "The Know-Nothing Class of 1996" demonstrates these trends using a more street-level approach. The report surveyed 500 college seniors and asked them twenty questions drawn from fifth-grade-level examinations. Examples of questions include:

- What two countries were allied with Germany in World War II?
- Name four countries in Africa.
- What is the area of a room measuring 14 feet by 7 feet?

On these three questions, correct response rates ranged from about 67 percent on the math question to about 35 percent on the Germany question. A large percentage of students could not get a passing grade (fourteen or more correct answers) and not a single student answered all twenty questions correctly.

On our own, we have conducted similar nonstandardized experiments, asking sixth- to tenth-grade-level questions of college students but giving the students an explicit incentive to get the answers correct. We found equally dismaying results. Only 44 percent of the students could identify the name of the war in which America won its independence from Great Britain and name one of the two decades in which it occurred. Just 66 percent could answer the first part correctly. Only 44 percent could correctly compute the length of the hypotenuse of a right-angle triangle. Less than 40 percent could identify the decade in which the Civil War occurred, even with a plus-or-minus one-decade margin of error.

Whether one views these statistical trends and anecdotes as showing small gains, no changes, or declines in academic achievement, the amount of bang for the buck is tiny, as shown by Figure 5.7. When adjusted by the consumer price index (CPI), spending per pupil in public schools has increased by more than four times since 1960 and by about two and a half times since 1970. As a percent of median family income, education spending per pupil has jumped from about 4 percent in 1960, to 6 percent in 1970, and to more than 15 percent in 1996. Taken together, the evidence on spending and learning is no cause for celebration about the state of U.S. education, but it also indicates that critics often overstate their case.

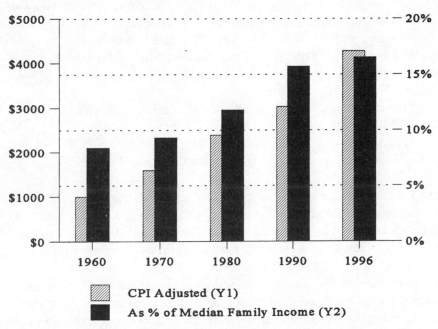

FIGURE 5.7   Spending per Pupil (elementary and secondary), 1960–1996

SOURCE: U.S. Department of Education, National Center for Education Statistics, *Digest of Education Statistics, 1996* (Washington, D.C.: USGPO, 1996), p. 164.

The Received Analysis

Many critics look to hand out blame for these trends in U.S. education. Frequently, the educational outcomes are laid at the feet of the educational production system and its participants: schools, teachers, and administrators. Whether emanating from academic units at universities, from the teachers' unions, or from political think tanks of different stripes, just about everyone has a prescription to cure these problems. Political conservatives, sometimes in league with more liberal thinkers, support the idea of school choice and public vouchers to allow middle- and lower-income students to attend different schools, including private schools. Teachers' unions and academics at more traditional education departments within universities promote an endless array of new teaching pedagogy, enhanced technology, different class structures, different evaluation methods, mentoring methods, smaller class sizes, and the like. People from all sides, including many legislators, have pushed for more accountability in terms of assessing student skills and teacher performance.

We are by no means apologists for educational systems in the United States; instead, we generally align ourselves with the critics. Still, as guilty as the educational system in this country may be of the many claims made against it, one can legitimately ask whether the education production system is a fundamental cause of poor or stagnant educational attainment or merely a reflection of even more basic causes. Whatever one may think is a better production system for education—and the evidence does support some of these efforts more than others—the data on the factors important to educational achievement point out a couple of key facts:

- Family socioeconomic status, as it intermingles with the importance placed upon education in a household, swamps the effects of educational production methods or systems as a determinant of academic achievement.
- Even if education production methods matter a lot, they are driven, or at least overseen, by various democratic institutions (school boards, legislative bodies, regulatory oversight bodies, parents as voters) and are thus not fundamental influences.[12]

These two points highlight the fact that if educational production systems were the preeminent and most fundamental influences behind flat achievement, families would find ways to address the issue either through public policy, private education, or home-based education. If the nineteenth- and early-twentieth-century ancestors of today's parents—working longer hours and living closer to subsistence without electricity and sometimes in racially oppressive locations, in the absence of sophisticated educational methods, and sometimes without schools—could motivate their children to basic literacy, other basic skills, and sometimes far beyond, then families today could generate higher academic achievement if education were truly high on their agenda.

In other words, if better production methods exist and individuals are collectively united in demanding a better education product, such changes can be made. Although oversight and legislative bodies trumpet the assessment theme, one might question the real commitment of any of these groups and society at large in imposing straightforward tests on eighth graders, high-school seniors, or college seniors at public universities that establish a strict minimum for advancement. Such questions would not have to test the full depth or breadth of knowledge; they might, as a starting point, help to show that these students have a level of knowledge at least as high as expected in a fifth grader. On the whole, however, the lack of educational attainment generates a lot of press but very little behavioral response by most families. To be sure, a small percentage of families have taken the bull by the horns in regard to education, but they represent a minority.

Seen in this light, much of the public rhetoric concerning educational problems—especially the most flaming rhetoric—smacks of political maneuvering on the part of one interest group or another. Teachers' unions want more funding. Social conservatives want more school choice. Professors want a greater hand in designing improved systems. Although the truth about academic achievement may arise in the midst of these political debates, the most critical questions are often shunted aside.

Affluence as a Fundamental Explanation

If better academic achievement is truly within our grasp, then why are we witnessing little growth, and maybe even decline, in academic

achievement? If the educational production system is not a fundamental explanation of the trends in education, then what is? These
questions bring us back toward the central aim of this part of Chapter
5: illustrating the link between rising affluence and academic outcomes. Although various criticisms of the educational process in
America may be valid, they overlook the most fundamental and ubiquitous influence on educational performance in the United States—
the lack of motivation because of high living standards. We propose
that the lack of better educational attainment in the United States
stems from America's rising material prosperity, influencing the basic
trade-off between leisure and work.

Economists have long talked of a college experience as a mix between investment and consumption—an investment in terms of the
time and effort designed to bring later rewards; a consumption (enjoyment) in terms of being around peers with similar interests, going
to ball games, or hanging out on nights or weekends. At the core, the
investment aspect is a form of labor and the consumption aspect is a
form of leisure.

This labor-leisure framework can be applied more broadly than
only to educational decisions made by college students. It extends to
decisions made by students at lower levels as well as to decisions made
by parents in regard to their children's educational pursuits. Workers
make choices that take account of their current living standards, their
wages and desired future living standards, the characteristics of the
job environment, and their taste for leisure. Students and parents, like
workers, make choices not based solely on monetary rewards expected from education but also on current and desired living standards, the set of characteristics of the educational environment, and
their taste for leisure.

Just as in the case of employment, the growth in American affluence over the past quarter century has altered the fundamental trade-
offs between labor and leisure in such a way as to make leisure—in its
various manifestations—much more affordable and pursued with
much greater fervor than in prior periods. Below, we discuss three
specific areas in which these manifestations of greater leisure appear.
These are illustrative rather than comprehensive examples.

One manifestation of the choice for more leisure—enjoyable educational environments—is the push by students and educators to
make learning more "fun." In fact, the emphasis placed upon "fun"
and even "technology" in many classrooms is little more than the

substitution of leisure masked as educational pursuit. This is not to say that specific teachers, professors, books, or devices cannot make learning less of a grind, more challenging, or rewarding. Teaching the ABCs and simple arithmetic may be successfully couched in terms of fun by the likes of *Sesame Street* characters, the TV show *The Magic School Bus*, and so forth. Looking at pictures in the Louvre over the World Wide Web may expand the walls of the classroom. Even aspects of a relatively boring subject like economics may be transmitted through in-class experiments rather than through traditional and often mind-numbing lectures or chalkboard diagrams.

However, acquiring in-depth and complex knowledge is ultimately work, whatever the educational vehicle or technical apparatus used, whether a book, a pencil, a slide rule, a calculator, Mathematica software, or an Internet site. Using the latest technical gizmos may ease tedious, computational burdens, but these aids do not fundamentally change the pursuit of more knowledge and bringing high-level analytical skills into play. The educational vehicle may help lessen some of the burnout and boredom of acquiring complex knowledge, but it cannot change the inherently demanding task of mastering a complex concept or skill into a pursuit of pure joy.

To promote education as akin to watching one's favorite team play baseball, playing a pickup game of basketball, reading a good novel, or sitting down for a romantic dinner merely dresses leisure up with an educational bow tied on top. It is hard to imagine ever making the mastery of the writings of Immanuel Kant a knee-slapping good time or transforming a classroom in a way that makes tackling one of those "word problems" in algebra or calculus a moving emotional experience. A few truly gifted teachers with the right set of students may find an especially productive balance of fun and work, but to expect this to be replicated en masse distorts the meaning of work and leisure. The interest among educators, even at the college level, in pandering to the "education is fun" mentality, latching onto anything with the prefix "techno" added to it, and trying to transform the study of Kant or physics into a joy ride just thinly veils the substitution of leisure for work in the educational system to meet the demands of consumers. Over the past quarter century, "science-lite" courses—scaled-back and cursory studies of astronomy, meteorology, geology, and the like—have taken the place of standard physics, chemistry, and biology courses in the core curriculum of most public universities. Students at many universities may not be able to solve a

basic algebra problem or write an interesting and grammatically correct short paper, but they have received an "A" or a "B" for courses
that may require little more than Web surfing.

A second manifestation of the greater emphasis on leisure in education-related decisions is the willingness of students and their parents
to spend more time and money pursuing degrees. Again, the stagnation groupies often interpret the extended careers of many college
students as exhibiting the effects of their trying to make progress
through school while working desperately to make ends meet. However, students of the 1950s, or even the 1970s, attended college and
completed programs of studies in shorter time frames, in spite of
demonstrably lower standards of living.

An alternative interpretation of the same data again turns the stagnation message on its head. High and rising living standards for students and their families allow students to pursue longer education careers without suffering as much economically. Given typical amounts
of family support for students, along with the kinds of wage rates paid
even for part-time workers now, students are in no hurry to move on
into full-time work. This incentive to remain in school joins hands
with reduced rigor and grade inflation within universities helping to
tip the scales between leisure and the work of attending college more
toward the side of leisure.

A third manifestation of the effects of affluence on the education-
leisure relationship is the willingness of students and parents to view
education as irrelevant. This is not meant to indicate that educational
degrees and certification are viewed with contempt or apathy. Rather,
the acquiring of knowledge and skills is often viewed with apathy or
contempt.

Certainly, an intense pursuit of the highest educational goals can
still lead a person to an income and consumption level far above the
average American. Net worth for heart surgeons remains on a level far
above that of most bank loan officers, carpenters, or lawn-care
providers. Lawyers, especially those ranked near the top of classes
from the top law schools, can expect starting salaries more than double someone hired as a management trainee. In fact, the income gap
between college-educated and non-college-educated individuals
seems to be getting larger. Our point is that even without a very impressive educational background, individuals and their families can
still have a prosperous existence relative to their forefathers. The tide
of economic growth has risen so high in the United States that a

college student can make a leisurely examination of the academic program, select a major with limited rigor, make relatively modest
grades, and still land a job that may supply plenty of income for a decent apartment, a color television hooked up to cable or a satellite
dish, a microwave oven, a late-model automobile, and designer-label
clothing, leaving plenty of time for softball, fantasy football, and so
on. Marriage and a little improvement in employment may lead to a
three-bedroom home, another automobile, and plenty of electronic
gadgetry—without much of an additional educational investment.[13]

Of course, it is not as if seven-year-olds are making this complicated
calculus about expected living standards. The same kinds of incentives, though, are at work on the minds of the seven-year-olds' parents, who influence thinking about educational pursuits. And even for
parents keenly interested in educational pursuits, children in their
teens can begin to get a rough idea of the kind of consumption levels
available for different degrees of educational effort.

More Leisure: Good or Bad?

In its treatment of employment issues, the stagnation-related literature often deteriorates into little more than moral philosophizing
about alleged descriptions of economic conditions in the country and
their relationship to employment. Although the foregoing pages may
appear to be a moral critique concerning work habits and educational
choices in America, our points are not primarily intended to motivate
changes in these choices. Rather, we seek to emphasize that many of
the employment and educational data that a lot of writers view as
negative can be explained by understanding the link between affluence and leisure. In doing so, we hope to help steer public debate
about the state of affairs, a public debate that is based on a clear understanding that choices to pursue more leisure are the ultimate
sources of many of the employment- and education-related statistics
so frequently used to work up emotion.

We, too, have opinions and moral philosophies. Our first inclination is to view the choice for more leisure in the face of greater affluence as a good thing—because people are able to pursue the activities
that give them the greatest satisfaction. Whether the time is spent
fishing, playing golf, shopping, or playing with one's children, we are
skeptical of public policy attempts to dictate where, when, and how

much people should enjoy their leisure. Our policy advice would be for policymakers to take a rest.

However, from a more paternalistic stance, the growth of leisure may not be an altogether good thing, especially in the long run. Ultimately, the choice for more personal leisure may entail spillover effects on society when accumulated generation after generation. Idle hands can lead to trouble and may result in genuine problems for families, a subject we discuss in the next chapter. Work can accomplish more than just putting more money in the bank. Even when and perhaps especially when work is onerous, important lessons can be learned from it that cannot be learned from leisure. As leisure becomes substituted for work or work and leisure become more intertwined in employment and educational settings, we wonder about the consequences down the road.

SIX

AFFLUENCE AND FAMILY PROBLEMS

Sometimes the sky really is falling.
—Charles Murray (on illegitimacy trends), *Wall Street Journal*

Prior to and during the 1992 presidential campaign, family issues began to pop up, highlighted most famously by the Dan Quayle–Murphy Brown affair.[1] By the 1996 primary season, issues surrounding American families had jumped from a topic used by a few Republicans to bash Democrats and Hollywood to an issue at the forefront of political debate. Alan Keyes and Bob Dornan, two of the 1996 Republican primary candidates, even made social issues relating to families the signature themes of their campaigns. During the 1996 convention period, both major parties were putting their own spin on how they could best address family issues. At their convention, the Republican Party stressed a return to old-style values, promoting public policy that would be stricter on crime and would diminish social program incentives for out-of-wedlock births. The Democratic Party allocated a larger role to government in addressing American family ills, with Hillary Clinton's *It Takes a Village* being one of the more highly publicized works promoting this theme.[2]

The Increase in Family Problems

In contrast to the hype about educational problems, the amount of attention directed toward issues related to and stemming from family problems could hardly overstate the problems. Statistics and stories showing social decay are liberally used in various books and articles. As an illustration of just how seriously these problems are now perceived, the fiftieth-anniversary issue of *Commentary* collected a number of writers' thoughts about contemporary social issues and the most pressing problems. A significant percentage of the contributors—including the likes of Elizabeth Fox-Genovese, William Bennett, Edward Luttwak, Gertrude Himmelfarb, and others—pegged the decline in American families as their main concern.[3] The United States has fallen victim to a potentially disastrous decline in stable families and the basic decency that stable families have traditionally fostered.

All kinds of figures directly related to family life and its erosion could be cited. Statistics focusing solely upon parenting trends or divorce do not sum up the whole story. Families that have two parents may not be functioning very well now, nor did they in the recent past. Some countries, such as Japan, have low divorce rates but high rates of female suicide.[4] As a result, it would be hard to contend that Japanese women are better off solely because of lower divorce rates. In unfortunate cases, children and spouses are subjected to abuse within households that may never break up. Again, in these cases, it would be difficult to contend that divorce signals a reduction in overall family welfare.

Nevertheless, the more measurable quantities such as single parenthood and divorce do say something about families, especially when taken together and when qualitative measures of family happiness do not contradict the quantitative measures. Further, all kinds of measures indirectly related to family welfare such as crime or suicides also confirm the conclusions drawn from the more measurable items.

Perhaps the single most alarming figure related to families is the number of children born out of wedlock. As Figure 6.1 illustrates, the percentage of all such births has rocketed from only 5.3 percent in 1960 to more than 30 percent in 1996. Much of the attention is directed toward births by unwed black mothers. Among black women, an alarming seven out of every ten children are born to unwed mothers, up from about three in ten in 1960. Much less documented, though, is the tremendous growth of out-of-wedlock births among white women. (A breakdown of births to unwed mothers by race appears in Table 6.1.) Births to unwed mothers were less than one in twenty births in 1960 and had grown by 1996 to one out of every

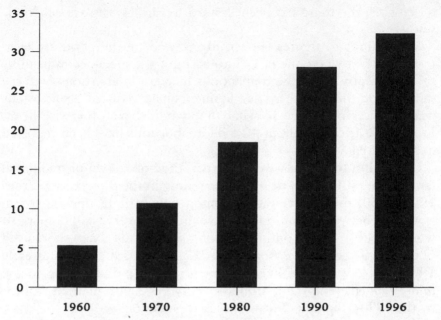

FIGURE 6.1   Births to Unwed Mothers, 1960–1996 (in percent)

SOURCES: U.S. Bureau of the Census, *Children's Well-Being: An International Comparison* (Washington, D.C.: USGPO, 1990); U.S. Bureau of the Census, *Statistical Abstract of the U.S.* (Washington, D.C.: USGPO), various volumes.

four births. As with the figures for black women, the rate among white women also varies greatly with socioeconomic status. For example, among white women with college degrees, the rate is still around the 5-percent level, whereas for white women below the poverty line, the rate is 44 percent.[5] Even with these cross-sectional

TABLE 6.1   Births to Unwed Mothers by Race, 1960–1996

	White	*Black*
1960	2.2	23.5
1970	5.5	37.5
1980	11.2	56.1
1990	20.4	66.5
1996	25.7	69.8

NOTE: Percent of total births. Data for 1960 were estimated from rates per 1,000 unmarried women and total percent to unmarried women.

SOURCE: National Center for Health Statistics, *Vital Statistics of the U.S.* (Washington, D.C.: USGPO), various volumes.

differences, the trend has been upward, regardless of socioeconomic status.

These kinds of figures concerning unwed motherhood are even more startling when one takes into account the increased availability of contraceptives and the tremendous increase in abortions over the same period. Both of these developments have reduced births to unwed mothers compared to what they would have otherwise been. From 1973 to 1996, about 40 million abortions have been reported in the United States.[6]

In addition to out-of-wedlock births, the breakdown of traditional family relationships can be seen in the jump in the divorce rate. From 1920–1960, the divorce rate exhibited only a slight upward trend, hovering between nine and twelve out of every 1,000 married women. The only blip during this long stretch was a very short-lived one around the end of World War II. By the late 1960s and early 1970s, the divorce rate began a much more rapid ascent up to the mid-1970s, flattening out around twenty per 1,000 married women by the 1990s. Figure 6.2 depicts these fluctuations.

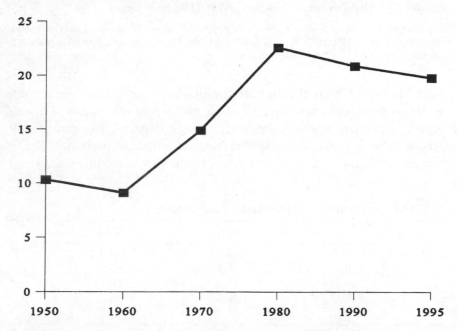

FIGURE 6.2   Divorce Rates per 1,000 Married Women, 1950–1995

SOURCE: U.S. Bureau of the Census, *Statistical Abstract of the U.S.* (Washington, D.C.: USGPO), various volumes.

As a result of both the increased out-of-wedlock births and the higher rate of divorce, more and more children now grow up in single-parent families. Figure 6.3 shows these changes. In 1950, 93 percent of all children lived in two-parent families. This figure was still holding above 85 percent in 1970 but had dropped below 80 percent by 1980. In 1996, less than 70 percent of children lived in two-parent homes. Of these children in single-parent homes, just under two-thirds are there because of divorce or separation, one-third because of out-of-wedlock mothers never marrying. Only about 5 percent of the homes with single parents are that way because of widowhood, historically the dominant reason for single parenting. Among black households, nearly 55 percent of children live with only one parent. Almost every European nation has shared in this upward trend of single parenting, with Sweden leading the pack at 50 percent, Denmark following at 46 percent, and France and England being right around the U.S. level of 30 percent.[7] The percentages in Germany and the Netherlands are about one-half this amount, with Italy being the only European nation still in single digits with 7 percent. Among wealthy

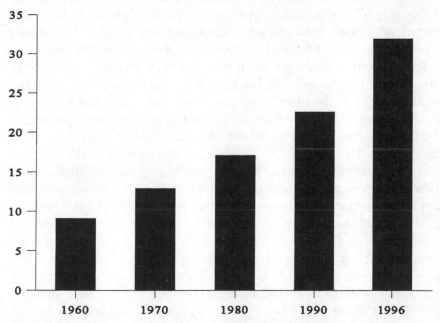

FIGURE 6.3   Percent of Children Not Living with a Married Couple, 1960–1996

SOURCE: U.S. Bureau of the Census, *Current Population Reports: Marital Status and Living Arrangements* (Washington, D.C.: USGPO), various issues.

nations, Japan is by far the lowest at 1 percent. These contemporary figures for the United States and several European countries are completely out of sync with the historical incidence of two-parent family relationships as the overwhelming norm, both in the United States and in other countries.[8]

Many explanations for the broken families, unwed and teenage pregnancies, crime, and overall moral bankruptcy of the country have been offered. The stagnation thinkers have sometimes attributed the decline to the necessity of two wage earners in a family and other economic pressures. Religious conservatives likewise point to two-wage-earner families but often stress the choice rather than the necessity of the arrangement while also imparting some of the blame to the diminished role of religion in American life. Social conservatives like to criticize the role of programs like Aid to Families with Dependent Children (AFDC) as actually supplying financial incentives for the erosion of traditional, two-parent families.[9] Social liberals tend to mark out any cutbacks in social programs or reductions in the rate of growth of social programs as the culprit. Social conservatives and religious advocates often point to the discarding of traditional values in the 1960s as well as the decline of religious values as a source of society's flaws. Other social commentators attribute the situation to a hodgepodge of these and other factors, such as the earlier onset of puberty in modern times.

Still, no one talks about the contribution of growing affluence to these family breakdowns. At the most fundamental level, rising living standards may be the most important contributor. By "fundamental," we mean that although influences stemming governmental programs, the erosion of religion, and other sources may play a role, these influences themselves are often the product of the growth in affluence, so that the negative outcomes we have experienced are due, directly and indirectly, to increasing wealth. The mechanisms by which affluence can lead to negative family outcomes are discussed in detail below.

The growth in family problems also marks one of the greatest, yet unacknowledged, flaws in the stagnation dogma. According to that camp, economic hardships have contributed heavily to family problems of the sort we discuss here. Yet if one looks at data on teenage pregnancy or divorce, the statistics improve all the way back into the 1950s. Just about anybody—even the staunchest stagnation writers—will admit that economic conditions have improved in comparison with the early 1950s. Additionally, the 1950s were an era of open, government-backed racial and gender bias. If economic problems were at the heart of the family problems, we might ask, why did they not show up until the 1980s and 1990s?

We offer a few important qualifications. First, our attention to the negative family-related consequences of greater affluence does not mean we do not recognize important family-related benefits from greater affluence, nor do we think the negative consequences necessarily outweigh the positive consequences. Lower infant mortality rates due to greater material affluence certainly benefit families, as do many life-extending procedures such as heart-bypass and heart-transplant surgery, which owe their existence to greater affluence. The growth of leisure time affording the opportunity, if seized upon, for parents to increase time spent with children emanates from greater affluence. Many, many more examples could be cited to underscore the beneficial effects on families of greater material wealth.

Second, we do not suggest that affluence is the only reason for the upward trends in social consequences. We emphasize the importance of affluence to these trends here because so few have examined this mechanism. Additionally, although other factors we have already mentioned such as welfare or religion may have impacts separate from wealth, it is unlikely that these factors are completely independent of the effects of massive increases in wealth.

Last, a few critics might quibble with our definitions of basic morality and decency. Our main interest is showing the link between affluence and behavior. In a country with the diversity of the United States, we expect that some would view what we call "negative" consequences as positive. We think we are safe in assuming that the vast majority of readers would agree with our definition of negative outcomes in this chapter. If anything across historical civilizations is constant, it is the small core of behavior that is viewed as acceptable and unacceptable to societies. Although the circle surrounding items included in basic morality and decency may have been drawn a little bigger or a little smaller by various societies, almost all cultures—Western or Eastern, primitive or advanced—have punished murder, assault, and theft. Other ethical areas such as sexual behavior have been more malleable, but even subjects like out-of-wedlock births, divorce, lying, and the like have usually been held in disrepute, at least for common citizens. These core values might not always be equally extended or enforced across all individuals in a society—to both slaves and masters, for instance—but these inconsistencies in application notwithstanding, the standards have been ubiquitous.

Affluence and Family Breakdowns

What would *rising* affluence possibly have to do with increases in single-parent families, out-of-wedlock births, divorce, and related matters? Many among the supporters of the stagnation doctrine would interpret the decay in American family life as a direct extension of economic pressures upon contemporary families. Moreover, the tendency for these family problems to be more frequent as one looks down the economic ladder is usually taken as prima facie evidence of falling affluence causing family troubles. For instance, cross-sectional evidence drawn from family data around a given point in time—1990 census data, for instance—shows that higher socioeconomic status reduces the likelihood of divorce. Poorer families are more likely to experience family splits and single parenthood than are wealthier families.[10] Yet, as we discuss below, this received view of economic status and family problems is partial at best.

Before proceeding, we want to clarify our focus in explaining long-term trends in these problems rather than cross-sectional regularities. Whatever precise role economic problems play in explaining family decay across families in 1990 or 1970, this is a different matter than the one we consider here. We ask: What effects would substantial increases in living standards between 1970 and 1990 have on trends in family problems? Our question extends to all families—poor or rich, old or young, black or white—and is independent of whatever cross-sectional differences may be present. We are not investigating the effects of affluence across different income classes at a given point in time; in cross-sectional studies of affluence and family disruptions, it is difficult to determine the extent to which lower affluence is causing family problems and the extent to which family problems are leading to lower levels of affluence.

Family Decisions

To understand the link between affluence and family outcomes in general, we must first view intrahousehold decisions as sensitive to the traditional economic influences of prices and incomes. When deciding on how to divide work among family members, on how many children to have, on when to marry, on whom to marry, on whether to remain married or not, on whether to have extramarital affairs, and the like, the costs (prices) of alternatives along with the income or wealth that makes them affordable will play a role. We are not insisting on a view of identical, robotic households where people are exactly alike and where other influences never come into play; instead, we merely suggest that the affordability of various alternatives based on costs and income will make a difference when looking at many households. In fact, University of Chicago economist Gary Becker won the Nobel Prize for this and related applications of economic ideas to areas typically left to sociologists.[11]

Several relatively noncontroversial examples of the importance of prices and incomes to intrafamily decisionmaking already exist. For example, diminished birth rates over the twentieth century in the industrialized countries are a manifestation of family decisions being influenced by economic prosperity and opportunities for economic prosperity. Higher wage rates and incomes in cities drew more people into cities, reducing the contributions of children to household income. On farms, children became net contributors to family incomes as they grew older by feeding animals, working the soil, picking crops, and so on. However, with their families living in cities, children had few substantial chores and quickly became a net drain on household income. In other words, the price of having children increased, and as a result, birth rates diminished. The idea is not cynical and does not imply a kind of superrationality within households. In contrast, it makes the modest claim that as children become more expensive relative to their contributions, couples produce fewer of them.[12]

The move from primarily extended family households to predominantly nuclear family households is another example of the effect of affluence on household decisions. Academics might be inclined to hypothesize about changing cultures and invent labels for one era or another. Still, the idea that people in any age or at any time enjoy living right on top of each other in crowded conditions more than having ample space for all family members hardly seems worthy of discussion. The switch to nuclear households came about very simply because greater economic fortunes allowed couples the financial strength to move out of the extended-family dwelling or village. Also, financial incentives in terms of salaries and wages arose to encourage movement not just out of the house, but out of the community.

Still, skeptics may think the connection between affluence and family breakdowns may appear to be a stretch. Even if we observe families moving off farms, more wives working, or families producing fewer children due to economic motivations, this does not directly link

unwed pregnancy and divorce to affluence. Specifically, how can affluence and financial incentives affect decisions that lead to more single-parent families?

Trends in Single-Parent Families

Simply put, these outcomes for families are the by-products of rising
living standards, making objects of desire such as sex, free time, diminished boredom, and the like more affordable. Engaging in extra-
and premarital sex and pursuing leisure activities or escaping problems are not free goods—they come with a price tag. The price tag
may include purchases of market goods such as movie tickets or a
restaurant dinner, but it also includes psychological costs on families
and effects on family living standards. Although subject to the same
desires, most people of past eras found the price too high in relation
to their family living standard to pursue these objectives with great
frequency. The gains in economic welfare over the past quarter century have brought these possibilities within the grasp of nearly everyone in society.

We will use sexual activity as the source of family problems to illustrate our point, but we could apply the same ideas to other sources of
family problems. That sexual experiences are pleasurable and sought
after by people is hardly earth-shattering news. Sexual encounters
may be sought in premarital, marital, extramarital, and postmarital
contacts, and all of these encounters involve a calculus of their costs
and benefits—a calculus not necessarily, though sometimes, made explicitly in terms of dollars. This does not imply that all people will increase sexual encounters of some type as they become more affordable or increase them by the same degree. Just like changes in the
affordability of Pepsi or Coke will have a much bigger impact on
some individuals than others, so it is with sex.

Increasing affluence from the 1960s onward has made sexual experiences outside of marriage more affordable by reducing their consequences and thereby reducing the disincentives to engage in them.
Bluntly stated, the economic viability of single-parent families in recent decades has increased certain forms of sexual behavior—pre- or
extramarital sex—which ultimately helps to explain the upticks in single parenting and divorce. In societies where everyday life is a struggle for survival, unwed pregnancy and family breakups present potentially life-threatening hardships. To bring a child into the world in a

single-parent home or to break the marital bonds in these societies is akin to economic suicide or homicide for at least some members of the family. In these more brutal economic circumstances, the incentive to make things work in the family is very strong. Over the past hundred years in America, economic gains have substantially reduced this incentive. The material growth in American society over the past twenty-five years, to the point where virtually no families are in poverty according to the worldwide standard, has shifted Americans into the position where decisions about their families can be made separately from considerations about whether family members are likely to face life-threatening outcomes.[13] In contrast, anthropologist Desmond Morris has noted that the hardships imposed on single mothers in many circumstances have led to starvation or prostitution, especially if extended family support was lacking or withheld.[14]

Single parenthood in America today still substantially reduces family economic well-being in the case of women and children. (Household income may increase for divorced fathers.) The best current estimates place the reduction in income at a whopping 70 percent of prior income for divorced mothers.[15] But because of the vast improvements in income and wealth since 1990, a single mother now may well be able to provide an existence that allows for many of the typical "luxuries" of American life—microwaves, color television, CDs, video games, fancy basketball shoes. In this environment of material abundance, decisions about sex outside of marriage and separation from families to find greater personal fulfillment take on a whole different slant.

To be clear here on the mechanisms behind the effects, young women do not have to think to themselves, "Oh, I'll become a single parent because I can afford it more easily than my great-grandmother could have." Nor does a married man picking up a woman in a bar have to think, "So what if my behavior leads my family to break up; my family won't starve," for our theory to be correct. Instead, all that is necessary is for less care to be taken in avoiding single parenthood. The reference to decisions made by married couples to diminish fertility as more of these couples moved to cities also holds here. It is not likely that very many husbands and wives sit down and make precise calculations concerning the cost of children and the household productivity of children, and even further, they probably do not calculate the optimal number of children based on their financial situation. However, families could certainly gain a broad perspective on the reduced financial viability of large households in urban versus rural settings. And these families could exercise greater, though not perfect, care in avoiding pregnancy.

Our explanation of the growing number of unwed pregnancies and divorce falls right into step with the data shown at the beginning of the chapter: tiny unwed pregnancy and divorce rates in the 1950s that have rocketed since that time. Any stagnation-based explanation must not only face up to the lack of evidence for stagnation over the past twenty-five years but also somehow account for the lack of family breakups in an era of much lower affluence.

Our proposition concerning the role of affluence also helps to explain the tremendous growth of unwed pregnancies among whites and not just poor blacks. It generalizes the analysis of many social programs like AFDC forwarded by social conservatives.[16] These authors contend that such programs encourage single parenting by raising the incentive (or reducing the disincentive) for single motherhood and diminishing the importance of financial contributions by males. Implicitly, these programs subsidize behavior that leads to family dissolution. As a result, the nation ends up with the epidemic of social pathologies such as astronomical teenage pregnancy among poor blacks and abandonment of poor families by black males. In essence, it is a generalization of this same point that we forward here: When an activity is made more affordable, the amount of the activity will increase.

The promotion of undesirable behavior because of increased affordability is at work not only through the redistribution of income by means of the public sector. The same kinds of incentives are also being supplied by the private sector because of the tremendous growth of incomes. AFDC and associated welfare programs may indeed make a contribution to the unthinkably high teenage pregnancy and single-parenthood rates among poor blacks in this country, but they do not explain why out-of-wedlock births among much more affluent blacks and whites have risen so dramatically. Once the effects of private-sector material growth on incentives for behaviors leading to family breakdowns are recognized, we will get a clearer picture of the link between the personal and social pathologies we are focusing on.

In fact, the ability to subsidize irresponsible behavior because of higher living standards extends well beyond issues of single parenting. Much has been made of the 1960s as the era that opened the trap door for family problems because of the promotion of antitraditional values—"dropping out," experimentation with drugs, and more casual attitudes toward sex. Mixed into this pot were protests concerning the Vietnam War and civil rights. Yet the youth of the 1960s were not the first to want to reject society's constraints. They were not the first to oppose an unpopular war effort—the Korean War was also highly unpopular. Mostly propped up by parental affluence, the youth of the 1960s generation were the first—at least by the millions—to be able to afford to just hang out and pursue alternative lifestyles.

Indirect Effects

Both directly and indirectly, rising affluence has contributed to family problems by promoting more "outsourcing" of parental duties to formal and informal day-care arrangements. Indirectly, the growth of single parenthood promotes outsourcing of parental duties for the simple fact that without another wage earner in the family or public assistance, the single parent must usually seek employment.

The same kind of growth in outsourcing of parental duties has also occurred due to the more direct influence of rising living standards discussed back in Chapter 5—that is, the big jump in female participation in the (out-of-home) labor force because of higher wages becoming available to women. Outside incomes grew to very attractive levels at the same time that technology and automation reduced the net contribution of women to household production. As this cost-benefit balance between staying at home and seeking outside employment tipped more heavily toward outside employment, households experienced greater consumption possibilities, but at a price of reduced parental exposure in child rearing. Beyond the parenting practices, material affluence has also indirectly contributed by reducing the social stigma attached to unwed motherhood and divorce in America. Along with the trends in these activities themselves, attitudes among the general public toward unwed pregnancy and divorce have dramatically shifted.

In past eras of meager living standards, the extreme hardships imposed on families, along with religious values, helped contribute to the social stigmas attached to unwed motherhood and to males or females who separated from their families. One would not have to defend the appropriateness of the social harassment to still recognize the role that it played in reducing extra- and premarital sex or divorce. At times, public knowledge of sexual promiscuity or family abandonment could mean nearly complete ostracization from mainstream society. In the 1990s, it garners little more than whispers. One study showed that only 37 percent of respondents viewed having children out of wedlock as "not OK" in 1992—down from 54 percent in 1980. The percent who viewed it as "OK" had grown from 34 percent to 49 percent.[17] Social harassment and changes in social attitudes have been established as a strong motivating force behind the individual choices made. One example is the tremendous growth of the X-rated entertainment industry, a result of people becoming free to watch such movies on home video rather than having to venture to X-rated theaters to see them.[18]

One of the key channels of this reduction in social stigma has been through affluence's effects on religious practices. Rising affluence usually leads to a decline in religious affiliation or, at least, in active religious participation. For those who maintain a nominal affiliation, the character of religion often changes from one with strict moral standards to one with much more lenient standards. As Robert Bork put it: "Religion tends to be strongest when life is hard, and the same may be said of morality and law. A person whose main difficulty is not crop failure but video breakdown has less need of the consolations and promises of religion."[19] The exact reason living standards play a role in religiosity is not altogether determined, although many explanations have been suggested. Whatever the factor or combination of factors, the pattern of religious decline in the face of long-term economic growth is an empirical regularity.[20]

No doubt, the public image of religion, or at least some religiously inclined people, has not always been stellar. Intolerance stemming from religious views has led not just to opposition but to ridicule for diverse points of view and in some cases to physical violence against people. Historical episodes such as the Inquisition and the Crusades, as well as contemporary struggles in places such as Northern Ireland, demonstrate the intolerance that can be associated with religion. Fear of religious intolerance and the dominance of religious institutions in parts of Europe prompted the political founders of the United States to lay roadblocks in religion's path. In particular, the founders tried to permanently restrict the political means open to religious leaders or groups to clamp down on personal liberty by constitutionally mandating a separation of church and state. In addition, many people have pursued religion on formal or even hypocritical bases, publicly advocating the importance of religious values while pursuing personal lives inconsistent with their avowed religious views.

Still, whatever its excesses and inconsistencies, the role of religion in supporting traditional family units by limiting out-of-wedlock parenthood and divorce is undeniable. Part of religion's influence arises directly out of the set of values that it promotes. For the most part, religious groups with strong beliefs foster the importance of and the commitment to one's family even in the face of difficult circumstances. They have also, generally, promoted beliefs about sex belonging exclusively within marriage. To the extent that people became indoctrinated and committed to these and other beliefs, they usually worked to sustain traditional families.

Religion not only provides a set of values that people hold to with varying degrees of intensity but it constrains behavior by raising the stakes of certain actions—raising the social stigma of out-of-wedlock birth or divorce among neighbors, peers, and friends. As the social stigmas imposed both by religious and purely secular sources have diminished, part of the cost of engaging in acts that lead to family breakups has been reduced.

Crime, Delinquency, and Affluence

A person hardly needs to dig any deeper than the family troubles discussed above to understand the source of many of the problems like crime, delinquency, disaffection, and lack of motivation for educational attainment that threaten American society. Several studies that look at parental makeup of households and take into account other factors confirm the obvious: Family breakdowns contribute to higher rates of drug use, larceny, arrests, truancy, discipline problems in school, violent and aggressive behavior, sexual activity, and other problematic outcomes. One set of authors put it plainly: "The major reason for the increased deviance in youths in mother-only households is the absence of the second adult."[21] William Comaner and Llad Phillips found that the most important factor for predicting male teenage delinquency between the ages of fourteen and twenty-two is the absence of the biological father in the house.[22] Naturally, those who might hold an interest in protecting a particular agenda might dispute the importance of traditional families. We could hardly imagine that most citizens arrogantly think—if really pressed on the subject—that child rearing within traditional, two-parent family relationships can be so flagrantly tossed aside without disastrous consequences.

A few social commentators do attempt to reject the notion of an increase in crime. Certainly, politicians try to put the best spin on the latest year's crime statistics, especially if they show a hint of improvement. And it is true that if we focus on crime rates over the very recent past, the uptick in crime may not be readily apparent. The rate of offenses bobs around from year to year, prompting great pronouncements concerning the drop in crime, when, in reality, the drop may be trivial and due to little more than reporting errors.[23]

A quick look at violent crime rates since 1960 illustrates just how much crime has skyrocketed. Figure 6.4 depicts the sad state of affairs. In 1996, the last year for which nationwide figures are available, the violent crime rate, which includes murder, rape, robbery, and aggravated assault, was a little above 630 offenses per 100,000 people in the United States. It is true that this is down from the peak of 758 per

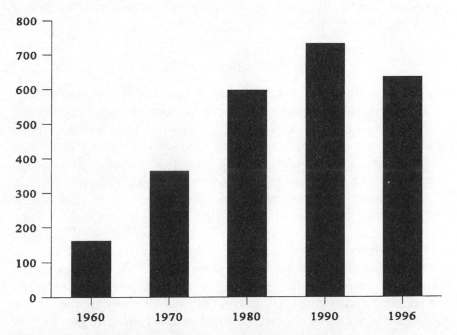

FIGURE 6.4   Crime Rates per 100,000 People, 1960–1996

SOURCE: U.S. Bureau of the Census, *Statistical Abstract of the U.S.* (Washington, D.C.: USGPO), various volumes.

100,000 in 1990, but it is nearly double the 1970 rate and more than triple the 1960 rate. Subsets of the U.S. population live in environments barely short of anarchy. People unfortunate enough to be residents of crime-infested housing projects and urban ghettos sometimes live in conditions where one murder per day occurs in their immediate neighborhood. Although black Americans make up just over 10 percent of the U.S. population, they fall victim to over 50 percent of murders committed.[24]

As Table 6.2 shows, crime by teenagers is a major source of the growth in overall crime rates. For each of the groups from thirteen to twenty years old listed in the table, murder and non-negligent manslaughter rates have more than doubled since 1970. When looking at these and many other statistics, we find it incredible that anyone would question whether crime is an increasing problem in our society. Even allowing a healthy margin of error in these figures due to the difficulties of obtaining accurate victimization rates, the long-term trend in crime is disturbing. Princeton professor and Brookings Institution associate John DiIulio views the current confluence of rising teenage population and deviancy as a time bomb of "superpredators."[25]

We could easily describe crime in the 1990s—whether general or juvenile—to the point of numbing readers' minds. We could include many detailed summaries of crimes by prior offenders, of violence by parolees, of violent crime perpetrated by and against preteen children, of the utter brutality of many criminal acts. However, most Americans have a strong sense of these problems from television reports, incidents in their own communities, problems in their own neighborhoods, and even personal experiences.

TABLE 6.2   Murder and Non-Negligent Manslaughter by Juveniles and Young Adults, 1970–1993 (per 1,000 population)

Age	1970	1980	1990	1993	Rate of Increase 1970–1993
13–14	4.2	5.4	8.8	10.5	6.3
15	17.2	13.5	31.0	36.2	19.0
16	26.8	24.6	56.5	66.4	39.6
17	32.9	38.2	72.4	84.8	51.9
18–20	44.5	46.4	73.5	91.3	46.8

SOURCE: U.S. Department of Justice, *Sourcebook of Criminal Justice Statistics* (Washington, D.C.: USGPO), various volumes.

In spite of the shocking trends evidenced by the crime data, they understate the problem in that Americans have altered their behavior in efforts to avoid being victimized. Some avoid going out at night; others avoid certain streets or parks; some invest in bars, locks, and electronic security equipment; and others purchase private security personnel. As Senator Daniel Moynihan points out in his essay "Defining Deviancy Down," a complete picture of how bad crime is in America must take into account the adjustments that help to keep the crime rates lower than they would otherwise be.[26] John DiIulio points out that there are two parts to the crime rate—the "crime numerator," or possible criminals, and the "crime denominator," or possible victims. He notes that the "crime denominator" is definitely falling because of movement to suburbs and private security measures. All else being equal, this effect causes crime rates to fall as the number of potential victims decreases. However, as he observes, important contributors to the "crime numerator," such as the number of youths, will rise dramatically in the near future, with real and tragic results.[27]

Without a doubt, Americans are not nearly as safe on their own streets and in their own homes as they were even twenty-five years ago. Even if the stagnation supporters were correct about living standards and income inequality, these numbers would be hard to fathom, but in light of an accurate picture of trends in affluence over the same time frame, the amount of criminal deviancy becomes surreal. The United States is the mightiest economic power in history, its citizens enjoy wealth beyond the dreams of even most citizens of one or two generations past, and yet the streets of some Third World countries are safer than many city streets in America. Why does the most affluent country in the world still experience significant levels of violent crime? Why are many American cities nearly uninhabitable for law-abiding citizens?

Affluence and Crime in General

Much like problems within families, the first inclination when considering crime and affluence is to suspect that higher living standards lower criminal activity by diminishing the economic pressures that sometimes lead to crime. As in the case of family breakdowns, the trends in criminal activities across families at a given point in time must be separated from the trends in criminal activities over time for society at large or any given socioeconomic subset. There is little doubt that individuals growing up in poorer economic conditions are more likely to commit serious crimes than their more affluent counterparts. Still, one must ask why crime rates within a socioeconomic group or across all groups would grow over time, especially when living standards are improving substantially.

In other words, a low level of material well-being may put some people in more desperate or frustrating circumstances than others and make them more likely to engage in crime, but this is only one aspect of affluence's impact on crime. If it were the only influence, then we should observe lower crime rates as material well-being improves—as it has in the United States. Since crime rates have vaulted in the opposite direction over the past quarter century, some other factors may be exerting important effects on them, and perhaps the links between affluence and crime are more complicated than simple cross-sectional evidence might indicate.

Several specific avenues for the effects of affluence on crime can be identified. These affluence-based effects include: (1) the effect on families, (2) the effects of allowing people to afford to obfuscate criminal justice, (3) the effects on people's taste for punishment, and (4) the effects on incentives to pursue enforcement.

Family Breakdowns and Crime

The role of affluence in leading to family breakdown and thereby to more crime is possibly the biggest contributor to crime, especially among young people. Seemingly, the contribution of family breakdowns to crime to which we alluded at the outset of this section is not controversial. A 1991 survey of state prison inmates concluded that 43 percent of all inmates grew up in single-parent homes and another 14 percent grew up either with a relative or in foster care. In total, 57 percent of these inmates grew up outside of traditional, two-parent environments, in comparison to 27 percent for the population as a whole. Fifty-three percent of African-American inmates grew up in single-parent households.[28] Study after study shows links between family breakup and severe family problems and juvenile delinquency and adult criminality.

Much more than poverty, racial prejudice, or any other factor, it is the stable home that determines whether increased crime will follow.[29] Besides supplying love and affection, good mothers and fathers also provide examples for their children regarding work and morality. Also, through whatever means they may choose, parents are important in restraining the undesirable behavior of their children. Where one parent is left with all of these jobs, difficulties frequently arise. In homes without fathers, adolescent boys may often be left without the role model they need or the masculine authority figure necessary to restrain them. Charles Murray says of this situation, "The culture must be *Lord of the Flies* writ large, the values of unsocialized male adolescents made norms—physical violence, immediate gratification, and predatory sex."[30]

Affluence and Due Process

Increases in living standards bring about a transformation in people's thinking about criminal justice. The framers of the U.S. Constitution were sensitive to issues of appropriate means of law enforcement and acceptable methods of punishment, including guarantees of due process and prohibitions on "cruel and unusual" punishment in their document. The provisions for due process—courts, juries, rules of obtaining and presenting evidence—were included to pursue an obvious goal, the protection of innocent people from arbitrary and rushed judgments. The restrictions on methods of punishment are more of an end in themselves, apparently owing their existence to the preferences and sensibilities to the late eighteenth century. In 1789, the due process provisions were attempts to limit the ability of any particular public official or other person to act as prosecutor, judge, and jury and to limit the ability of an enraged crowd to pull a person out of jail and exact punishment on the spot. Additionally, the framers wanted to limit the ability of enforcement officials to keep people under guard for no reason. Under the British, colonists had witnessed the excessive power of British military commanders and governors in regard to these very points.

The rise in the affluence of average citizens in the United States has markedly increased the ability of accused individuals to use the due process provisions of the Constitution in ways that the framers of that document could hardly have imagined In writing the *Federalist Papers*, Madison, Hamilton, and Jay certainly did not contemplate the ability of accused individuals to obfuscate the facts and justice by using the due process provisions. They did not foresee turning out murderers and assailants because of violations of technical and rigid rules of evidence. Instead, they tried to hammer out a system that guaranteed little more than ensuring trials before juries and making sure that those juries were made aware of questions concerning the gathering of evidence. They did not foresee trials lasting months because of hundreds of motions related to due process or to execution of judgment being delayed for years because of appeals.

Yet obfuscation and delay are just where affluence has brought the criminal justice system. Whether paying for the highest-priced defense attorney or relying on a low-paid public defender, defendants in cases today can pursue a strategy of veiling and obstructing the trial process through the due process provisions. For example, in the few cases where states have imposed the death penalty since the mid-1970s, the average amount of time that elapses after sentencing—not after commission of the crime itself—and before execution is almost nine years. The benefits to the criminal of using this process are large, whereas the costs to (affluent) taxpayers, though large in total, are small enough to individual taxpayers so as to elicit no significant backlash. In the case of public defenders of poor clients, the impact of rising living standards may not be nearly as obvious as in the case of a celebrity able to spend millions on a defense team. However, even though public defenders may not make a lot of money, they face little or no personal cost in delaying cases. The costs associated with delays are borne by the taxpayers. And although the defendant may certainly desire freedom sooner rather than later, months of delay in obfuscating the process or in appealing decisions may be a small price to pay if the defendant is truly guilty and the evidence is very damaging.

Whatever the cause of spreading cases over longer periods of time, there is little doubt that doing so is a costly exercise available only to wealthy societies. During earlier periods in U.S. history, neither defendants nor the public purse could afford the sprawling applications of due process available today—applications in which it is no longer clear whether due process is a means to an end or an end in itself. Even though the focus here is on the criminal justice system, the same kind of effect can be seen in the civil court system. The explosion of civil litigation that has taken place in the United States can only be available to a very wealthy society—if for no other reason than that such a society can afford the time and money chewed up by litigants and their lawyers. Any society in which people must scratch and paw for survival or live a modest existence hardly allows them time to litigate endless disputes, much less the financial wherewithal to fund the litigation. Whatever disputes arise in these societies must be settled in a much less costly, more time-efficient manner.

With respect to affluence's ultimate effects upon crime, the endless pursuit of due process has reduced the effectiveness of the criminal justice system in bringing perpetrators to justice, as compared with the situation in the eighteenth, nineteenth, and early twentieth centuries. As a result, crime has increased. Some may argue that the fleshing out of due process has also reduced the number of innocent people falsely convicted. To be sure, this effect goes hand in hand with reducing the effectiveness of catching criminals. However, at some point, diminishing returns for increased due process must set in. The benefits in terms of fewer wrong convictions gained by the earliest extensions of due process may have been substantial. But now, how much more is gained by the umpteenth extension of due process?[31]

Affluence and Punishment Preferences

On top of the crime-increasing effects of affluence through the operation of the criminal justice system, rising living standards have also altered sensibilities about appropriate punishment. For whatever psychological reasons, wealthier societies lean in the direction of an increasing aversion to punishment. Although the framers of the Constitution were concerned with "cruel and unusual" punishment, the meaning of this phrase in the colonial and early republic days differed widely from today's meaning. For example, as late as 1783, three men were executed for robbery in Pennsylvania. Even when Pennsylvania's code was revised in 1786, capital crimes included not only murder and treason but also rape and arson.[32]

Within the twentieth century, the history of federal prison policies on Alcatraz Island is a case in point about changing attitudes toward punishment. When built in the 1930s, the prison represented a "get-tough" attitude toward crime, especially violent crimes committed by people seemingly incapable of rehabilitation. Alcatraz made no pretense of rehabilitation—it practiced punishment for the sake of punishment. Prisoners received very limited privileges in terms of time spent outside their cells. By the early 1960s and following a possible successful escape attempt from Alcatraz, public opinion toward facilities like Alcatraz had swung in the opposite direction. "Tough" prisons like Alcatraz had fallen out of favor, and in 1962, the prison was permanently closed. The Alcatraz example, though, extends beyond

1962. In the decades since, several movies have been made about the supposed successful escape attempt. The interesting point about these movies is that the prisoners involved in the escape are treated, more or less, as heroes, not for their criminal past or renewed spirits but because their escape helped shut down Alcatraz.

The anti-Alcatraz sentiment illustrates much of the public discussion and attitude about punishment of criminals from the mid-1960s onward. Many writers, commentators, and politicians began to actively sympathize with even criminals who had committed very violent acts. According to this viewpoint, whether the cause of criminality is poverty, race, urbanization, alienation, or whatever else, law-abiding citizens should bear at least partial responsibility for the acts of criminals.

Punishment as a deterrent to criminal behavior and certainly as the just deserts for criminal acts fell out of favor. Many social analysts and policymakers turned their efforts toward rectifying poverty, race relations, and so on as the remedy for crime rather than supporting punishment as the remedy. Executions diminished, falling from more than 1,600 in the 1930s to just over 700 in the 1950s and fewer than 200 from 1960 to 1967, when executions were halted until 1977 because of court challenges. As a result, this most severe of penalties ceased for a time to be a means of punishment, and even when revived, it hardly took on the role of a likely and swift punishment for even the most premeditated murderers whose cases showed the most clear-cut facts about guilt. In response, movements arose in the 1980s and 1990s to stiffen punishment standards by mandating sentence length, imposing stronger penalties for repeat offenders, and other measures.[33]

In spite of the moves toward toughening penalties for violent acts, committing these crimes hardly brings swift and sure punishment. In a study for the National Center for Policy Analysis, Morgan Reynolds calculated the probability of actually spending time in prison for the commission of various acts in 1993.[34] The probability of serving prison time for committing murder or non-negligent manslaughter was only 33 percent; for rape, 16 percent; for assault, 4 percent; and for burglary, about 3 percent.

In an even more enlightening finding concerning punishment trends over the past forty years, Reynolds used the probabilities of being caught, prosecuted, and convicted along with the median prison sentence applied if convicted to compute a measure of the "expected prison time" for committing various crimes since the 1950s.[35] "Expected prison time" is a much more accurate measure of the behavior-influencing aspects of punishment than average sentence length because it takes account of both the likelihood of going to prison and sentence length. The results appear in Table 6.3. Expected prison time for murder/non-negligent manslaughter from the 1960s through the 1980s fell by over one-half its 1950 level. By 1992, the "get-tough" measures of the 1980s and 1990s had raised the expected prison time to near its 1950 figure. Expected prison time for other categories of serious crime—rape, robbery, aggravated assault, and burglary—also show dramatic reductions over the 1960s, 1970s, and 1980s, falling to between 15 and 30 percent of their 1950 levels. With the exception of rape, which is back to about 70 percent of its 1950 level, penalties for these crimes showed little "toughening" by 1992.

Ironically, the renewed use of the death penalty following its 1960s–1970s hiatus also illustrates the difficulties of stiffening penalties for serious crime. As of 1998, thirty-eight states had enacted death penalty provisions. However, most of these states permit death judgments only under "special circumstances." Under these special circumstances, imposing the death penalty requires more than the commission of first-degree murder; instead, circumstances such as multiple murders, killing of law enforcement officers, little likelihood of rehabilitation, and the like must be present. In effect, cold-blooded murder is not sufficient cause for enacting the death penalty, unless the victim wipes out a preschool, commits a string of grisly murders, kills a police officer, or adds some other especially heinous feature to the crime.[36]

TABLE 6.3   Expected Prison Times, 1950–1992

	1950	1960	1970	1980	1992
Murder/non-negligent manslaughter (years)	2.3	1.7	1.1	1.2	2.1
Rape (days)	136	154	67	42	93
Robbery (days)	140	93	30	34	36
Aggravated assault (days)	25	19	8	7	11
Burglary (days)	25	14	3	4	6

NOTE: Expected prison times are computed based on likelihood of prison time for an offense, along with the average time spent in prison.

SOURCE: Morgan Reynolds, "Crime and Punishment in America," National Center for Policy Analysis, Policy Report No. 193 (June 1995), Table 4. Reprinted by permission.

The facts concerning the use of the death penalty in the United States bear out our point. From 1977 to 1996, about 400,000 reported homicides took place. Over the same period, only about 5,500 convicted murderers were executed—only one execution for about every 1,000 people murdered.[37] In the cases where execution was the end result, efforts of the accused, the accused's attorneys, and opponents of the death penalty are usually successful in delaying executions for a decade or more after the final judgment is offered. As noted earlier, the average time between sentencing and execution was about nine years. Using the figures for the likelihood of execution and the time until execution, we computed the average reduction in life expectancy due to the death penalty across all murderers over 1977 to 1996 to be between ten and fifteen days.[38] These data reinforce the idea that aside from a few individuals unlucky enough to have their death-penalty number come up, the whole debate about the death penalty is really more about symbolism than deterrence.

Even for punishment below the severity of the death penalty, criminal justice in the United States is incredibly lenient compared to bygone eras. For example, although roughly 600,000 murders were committed from 1965 to 1997, only about 100,000 people were in prison for murder in the mid-1990s. More than ten times the number of murderers have been paroled than executed since 1965. The average time spent in prison for murder was about the same in 1960 as in 1992.[39]

Similar moves for stiffer punishment standards for repeat offenders also help illustrate the distaste for punishment in America. California adopted the "three-strikes-and-you're-out" rule in a 1984 ballot initiative. This law attempted to mandate longer sentences for habitual, serious offenders by making a third-felony offense automatically punishable by twenty-five years to life in prison regardless of the exact nature of the felony. By the 1990s, the law was under heavy attack from opponents who saw it as too harsh, as it could mean sending a person away for a long time when the third offense might be "merely" stealing a TV.

Affluence and Enforcement Incentives

Affluence also diminishes the incentive to pursue enforcement against some kinds of criminal activity. As a society becomes wealthier, citizens and their enforcement agencies become more tolerant of crimes that impose increasingly smaller dollar costs as a percentage of total income and wealth. For example, theft involving less than $100 might be designated as a misdemeanor offense in most states, prompting police to devote few resources to track down evidence and suspects. Unless the criminal is caught right in the act, the crime may never be addressed by the criminal justice system. Even if it is, the penalties for an act deemed so trivial are usually very minor.

In contrast, if families are struggling to make ends meet, the theft of the equivalent of $90 is no trivial matter. In a society living very near subsistence, the amount of monetary harm necessary to bring strict punishment is likely to be much lower. As a result, countries like the United States may experience more criminal activity simply because the citizens can afford more of it.

Over decades of tolerating increasing amounts of "trivial" crimes, society will begin to pay a higher price in terms of crimes becoming more serious. The tendency for petty offenders to later turn into more serious and sometimes violent offenders is well established.[40] Unpunished "small" crime usually leads to more "small" crime and eventually to "big" crime because the perpetrator observes that it goes unpunished. By overlooking greater amounts of misdemeanor-level actions because of affluence, American society has helped to build the skills of many in criminal activity—which can be termed creating criminal human capital.[41]

Whatever one may think about appropriate means of punishment, more stringent punishment swiftly applied is an undeniable force in reducing criminal activity. To think otherwise is to deny one of the most basic facts about human behavior: People respond to important incentives and to significant changes in incentives. To borrow an example from University of California–Los Angeles economist Armen Alchain, if Congress mandated that all cars be equipped with a large hunting knife strapped to the steering wheel, with its tip pointed at the driver's chest, no one would contend that driving habits would go unchanged. Reductions in the certainty and swiftness of punishment because of the criminal justice system, coupled with reductions in the severity of punishment, are as certain a recipe for more violent crime.

Affluence and Anxiety

To this point, the fact that families are so anxious, not just about crime or divorce or other social ills but about economic well-being, has been ignored. For those promoting and profiting from the stagnation message, the anxiety statistics themselves, as cited in Chapter 2, are evidence enough of the flattening and decline of living standards in the United States as well as proof of the bleak prospects on the horizon.

This widespread economic anxiety cannot generally be attributed to bad economic conditions. Whatever the trends in living standards have been in the United States over the past few years, one point can hardly be disputed: Average Americans enjoy living standards far above the standards for average citizens of most of the world's nations. In the simplest of terms, Americans enjoy more protection from cold, heat, wind, and rain; they enjoy a complete absence of the threat of starvation to the point of being able to concern themselves with pleasing their palates more than filling their stomachs; they have access to by far the best medical care in the world; they select from a virtual cafeteria of recreational pursuits. And still, when asked about current and future economic conditions, they are anxious. Once one is reminded of these worldwide comparisons of living standards and adds to them the recognition of the more detailed trends in U.S. affluence over the past quarter century emphasized here, the cause for American anxiety must come from something besides current problems associated with material well-being. What are these alternative causes? We do not pretend to be psychologists, but we do think that explanations in harmony with our general theme about the effects of rising affluence are plausible. Rising affluence is not the only answer, but it does point out a *neglected cause* of social decay and anxiety.

In part, the fact that anxieties about material well-being do not decline even as affluence increases fall into step with the never-ending desire to improve one's lot no matter how good that lot may be right now. One of the most basic premises of economics is that the desires of people are unlimited with regard to consumption of goods and services as a whole over time. A primitive villager desires a hut that is a little more comfortable than the current one. The family in a comfortable three-bedroom home imagines the same home or a different one with a little more room, a swimming pool, a game room, a home theater, and improved decor. The estate owner yearns for more luxurious appointments, a second home by the sea, a summer house in the mountains. The nineteenth-century Native American who is a single-horse owner thinks of having two horses or a better-bred one; the Acura owner dreams of the Lexus.

   This is the way of the world. A few people through great personal effort may acquire the ability to be completely at peace with their current situation with little desire for change or improvement, but most people never attain this kind of inner contentment with their material possessions. Most people are continually observing or imagining new products and services that would provide more personal pleasure and satisfaction.

   This may help to explain why stress levels about living standards have not dropped, but why would they increase? Increasing affluence may only serve to fuel the fires of desire for "more" by making "more" not only seem attainable but by getting people in the habit of feeding the material addiction. The answer may lie in how people build skills in consuming thing—consumption capital, in economic parlance. As we mentioned in Chapter 1, Nobel Prize–winning economists Gary Becker and George Stigler explained how skills in consumption can play a role in developing and altering what may appear to be merely matters of taste.[42] The extension of their insight here is that people may not just build skills in consuming some particular items but may also build skills in consuming in general.

   Primitive villagers living in a grass hut and eating berries may have the same basic desire for improvement as does a modern family of four with a thirty-two-inch TV and two cars. Villagers living in a time when the consumption ability of the average family for their society did not change over a whole lifetime may have become resigned to their material lot and may not have let the desire for more become an all-consuming fire. Modern family members, in contrast, observing and experiencing nearly continual improvement in their consumption ability may build up their skill in consuming more so that, like an addict, they may not only need another fix but may need a more powerful fix.

   Seen in this light, the difference between the villagers and the modern family members is not one of basic psychological makeup, nor is it based on different underlying cultural values. Instead, it is more a matter of habit and practice. The lower levels of stress over economic matters that the villagers experience may have little to do with fundamental psychological differences between them and modern people or with a life lived closer to nature or other such anthropological explanations; rather, the difference in stress levels may largely be due to modern people living with growing affluence and becoming practiced in feeding their desires. If one were to expose these villagers to modern society for a lengthy period, it would not be surprising to see stress levels about material gains grow, if not in their own generation, then very likely in the next.

Beyond "addicting" people to consumption, growing affluence may have contributed to stress that individuals attribute to economic anxieties, but stress that may arise partly out of noneconomic matters. Certainly, deterioration of families through unwed pregnancies, higher juvenile delinquency, higher crime rates, and the like are all serious matters that can lead to unhappiness and anxiety. Through contributing to increases in these other kinds of family problems, growing affluence may have in fact contributed to anxiety levels. However, this contribution is due to the indirect influence on social ills rather than being a result of the alleged flattening of living standards.

Finally, rising affluence may have contributed to rising anxiety because anxieties themselves are something that greater wealth allows us to indulge to a greater extent. We do not propose that serious mental illness is related to affluence. Instead, we propose that people in a society with tremendous material abundance can dwell much more extensively on their fears, disappointments, and problems than can the citizens of a very poor society.

We can illustrate the importance of affluence to indulging anxieties by using a polar extreme: The residents of Third World nations do not have the resources to spend time on a therapist's couch discussing their frustrations and trying to find their true inner being. In contrast, America is the land of counseling. From 1983 to 1996, the number of employed psychologists grew by 81 percent in the United States, as compared with overall occupational growth of 26 percent.[43] Mark Smith, a member of an alternative rock band named The Fall, put it aptly: "Having a problem is like a professional career these days. It's become really hip. People actually don't like it if you haven't got a problem."[44] In an environment in which psychotherapy and counseling are major growth industries and cater to the variety of anxieties of Americans, it is hardly surprising to find anxiety concerning the economy as part of the mix.

SEVEN

AFFLUENCE AND POLITICS

*Civilization, in fact, grows more and more maudlin and hysterical;
especially under democracy it tends to degenerate into a mere com-
bat of crazes; the whole aim of practical politics is to keep the popu-
lace alarmed (and hence clamorous to be led to safety) by an endless
series of hobgoblins, most of them imaginary.*

—H. L. Mencken, *In Defense of Women*

In his widely cited 1958 book, *The Affluent Society*, John Kenneth
Galbraith explored American living standards and their seeming effects. He eloquently expressed how, for most Americans, concerns
about life's most essential goods and services no longer dominated
consumption decisions as they had done for most of the world's population up to that time; rather, by the late 1950s, most household decisions boiled down to choices between one luxury item or another.
Of course, Americans did not always see their own decisions as
choices between luxurious alternatives; nonetheless, on worldwide
and historical scales they were living in the lap of luxury.

Based on his observations about typical living standards in the
United States, Galbraith concluded that Americans had grown too
prosperous to worry about soaking the rich and enlarging the public
sector for purposes of income redistribution. In his own words, "The
arithmetic of modern politics makes it tempting to overlook the very
poor"; "the concern for inequality had vitality only so long as the

many suffered privation while a few had much. It did not survive as a burning issue in a time when the many had much even though others had much more."[1]

Although Galbraith's analysis of living standards hit the mark, his observations about the public sector involvement in the politics of poverty could not have been more off base. Less than a decade after his dismal outlook about care and concern for the poor in society, the Great Society program of President Lyndon Johnson and its budget-bulging expenditures blew the top off government spending. A multitude of programs and government bureaucrats marched in, with the explicit intent of helping the economically disadvantaged. Beyond just poverty, though, the Great Society initiated an explosion of public-sector involvement by all levels of government in all kinds of pursuits. Just like poverty expenditures, much of the growth in government spending reflects not just more spending on the same old programs but the invention and growth of entirely new public-sector ventures.

Galbraith correctly identified a critical link between affluence and politics—he just misunderstood the direction of the effect. In contradiction to his predictions, greater affluence has actually led to an increase in programs such as those directed toward the poor rather than a diminishing of those programs. The link between large gains in material well-being in democratic societies and accompanying jumps in the size of the public sector is sometimes referred to as "Wagner's Law" by economists.[2] Every major democracy has experienced a sizable enhancement of the public sector over its midcentury level, while at the same time living standards have improved substantially. The purported relationship between growing personal incomes and the relative size of the public sector has been challenged. However, most of these challenges are based on studies that use state and local rather than national data. Additionally, this literature usually does not take into account regulatory growth.[3]

To be sure, many other factors contribute to public-sector growth. Economic and social crises such as the Great Depression and World War II are among the leading contributors to spurts in government growth.[4] Often, very poor countries become susceptible to massive gains in government power especially when they become subjected to dictatorial regimes. Still, growth of private-sector income in democracies has fostered the tendency for the public sector to bite growing chunks out of the private sector.

Public-sector growth in the United States illustrates this tendency as well as in any country. Figure 7.1 depicts the growth of average tax burdens on U.S. families—government revenue as a percent of national income—for all levels of government from 1950 to 1996. Up to the early 1960s, the federal government accounted for most of the growth of these tax shares. After the early 1960s, state and local governments accounted for most of the growth, although some of this spending is from federal government mandates for medical care, pollution control, and so forth. Americans now funnel more than one-third of their income through the public sector, in contrast to less than one-fourth in 1950.

Although the share of income paid out in taxes is a mild illustration of the public sector growing along with affluence, much of the growth in tax burdens occurred between 1950 and 1970—before the improvements in living standards that have been our main focus. Further, in terms of taxes and spending, the U.S. public sector still lags behind those of many other highly industrialized nations. This might

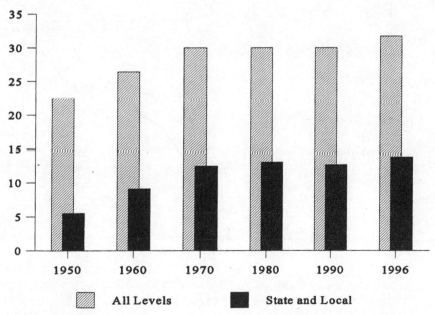

FIGURE 7.1   Average Tax Burden on Households, 1950–1996 (in percent)

NOTE: Figures are computed by dividing tax revenues by GDP.
SOURCE: *Economic Report of the President, 1997* (Washington, D.C.: USGPO, 1997).

create suspicion about the public sector–private sector link we are asserting, especially for the post-1970 time period.

However, an analysis of government growth based only on taxation and spending vastly underestimates the magnitude of the U.S. public sector and its affluence-inspired growth, because it omits the area of U.S. public-sector growth that has made the largest leap since 1970—regulation of the economy. Figure 7.2 displays a composite index of the total amount of federal regulation. The index is based on several measures that indicate growth in regulation: number of pages in the *Federal Register*, Environmental Protection Agency (EPA) employment, U.S. Department of Agriculture employment as a ratio of private-sector agricultural employment, the ratio of lawyers to the population, the ratio of civil cases to criminal cases in federal courts, and noneducation state employment per capita. According to this index, the amount of regulation took off right around 1970 and has rocketed upward ever since, with only a minor abatement of this trend occurring during the early Reagan years.

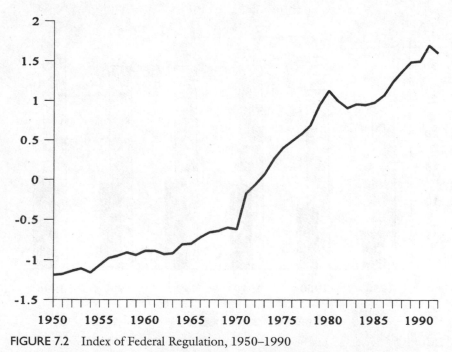

FIGURE 7.2   Index of Federal Regulation, 1950–1990

SOURCE: Brian Goff, *Regulation and Macroeconomic Performance* (Boston: Kluwer Academic Publishers, 1996), p. 99. Reprinted by permission.

Beyond this composite index, one need only have a passing knowledge of the *Code of Federal Regulations (CFR)* to gain a sense that this is the area of massive government growth. The *CFR* is the storehouse of government rules and now bulges to around 150,000 pages. This does not count the thousands of regulatory pages contained in the state equivalents of the *CFR*. Of course, we do not assume that government regulation is always bad; the benefits must be weighed against the costs. Yet, the massive extensions of regulation's reach in the United States now means the costs are often much greater than the benefits. As evidence, Washington University economist Murray Weidenbaum estimates that private-sector spending to comply with federal regulation is nearly $700 billion per year.[5] Thomas Hopkins of the University of Rochester has estimated that it will pass $700 billion by the year 2000.[6] By another estimate, the ten-year net reduction in income from federal regulation now amounts to nearly $1 trillion.[7] Public-sector activity can grow by taking more private-sector income, by nationalizing more private-sector assets, or by controlling more private-sector decisions. The data cited above emphasize how much this third avenue of public-sector growth has exploded since 1970.

Time and Money on Our Hands

Why is there a relationship between government spending and affluence? At the broadest level, a slight amendment of a statement made by philosopher Joseph de Maistre would seem to fit. He said, "Every nation has the government it deserves."[8] In our version, this would read: "Every nation, at least among democracies, may well have the government it deserves, but it also has the government it can afford."

Still, this broad explanation does not pin down the precise linkage between private-sector and public-sector growth. Why do citizens elect politicians who build and uphold a public sector that continues to gobble up a greater share of the economic pie as these citizens grow wealthier? The answer to the question cannot rest solely on the fact that people have more money with which to help other people. Although wealthier people obviously have more money at their disposal to help others, this answer begs the public-sector part of the question. Why would wealthier people, if only concerned about redistributing part of their income, choose to do so through public-sector mechanisms, especially with all of the waste and political chicanery involved?

The answers we provide below view political markets as sharing similarities with typical economic markets.[9] The same "supply and demand" framework that is useful for analyzing economic markets in general can conveniently be applied to condense and organize thinking about the effects of wealth in political markets. On the demand side of political markets, growing affluence stimulates changes in voter preferences or at least in the expression of those preferences as well as changes in the information set held by voters, resulting in changes in the mix of voter interest in issues on broad versus narrow issues. On the "supply side" of political markets, greater material wealth alters the information supplied to voters as well as supplying funding to organizations (interest groups) within and outside of government. These wealth-based influences are developed in more detail below.

Affluence and Ideology: The Support for Dolphin-Free Tuna

The role played by rising affluence in relation to ideology is the simplest to explain of the three wealth-based influences on politics. Referring to the basic wealth effect discussed in Chapter 1, we mean that greater economic prosperity allows individuals to indulge themselves in behavior and even the contemplation and support of ideas that people in very poor societies could not afford. It may be that individuals in poorer societies hold the same concerns about such issues, but they must lie dormant until incomes rise sufficiently so that acting upon these concerns becomes affordable. The stir about dolphin-free tuna in the United States is just one example. Barring some kind of religious prohibition, one could hardly imagine a Peruvian fisherman making the equivalent of US$2,000 per year concerning himself with whether a few dolphins get caught in his nets when he fishes for tuna. Whether resulting in new legislation or administrative edicts or not, the mere debate over dolphins in tuna nets says something about affluence and its effects on preferences or at least on the indulgence of preferences.

We could have titled this subsection "Why We Save Whales When Our Ancestors Ate Them." This would be yet another example of an activity that reduces potential material well-being in favor of a purely psychic benefit. The peace movement of the 1960s is another expression of the affluence–political preference nexus or, at least, the link between affluence and the expression of preferences. The generation sponsoring marches, sit-ins, underground newspapers, and the like had definite issues that sparked support, most important among them the war in Vietnam and civil rights. As we pointed out in Chapter 6, this was not the first generation of people in their teens and twenties to strongly disapprove of public policy. The Korean War was also not a popular venture. However, the youth of the 1960s were among the first to be propped up by an economy and parental households with enough financial strength to allow massive numbers of young adults to "drop out of society" and still be able to live a comfortable existence. Again, in an economy with little in the way of material success, "dropping out" of society is not a choice about whether to pursue "establishment" values but is a choice about living and dying.[10]

We should note that the link between affluence and public expenditures starts at incomes barely above subsistence. For instance, a World Bank study has shown that societies that have per capita income per year as low as $1,375 are willing to pay to reduce unsanitary conditions.[11] However, the nature of affluence-induced expenditures in countries as wealthy as the United States extends far beyond basic health and safety considerations. Additional examples are provided in the applications sections below. The point is not that pursuit of psychic benefits at the expense of material gains is necessarily a bad thing; rather, political ideology—for good or bad—is sensitive to incomes and affluence.

Affluence and Information, Part I: Apathy

Whether the people being considered are consumers in everyday markets or voters who make up the basic "consumer" units in political markets, information is a critical determinant of their behavior. In political markets, the influence of wealth upon consumer activity is relatively complex. Higher levels of affluence alter both the information supplied to voters and the information that interests them the most. Wealth leads voters to become informed about or at least aware of certain issues while becoming less informed about others. Although this sounds paradoxical, the dual effect of affluence on voter information fits into the main themes of the book.

For one thing, the impact of affluence upon voter information and participation resembles what happens within many families as they experience increases in wealth. With a boost in household incomes and wealth, parents can choose to use the greater economic rewards by increasing their leisure time with their children. However, the increased economic power also allows wealthier parents to afford to buy hours of freedom away from their children through baby-sitters, toys, cars, and other means. These hours may be spent pursuing other kinds of leisure time or producing even more wealth. If persistent enough, this kind of parental behavior generates negative consequences for child behavior, even though the parents feel better off because of their free time. In the same way, voters can afford to neglect more public-sector decisions and forgo the time they need to spend to become informed about such decisions.

Without a doubt, greater affluence has contributed to greater apathy by average voters in terms of many political outcomes and the relevant information pertaining to these outcomes. Voter participation rates, which have sunk to all-time lows, testify to the indifference of the voter to everyday political issues. As a result, the legislators elected by voters may pursue the objectives of narrow interest groups to a greater extent. If fully informed, voters might balk at the redistribution of their wealth toward these interests, but the "rational" neglect of political issues means they will never obtain this information.[12]

Whether the subject is congressional acts, federal agency rules, or state legislative or agency outcomes, Americans know very little about their own public sector. As we noted above, the *CFR* contains around 150,000 pages, but how many people have even heard of this publication or, even less likely, know its provisions? What percentage of Americans know about the recent EPA proposals for stiffening clean air restrictions, much less the potential gains and losses from these proposals? What percentage know anything about Medical Savings Accounts?

All of this ignorance and apathy is perfectly rational from the standpoint of any given individual. Not only is the impact of any given individual muted in such a large society but the relative affluence means most Americans can absorb the hit on their wallets and not blink twice. So what if a person's take-home pay is reduced by an extra $100? It may stimulate a little grumbling about Newt Gingrich, President Clinton, or Congress for a while, but turning off the thirty-five-inch television with surround sound, getting off the couch, and finding out what is really going on is hardly worth the savings.

Affluence and Information, Part II: The Jerry Springer Generation

At the same time that Americans are generally apathetic and ill-informed about public policy, they are disproportionately aware of—

though not necessarily well-informed about—other kinds of public-policy issues. These might be labeled "trendy" public-policy issues that dovetail with their leisure interests and with technological changes. The kind of leisure time enjoyed by typical American citizens since the 1950s permits personal junkets into all kinds of pursuits that were just not possible for our predecessors, who worked much longer hours. U.S. voters began to have more and more time to fill and could spend it as they wished, whether in reading, engaging in a sport or recreational activity, or taking advantage of technologically advanced entertainment media.

When leisure time became coupled with the kinds of technological breakthroughs that made television ownership nearly universal in the country and now puts hundreds of channels at the touch of a remote control device, a powerful mixture of politically charged ingredients entered the home on a regular basis. As part of this information explosion, in addition to the time to devour some of it, the "tabloid" television news shows proliferated, along with radio "talk shows." Viewer-voters can gorge themselves on a feast of problems, many of which unabashedly plead for public intervention. The personal has now become the political. Everyone can take personal problems and have them spread far and wide on television and radio. It is economic advances that have made both the higher amount of income and the leisure time possible, as well as the technological breakthroughs with their mountain of information—facts, perceptions of facts, distortions of fact, and outright fabrication of facts.

These factors woven together have developed an electorate that is not necessarily more informed about political debate in general than its predecessors but one that attaches itself to the cause of the month. The impact of technology and leisure time multiplies when facts are distorted or confused—in particular, when people misunderstand or misrepresent what is happening to living standards. For example, the perception of a decline or stagnation in living standards becomes the very basis for promoting political action or an unfortunate but isolated accident becomes the basis of an entirely new regulatory movement. In essence, this is the effect that H. L. Mencken conjures up in the epigraph at the beginning of this chapter, the magnitude of which may now even exceed his predictions.

One recent example is that of silicone breast implants. The daytime talk shows and evening newsmagazines inundated the public with the personal traumas of women who had silicone breast implants. The women interviewed related their implants to episodes of connective

tissue disease, immune system breakdown, and other physical problems, with some going so far as using razors to take out their implants
themselves. On television and radio, these people repeatedly told their
stories, dramatic evidence of the harm caused by the implants. The
problem with the stories was that medical studies had not been able to
find a link between silicone breast implants and serious physical ail-
ments.[13] Nonetheless, the popularization of these stories led to continued political pressure, ultimately ending in a ban on silicone implant use issued by the Food and Drug Administration. John Stossel, a
reporter on ABC, has become an outspoken critic of the kind of media
coverage that panders to what may be remote dangers to society but
dangers that provoke great outrage and response.[14]

Even though media outlets such as C-SPAN provide the opportunity for in-depth knowledge about political issues, these outlets appear
to be supported only by a devoted few, while the rest of Americans
watch Jerry Springer, Oprah, Sally Jesse Raphael, and Geraldo. Even
supposedly "respected" news coverage frequently dips into isolated or
distorted events magnified to give the impression of a problem. A
story where CNN reporters tagged along on a U.S. Fish and Wildlife
Service arrest is a case in point. The Fish and Wildlife Service assem-
bled a large, heavily armed force to search the ranch of a sick, seventy-
two-year-old man for suspected poisoning of eagles. The reporters
dressed like the agents and developed a story concerning the poisoning of eagles, even though no eagles were found and the man was ac-
quitted of charges of poisoning eagles in spite of two extensive
searches.[15]

The trend in news coverage pandering to special interest may not
only result from consumer preferences for this kind of information but
also from the ease with which it can be communicated. A large oil spill
with dying animals and oil-drenched rocks can be displayed in a few
seconds with full impact. However, attempting to explain complex relationships among risks, accidents, prices, and the environment can
put most economics classes to sleep, much less a family with remote
control in hand.

The impact of affluence on voter apathy and voter leisure has led to
less awareness of political debate in general and, in the process, less
participation on major political issues, while spurring greater and often superficial attachment to sensational causes. The voters of bygone
days barely had time to keep the cows milked and surely lacked the
time or the inclination to sit around and absorb a show concerned

with faulty bungee-jumping equipment; but they were very much interested in whether the public sector was draining their take-home pay and kept their lawmakers on a tight leash in this regard. Politicians who took more of it or allowed agencies to effectively control more of their resources stood to pay the price exacted at the polls by voters. These voters of past times may not have been informed about subtle policy nuances, but they could not afford the luxury of letting lawmakers play around with their money with impunity. However, voters today can afford to be much more casual about their lawmakers' tinkering with their take-home pay and are much more interested in a cause célèbre than their predecessors.

The shift in public policy resulting from the information effect is not very hard to trace. Each new cause of the month exploding into the public forum leads to congressional action, state legislative action, or federal/state agency action. The 70,000 pages in the *Federal Register* each year proposing new federal regulations illustrate the process: Have a problem? Get it on *Nightline* or *Dateline,* get a new regulation proposed in the *Federal Register*. At the same time, major debates over the direction of public policy seldom crop up. Whether good or bad, the New Deal era legislation and the civil rights and Great Society legislation of the 1960s illustrate a very different kind of public policy process than today, when there are few major debates, though nearly 200 new pages in the *Federal Register* are generated per day.[16]

Affluence and Interest-Group Politics: Funding Save the Whales

The growth in voter interest in special and fairly narrow causes has spilled over not just into government but also into organizations that attempt to influence government outcomes. Whatever the ancestors of modern Americans thought about particular issues of public debate, these people living closer to the nub hardly pocketed the kinds of income allowing them to fund all sorts of political causes. When families must scratch out a daily existence, very few dollars are left over to support broad charitable causes, let alone the narrow agendas of groups like the World Wildlife Fund, People for the Ethical Treatment of Animals, or Save the Whales.

In contrast, the robust economy over the past fifty years provided the material abundance necessary to support all kinds of political agendas. This ability to support causes has worked simultaneously with the voter-information effects just discussed to provide the fuel for relentless efforts by interest groups to extract their pound of flesh from the public sector. These interest groups and the legislators in league with them continually trade votes behind the scenes, making deals about which most Americans—even those funding a particular cause—are unaware. As a result, the froth is continually kept boiling over the public-sector pot as a result of the attention and funding Americans give to particular causes and the efforts of interest groups, which combine with the apathy and ignorance of voters about the ultimate legislative and regulatory costs of successfully pursuing a particular cause.

Curiously enough, this path, through which wealth has most directly influenced politics, has not supported spending on political campaigns. One often hears editorial writers and "public-interest" groups like Common Cause bemoan the negative effects of money on political contests and call for a massive overhaul of campaign finance laws.[17] But on closer scrutiny, it is the diminutive amount of money spent on campaign finance laws that they speak of. The combined expenditures by incumbents and challengers for all House, Senate, and presidential races in 1996 totaled around $1 billion. That is a lot of money for any individual, but is it a lot to spend on capturing control of the political helm of the most prosperous and powerful nation on earth?[18] The amount is pocket change when compared to the $2-trillion federal budget. This level of campaign spending means only $1 out of every $10,000 of the $8 trillion the economy will generate in final goods and services in a two-year congressional term will be directed toward campaigns.

Such figures may make one wonder if incumbents have rigged the spending laws so as to limit challenges to their positions, but it should not cause consternation about overspending on campaigns. In contrast, it should direct attention toward the real source of the direct influence of wealth upon politics—the efforts to influence legislation and regulation. Somewhere in the neighborhood of $300 billion is spent annually for various kinds of lobbying efforts.[19] These efforts include those attempting to push through new legislative agendas as well as money spent to avoid or reduce the negative effects of various legislative agendas.

Examples of Affluence-Driven Public Policy

Although the public sector is absolutely stuffed with spending policies, tax policies, and other kinds of regulations that are, at least in part, an outgrowth of affluence, a few of these make the links between affluence and politics discussed above transparent. All of these political agendas have developed as a result of wealth's impact on ideology, information, or interest group activities. Often, wealth's influence has combined the effects of two or all three of these pathways.

Recent Environmentalism

Few public-sector policies can illustrate the tremendous effects of affluence on political markets as clearly as environmental policy. Figure 7.3 opens a small window on the magnitude of this growth by displaying employment in the EPA. This agency did not even exist in 1970 and more or less pulled together environmentally related jobs from various parts of the bureaucracy when it started up. Its employment over the past quarter century has nearly tripled. Many of the more aggressive state environmental bureaus, such as that in California, have rivaled or even exceeded the EPA's growth. Rising wealth

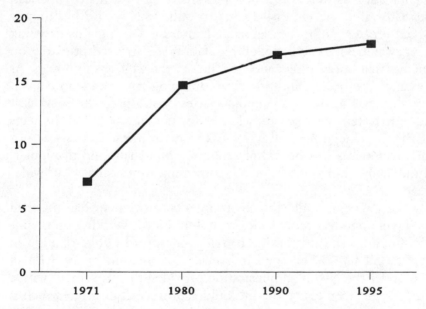

FIGURE 7.3 Environmental Protection Agency Employment, 1971–1995 (in thousands of employees)

SOURCE: U.S. Bureau of the Census, *Statistical Abstract of the U.S.* (Washington, D.C.: USGPO), various volumes.

has combined all three of the political effects discussed above—*ideology changes, information-leisure time links,* and *funding of lobbying efforts*—to produce the massive growth in environmental regulation in the United States.

Dating back to conservation movements of the nineteenth century, environmentalism in the United States attracted many advocates—occasionally very influential ones such as Theodore Roosevelt or Henry David Thoreau. These advocates pushed for maintaining a few wild areas in conditions as near as possible to their natural state. They garnered enough public and political support to designate these areas as national parks, starting with places such as Yellowstone in Wyoming and the Grand Canyon in Arizona.

Save for these kinds of attempts to preserve a few awe-inspiring locations, environmental issues failed to gain widespread attention or support until the 1960s, when obviously polluted streams and smog-shrouded cities caught the attention of many more Americans. The famous incident of Ohio's Cuyahoga River catching fire due to severe contamination as well the dirty haze hanging over many American cities illustrated the kind of threats to public safety and health that sparked greater public awareness and interest. During this dawning era of awareness, environmental regulation still focused primarily on remedies that bore a direct and clear link to the welfare of humans. As an example, restricting industry from dumping raw sewage into a waterway did not just help an animal species or subspecies to survive, it made the waterways safer and cleaner for the uses to which humans put them. Generating political movement on these issues was not nearly so much a task of skillfully juggling politicians and manipulating public opinion as it was merely informing Americans about widespread problems.

By the 1970s, though, the environmental movement had pumped itself up enough to become a major political force working on the inside of politics and not having to rally widespread public opinion in order to get its way on specific issues. The creation of the EPA in 1970 under the Nixon administration provided the movement with a distinct regulatory entity that it could capture and through which it could pursue a much broader agenda. As these political events transpired, interest in environmental policy expanded far beyond securing protection for relatively small acreage, prohibiting the dumping of raw sewage into waterways, or allowing the unabated pumping of toxins into the atmosphere. It branched out into saving spotted owls and snail darters, restoring and preserving "wetlands," prohibiting the cutting of trees over millions of acres, and insulating "ecosystems" from man's dirty hands. In short, the target of regulatory action moved away from human-centered concerns to nature- and animal-centered concerns and away from concerns with broad public support to those with only a very narrow base of support.

Legislation like the Endangered Species Act of 1973 and related regulations began to surface that promoted the welfare of various animals or habitats with only indirect or tenuous links to the welfare of humans. Saving an animal species or prohibiting the cutting of a stand of trees became ends in themselves divorced from the direct benefits that average citizens might gain because of the laws. Even further, these environmental agendas were ends to be pursued in spite of harm that they might impose on average citizens. The move to restrict landowner use of private property under the sweeping definition of "wetlands" is an example of this kind of environmentalism-against-mankind of the 1980s and 1990s. Maybe the most absurd example in recent years is the mandate to require "low-flow" toilets in residences for all new construction and replacements.

Of course, these kinds of causes attracted much lower levels of public support and even inspired very hostile responses from landowners, companies, and other individuals who felt their impact in terms of lost jobs, lost livestock, reduced revenues, and restricted choices. However, by the 1970s and 1980s, the environmental movement no longer needed broad public opinion in its favor in order to push through its ever-expanding agenda, since it was a major inside-the-game player in Washington, Sacramento, Albany, and other seats of power. Most of its activities and political deal making proceeded beyond the knowledge of average voters. Along with the growth of a federal-level environmental institution, as shown in Figure 7.3, the growth of employment related to environmental regulation has followed the same path in many state governments as well as in the private sector, especially as a result of EPA mandates.

Whatever good or bad one might see in the expanded and animal- or nature-centered environmental agenda, it splendidly illustrates the role of affluence in politics. First of all, it illustrates the effects of affluence on the ability to indulge the preferences of even a small number of citizens. Cleaning up a sewage-infected stream or limiting overfishing of an area can benefit average citizens in a society, whether they are very affluent or very poor. However, a society hovering around subsistence cannot afford many luxuries such as saving snail darters or spotted owls. About the only restrictions these societies impose are based on religious convictions, as in India, for example, with its protection of cattle. Second, it illustrates the effects of affluence on the ability of a well-organized and well-funded minority of people to push political agendas over on unknowing masses of citizens. This is the only way that regulatory actions of dubious merit such as restricting the water flow of toilets can be pushed through.

Although not all environmentally concerned ideas have a narrow base of support and result in inefficiency, there is ample evidence of many that are. For example, the proposed regulation by the EPA of benzine storage would have cost about $820 million for each life saved. An Occupational Safety and Health Administration (OSHA) regulation concerning formaldehyde was estimated to cost around $72 *billion* per life saved.[20] Naturally, disputes can arise about the precision of these estimates and the value of life and good health. Nonetheless, these figures point out that these kinds of environmental regulations have little to do with protection of humans and a lot to do with some other agenda.

Even the policies that originally attracted wide public support, such as pollution control, now illustrate the indulgence of special interest by an affluent society. The United States has spent over $1 trillion on pollution reduction since 1970. President Clinton's own administration estimates that the new ozone standards could cost as much as $80 billion. By the estimates of others, particulate matter regulations will cost society between $90 and $150 billion for full compliance.[21] Kenneth Chilton and Stephen Huebner of Washington University estimate that the Clean Air Act amendments of 1990 will force Americans to pay anywhere from $4 to $28 for each $1 in benefit received from pollution control.[22] These kinds of expenditures and trade-offs are not paying for skimming oil off American rivers or stopping the flow of raw sewage into an estuary; rather, they are more akin to searching the Atlantic to pick up a half-dozen floating bottles—the kind of environmentalism only a very affluent society can afford.

Just how far our society's wealth has allowed the indulgence of environmental preferences of a few to be taken can be seen in policies directed toward species that present significant dangers to humans or to their property. Can anyone imagine our ancestors attempting to repopulate large carnivores like the gray wolf or bemoaning the decline of the rattlesnake population? The idea that these creatures possess an inalienable right to an indigenous habitat upon which human landowners may not encroach was not dreamed up by a family eating a few beans and stale bread. Rather, professors, lawyers, and their associates decided these matters while dining in upscale restaurants or plugging away on their Pentium computers with seventeen-inch color monitors, full duplex microphones, and 24X CD-ROMs.

Possibly, the expense to which we will go to try to save not just a species but a single animal most vividly illustrates the effects of wealth. If a whale washed up on shore, could we imagine our distant ancestors spending thousands of dollars and hundreds of labor hours attempting to rescue it? It is more likely they would have viewed the animal's misfortune as good fortune and would have used the animal to their own benefit. The earlier movements to protect nature or to benefit humans were of a very different stripe than some of the more radical efforts today. The push for protection of national treasures like Yellowstone or the Grand Canyon resulted from a desire to preserve these areas for viewing by later generations of humans rather than from the desire to maintain the survival of a particular species or habitat for its own sake. In fact, in pushing to make the Grand Canyon a national park, Theodore Roosevelt explicitly identified the importance of saving the natural wonder so that it could be viewed by later generations.

In the name of wetlands preservation, today's environmental radicalism has been successful in extending the same kinds of restriction on a landowner's utilization of soggy pastureland as earlier movements extended to national landmarks like Yellowstone Park. Today, even though about one-third of the entire United States and about 50 percent of the land in the Western states is publicly owned, with more under special public protection,[23] challenges to the wisdom of the keep-it-all-public mentality meet with sneers: Privatizing even small sections is vilified as the equivalent of erecting an outlet mall on top of Old Faithful or building a water slide down the Grand Canyon. Clearly, such policy stances do not emanate from widespread public opinion about the best use of natural resources. Rather, they emanate from the affluence-altered preferences of the staunchest environmentalists.[24]

Again, the focus of the earlier, poorer America centered on facilitating and preserving a few highly valued natural sites and habitats for the recreational and educational purposes of humans. Our contemporary affluent society can afford to adopt provisions that not only extend protection to millions of acres of much less treasured sites but actually infringes on modest uses of private land by lawful human owners. The complete inversion of nineteenth-century standards based on our current affluence is obvious when advocates of restrictions on government takings and protection for private property owners are viewed as a kind of reactionary fringe, not just by environmentalists but also by supposedly dispassionate reporters, or when the practice of actually purchasing land to protect the environment as the Nature Conservancy does is viewed as just a minor sideshow in the environmental battle.

Politics of Income Redistribution

When the topic of income redistribution arises, most people automatically think of government programs intended to aid the poor. These programs do fit underneath the umbrella of redistribution, but the umbrella's expanse is much broader than that alone. The same forces are at work for the multitude of transfers that occur up, down, and across income classifications. Without a clear idea of the affluence of American society and the effects of this affluence on voter information, apathy, and interest group activity, many of the transfers of income by units of government seem paradoxical. If affluence and its effects are kept in mind, then the current politics of redistribution falls into place.

The first seeming paradox in income redistribution is a further expression of the dissonance between the rhetoric of economic despair and the realities of extravagant expenditures discussed in Chapter 3. On the one hand, Americans are continually exposed to heavy-handed political rhetoric about the problem of poverty and homelessness in the United States. On the other hand, the same public-sector officials schizophrenically chew up private-sector resources to maintain pristine habitats for owls or to maintain trade restrictions that prop up the prices of the milk, shirts, shoes, and cars purchased by the poor. If poverty is truly the continuing shame of America, then why have we pursued higher incomes for the dairy or textile industries and better lives for owls rather than improved lives for poor Americans?

The answer to this question and the resolution of the paradox rests squarely on the shoulders of rising affluence. To begin with, the very fact that income redistribution is accompanied by so many other agendas is, in and of itself, a testament to the affluence of Americans and the effects of this prosperity upon voter information and interest group funding, as discussed above. Whether it is the dairy industry, the textile industry, the automotive industry, the environmental lobby, or some other narrowly focused group, interest group politics dominate political outcomes. If Americans can fund all of these narrowly focused initiatives with so much fervor, this is in itself evidence of the widespread affluence enjoyed by most Americans. Only the tremendous affluence of the United States allows its citizens to "afford" to redistribute wealth toward special interest groups, lowly snail darters, and spotted owls. In a dictatorship, these kinds of redistribution might come about in spite of severe poverty. In a democracy, they can only indicate affluence.

In lumping so many other social agendas into the mix with redistribution toward the poor, it may appear as if Americans have fulfilled Galbraith's prophecy about the decline of interest in helping the poor. Although it is true that our more affluent society has grown relatively fonder of varied public crusades, redistribution toward the poor has certainly not suffered in an absolute sense. The growth of the varied public-sector agendas has come from an increased taking from the private sector—not from diminished funds for the poor.

Figures 7.4 and 7.5 provide evidence of this. The total share of national income devoted to income transfers—including federal, state, and local—had risen to about 15 percent, or over $1 trillion per year, by 1996. By contrast, in 1960 this percentage was less than 6 percent and was only about 8 percent in 1970. These are huge increases that do not even account for the spate of government spending and regulation that indirectly transfers income between families. At the same time, the total of spending on cash and noncash programs specifically for the poor comes to about $300 billion per year in the 1990s, or over $6,000 for each person—per person, not per family—officially listed in poverty. The amount spent per person in 1960 and 1970 was less than $1,000. Even after (over) adjusting for purchasing power differences, the mid-1990s figure is more than double the 1970 figure. Of course, this is not the same as $6,000 or its equivalent assistance eventually reaching each person; rather, it is the amount spent on poverty programs, including bureaucratic oversight of the programs as well as payments to producers providing in-kind goods or services.

This leads into the second seeming paradox regarding the politics of redistribution, and specifically, the rhetoric of class warfare: The

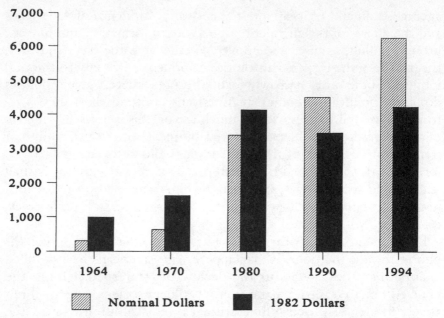

FIGURE 7.4   Cash and Noncash Expenditures on Poverty, 1964–1994

NOTE: Spending per person officially listed in poverty. Ten percent has been added to the 1964 and 1970 data to adjust for the omission of state and local data.

SOURCE: U.S. Bureau of the Census, *Statistical Abstract of the U.S.* (Washington, D.C.: USGPO), various volumes.

U.S. government spends over $300 billion every year to aid the poor—some in cash but most in goods and services[25]—and yet many critics claim that the United States is making little or no progress and may even be falling backward in the war on poverty. These critics would point to the decline in inflation-adjusted expenditures per person during the 1980s as depicted in Figure 7.4 as strong evidence.

This criticism suffers from several flaws. First and most simply, it does not account for the overadjustment in purchasing-power differences. Even more problematic, though, is that it ignores the tremendous differences in per-person expenditures on the poor from the 1980s onward versus the pre-1970 time frame. Even if expenditures per person fell after inflation adjustment, they fell from one high cliff to another—not down to the valley. We reported expenditures on poverty in this per-person way to gain a perspective on a sum as large as $300 billion. Looking at the numbers another way, means-tested assistance has increased from 1.8 percent of GDP in 1968 to 4.8 per-

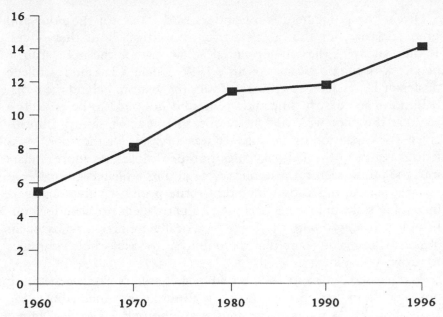

FIGURE 7.5   Federal, State, and Local Transfer Spending, 1960–1996
(as percent of national income)

SOURCE: *Economic Report of the President, 1997* (Washington, D.C.: USGPO, 1997).

cent of GDP in 1996.[26] Yet even with such sizable expenditures Americans are fed stories claiming that little or no headway is being made on poverty: The number of people below the "poverty threshold" has steadily increased since the mid-1970s from about 11 percent to about 15 percent of the population.[27]

To be clear on our point, poor people in this country may never touch anything close to cash or services that they would value anywhere near $6,000 per person, but this does not negate the amount spent. How can the rhetoric about the plight of poor people in America ever match up with these facts about expenditures?

The politics of class warfare derives much of its impetus from the very same source as the buildup in non-poverty-related transfers of income—the effects of wealth upon interest group politics. The affluence of Americans not only funds a whole industry with a vested interest in maintaining poverty as a major issue and maintaining funding but also props up an industry that wants to ensure that whatever funding is allocated continues to be doled out in the same way as before.

Often, the point here is misunderstood. It is not the poor and homeless that, for the most part, gain political clout themselves. Rather, many of the self-appointed advocates for the poor are the people with the political stake. In a 1996 article, Claremont College professor Harry Jaffa described this very mechanism behind the redistribution paradox when he said, "One did not need to be cynical to see that the poor were not the reason for the expansion of bureaucracy: the expansion of bureaucracy was a reason for the poor."[28] As rising wealth in the United States pumped more and more dollars into the public sector, the public sector and its affiliated groups—advocates for various causes including "the poor"—gained an ever-increasing stake in making "the poor" a permanent problem for public policy. In league with the "poor" advocates are people whose main interest is in making sure that the public sector as a whole continues to grow at a rapid pace.

As discussed in Chapter 4, these advocates are not above generating propaganda and systematic distortions about income inequality in the United States. As the facts bear out, some households in the United States in 1997 are poorer than other households, but poorer households are much better off in purely material terms than in the early 1970s and are better off by any material measures than the typical American household of the 1970s.

Our conclusions based on these facts should not be misunderstood. We do not propose an end to public assistance for the poor in the United States. Even though poorer households in the United States today stand above the poor from earlier decades and far above those who are poor on a worldwide standard, Americans would likely want to provide assistance to some households of substantially less material means than average. The point here is that advocates for the poor, especially those whose main objective is to increase the size of the poverty-administration industry, would find their jobs much harder if they uttered the truth about American poverty: We do not have many poor people in this country. We do have people who are not as wealthy as others, but on a worldwide basis, we have very few truly poor people.

Almost any assault on the rhetoric of poverty fires up contempt among those indoctrinated with the poverty message and those profiting from it. However, the real objectives of many poverty advocates in pursuing a poverty agenda rather than truly helping poorer households can be seen most clearly in their preferred methods of helping the poor. Not only is the amount of aid provided to poorer households a sanctified subject, but the means of providing the aid is just as holy. Attacks upon the traditional methods of doling out funds and services by means that require thousands upon thousands of federal, state, and local administrators are usually viewed as equivalent to attacking the poor themselves.

Where would most social workers be without an extensive bureaucracy to administer social programs for the poor? The political agenda of these workers as well as associated politicians and advocates would evaporate if the billions spent on noncash programs for the poor were converted into cash and distributed based on simple means and work tests. Such a program would provide money directly to the poor rather than supporting the current full-employment program for social workers.

Bringing the discussion here back to our main theme, rising American affluence, paradoxically feeds the politics of class warfare. Only a society bursting at its material seams can indulge a $300 billion social worker full-employment program disguised as aid to the poor and brush it off as hardly worth worrying about.

The Health Care Reform Agenda

One of the political hot buttons of the 1990s has been medical care and its reform. At the national level, this debate has only brought about the fairly modest changes in the 1996 Medical Reform Act that expanded the "portability" of insurance coverage. However, from 1992 to 1994, the likelihood of much more drastic moves, including much greater government intervention, loomed on the horizon. At the state level, more drastic reforms have been pushed through legislatures owing to the alleged crisis. Other reforms that would lead to less government intervention, such as Medical Savings Accounts (MSAs), escape the attention of most people. The intense political debate on some issues surrounding medical markets and the lack of knowledge about potential reforms reflect affluence-driven effects on information, voter attention, and basic misunderstandings of data concerning living standards.

As we discussed in Chapter 4, the usual interpretation of rising health care expenditures turns an indicator of affluence into an alleged indicator of decay. The wrongheaded analysis of what the growth in medical care expenditures means, along with the leisure time–information link, has created a fanatical commitment on the part of some. Usually, the reforms have steered much more in the direction of greater governmental involvement than toward a greater reliance on markets.

Beyond the wrongheaded views about medical expenditures and the mainstream debates about reforms, the 1996 debate, or lack of it, over MSAs vividly illustrates the voter indifference based on rational ignorance, discussed above. MSAs are like medical Individual Retirement Accounts (IRAs). Individuals make deposits into an account that will be used for routine medical practices. Typically, these MSA holders also purchase high-deductible catastrophic-care policies for nonroutine medical expenses. Any savings in their MSAs can be rolled over for future routine expenses or for retirement. It is argued that this will give individuals the incentive to spend their dollars prudently. Also, it is argued that if Congress extends the same tax deductibility to MSA contributions as insurance premiums receive, medical consumers would gain a viable, low-cost alternative to managed care systems—health maintenance organizations (HMOs) and their cousins—and retake control over their care decisions from corporate vice presidents and medical professionals on the corporate payroll. Big insurers behind HMOs fomented an anti-MSA lobbying effort, claiming that MSAs would benefit only the healthy and wealthy. The Clinton administration and powerful allies like the *New York Times* threw their hat in with the big insurers and ultimately limited MSAs to an "experimental" trial for qualifying small companies and individuals as part of the 1996 Medical Reform Act.

Whatever one might think of MSAs, one can hardly pass off the topic as of little importance to medical consumers and providers. The issue is hardly a minor legislative issue akin to the selection of congressional pages or Capitol elevator operators. Yet public opinion polls indicate that most Americans have no inkling what MSAs are and know even less about their tax status or the debate on Capitol Hill. This ignorance falls right in line with our discussion above: Americans are aware of all kinds of obscure incidents and push for political action based on these occurrences while they remain in the dark about political issues with widespread ramifications.

Exporting Affluence Politics

Affluence has combined all of its forces—ideology, information and apathy, and interest group funding—to produce the most insidious outgrowth of all of the political effects of wealth: the exporting of wealth-induced public policy beyond U.S. borders. American politicians and various do-gooders have taken up the cause of spreading a wealth-laden value system across the globe. What's more, the advocates of these various causes view themselves as the benefactors of the poor and unprotected masses, when, in reality, they help to keep the machinery of poverty and oppression firmly entrenched and sometimes go so far as to place people's lives in jeopardy.

For example, the crusade launched in the mid-1990s against U.S. firms that purchase products from foreign firms using child labor and making children work very long hours exposes the affluence-laden values run amok with the help of influential interest groups. Labor Secretary Robert Reich, among others, spearheaded these efforts. Columnists hung the morning show host, Kathie Lee Gifford, out to dry and prompted an apology from her over her sponsorship of a clothing line supported by child labor in overseas plants. She ultimately criticized Wal-Mart for purchasing materials from these foreign plants.[29]

At first glance, these charges of child extortion appear to make sense and elicit legitimate moral outrage. How can anyone justify an American company importing a shirt that was produced by twelve-year-old kids working twelve-hour days? Not only does the practice appear to take jobs away from adult wage earners in the United States, but it does so at the expense of defenseless children across the world.

Although this way of thinking is superficially attractive, it is a distorted view that comes from way up in the clouds of economic success combined with a healthy dose of interest group "what is good for me is good for America" politics. From the perspective of U.S. living standards, using an American child for labor in this way might truly be outrageous. However, would most Americans find it outrageous that preteens or even much younger children contributed to the incomes and survival of nineteenth- and twentieth-century American farm families in struggling to keep food in their bellies and their bodies warm? Are we to think that a ten-year-old child picking cotton on steamy summer days in the South in the 1930s or the 1940s is acceptable because of difficult family economic conditions but that a twelve-year-old Nicaraguan boy whose family is even in worse shape on the economic ladder is being exploited? This imbalance is nothing but inconsistent and in some cases deceptive.[30] A value system that permits such inconsistencies does not stand on unwavering moral precepts but is born of values weaned on economic privilege and protection of special interests.

Neither the ten-year-old farm boy in the 1930s American South nor the twelve-year-old worker in the Nicaraguan plant is necessarily the subject of exploitation. Both boys and their families are dealing with the fact that they cannot afford the luxury of a childhood involving minimal work—childhoods that now extend into the late teens and twenties for many American children. Further, all that the indignation and solutions forwarded by the critics of foreign child labor accomplish is less revenue to the firms hiring these children, less income for these children's families, and more wallowing in the mire of poverty, poverty as defined on a worldwide scale rather than on the much more affluent U.S. scale. A professor from Guatemala City put it this way:

> Desperately poor countries cannot afford to forgo jobs in the name of better working conditions. That is one of the luxuries of development. Per capita income in Guatemala is roughly one-twentieth that of the United States, and the gap in living standards is even more poignant when comparing the quality of nutrition, health care or plumbing. . . . Depriving developing countries, even with the best of intentions, of the capital and jobs needed to grow out of these centuries-old conditions of poverty will merely insure the indefinite perpetuation of misery.[31]

Politicians such as Robert Reich are the darlings of organized labor and others in the United States who want to see issues of low wages and child labor in other countries boil up into major brouhahas. These political skirmishes alleviate the necessity of defending U.S. trade restrictions and sanctions for what they are: protection for small groups of producers and workers in America at the expense of American consumers, rich and poor, and at the expense of the poor of other countries. Ross Perot and Pat Buchanan notwithstanding, American consumers having to fork over nearly twice as much for a shirt because of import restrictions does not lead to a net increase in U.S. jobs or better living standards in the United States. In terms of the foreign families involved, the title to an article by Paul Krugman says it best: "In Praise of Cheap Labor: Bad Jobs at Bad Wages Are Better Than No Jobs at All."[32]

We do not mean to sweep aside all of the moral dilemmas that sometimes crop up regarding child labor. For example, what about a five-year-old Pakistani child given over into slave labor to tie tiny knots in wool rugs? Would we support a standard that would impose limits on some kinds of child labor? Yes, we would, but we think that such a standard must take into account the economic conditions and practices deemed acceptable and unacceptable in the other country and not just those based on U.S., affluence-driven prejudices.

In addition to labor policy, environmental causes are among the more popular political exports from the United States. Through United Nations organizations and international treaties, environmental hawks like Vice President Al Gore have worked hard to impose the wealth-laden values of U.S. policymakers on the poor of the world. For instance, in negotiating toward NAFTA, many issues of environmental compliance arose. Could the United States receive assurances that Mexican producers would be held to the same standard as U.S. producers? If U.S. tuna boats were limited in their methods so as to reduce dolphin deaths, would Mexican tuna boats be under similar restrictions?

No doubt, agreements like NAFTA, if not accompanied by similar enforcement across countries, puts U.S. companies at a disadvantage. But who will pay the price for the luxury of animal- and nature-centered environmental policy in the United States? Will U.S. companies and workers foot that bill, or will it be passed on to the working poor of other countries? As Columbia University economist Jagdish Bhagwati pointed out in a debate about NAFTA's effects that appeared in *Scientific American*, "Would Americans stand for a restriction on meat purchases because Indians view cows as sacred?"[33] Should we expect Mexican fishermen making maybe one-fifth of the income of their American counterparts to take up the dolphin's cause and bear the economic price of its protection?

Beyond self-serving policies, some exports of U.S. environmental policy impose truly dangerous conditions on people in other countries, such as maintaining and restoring populations of various animals. In the United States, large, dangerous animals such as the gray wolf and grizzly bear, whose populations have been subsidized and protected in recent years, primarily threaten only livestock or very adventurous outdoor enthusiasts. In countries in Africa and Asia, the environmental exporters through U.S. and United Nations organizations and treaties have supported protection of animals presenting true threats to ordinary families and their livelihoods, such as tigers, crocodiles, snakes, and elephants. In places, these creatures are not just supported in remote habitats far from human dwellings but in areas very accessible to humans involved in their daily routines. As a senior associate of the Thoreau Institute put it, "Elephants are a marvel to us [U.S. citizens]; to Africa's struggling poor they are marauding pests. Elephants are cheap to us, costing only the price of the Discovery Channel; they are dear to the African farmer who must pay for land set-asides for wildlife parks and for lost crops, and who faces loss of life."[34] He notes that in a part of the world where human rights garner little respect, championing animal rights smacks of racism and imperialism. Rather than racism and imperialism as the root cause, we would suggest that these well-intended policies smack of affluence-indulged preferences.

The ban of the pesticide DDT, widely hailed in the United States as a triumph of environmentalism, is another example of exporting affluence-based politics in the United States to the Third World with tragic results. The United States banned DDT in 1972 because it killed birds and could cause cancer in humans. Nonetheless, no evidence shows large-scale reductions in bird populations or increases in cancer rates due to DDT, yet U.S. environmentalists exported this idea to low-income countries.[35]

The effects of DDT removal on Sri Lanka, for example, were devastating. After less than twenty years of DDT use, Sri Lanka had lowered malaria cases from 3 million to a mere 17. DDT killed mosquitoes and other carriers of malaria as well as lowering food prices by protecting crops from pests. In spite of these gains in food production and life expectancy, DDT was branded a danger rather than a savior and was banned. Within five years after the ban, Sri Lankan malaria deaths had climbed all the way back up to 2 million per year.[36]

Political humorist P. J. O'Rourke may have put these kinds of political exports in their place in his *Parliament of Whores*, in which he wrote:

> Contempt for material progress is not only unfair but dangerous. The average Juan and the average Chang and the average Mobutu out there in parts of the world where every day is Earth Day, or Dirt and Squalor Day, anyhow, would like to have a color television, too. He'd also like some comfy Reeboks and a Nintendo Power Glove and a Jeep Cherokee. And he means to get them. I wouldn't care to be the skinny health-food nut waving a copy of *Fifty Simple Things You Can Do to Save the Earth* who tries to stand in Juan's way.[37]

Cause for Concern?

These examples really only brush the surface of the specific effects of affluence upon American public policy. Again, we would not characterize all of the affluence-driven effects on public policy as bad. The ability to afford more government, just like the ability to afford more food or clothing, entails many advantages. A society may use its additional financial muscle to fund more research into basic science and certain public health problems that the private sector has little incentive to fund but may pay substantial dividends in terms of living standards and health. Or a wealthier society may find itself better able to defend its borders from foreign intruders and thereby forgo the devastating effects on society that come from foreign plunder. Even in areas where the problems may not be due to any lack on the part of private markets as much as to poorly defined property rights—such as with the polluting of streams and rivers or the air—a public sector that grows in an effort to stamp out such problems produces some positive results. More efficient means of solving pollution problems may exist than building up the EPA, but to the extent that the EPA and other organizations have played some role in reducing air and water pollution, one could say that the means of affording a bigger government has resulted in some gains.

Whether some policies are wasteful or fall into lockstep with conservative or libertarian political philosophies may be of little consequence in a society wealthy enough to pour whole dinners down the garbage disposal and where at least some policies have positive outcomes. So what if we take $500 more away from a family pulling down $70,000 per year and spend it on a poor family in such a way that the benefits received by the poor are really only worth $100 dollars in their own eyes? How much will the affluent family that blows $500 on a couple of days at Disney World miss the money? At least the poorer family is better off than it would have been otherwise.

We may not agree with such thinking, but we can certainly understand the reasoning. This way of thinking does have a certain logic to it. After all, it is certainly true that Americans frequently spend their money whimsically when left to their own devices. Then why should their government not spend it whimsically sometimes, as long as it provides occasional benefits along the way? Isn't this just the rewards of affluence?

Although in some ways appealing, the argument contains fatal flaws. For one thing, it overlooks such negative outcomes as affluence-driven preferences against low wages. Although they may not be American families, poor families across the world pay the price for this kind of indulgence of wealth by U.S. policymakers. Second, it does not account for the long-term incentive-altering effects of public policy. If the particular methods of public assistance for the poor induce many of these people into lifelong dependence on government assistance, are the policies really as innocuous as they might seem? Throughout the book, we have been pointing out the unintended consequences of growing wealth within a private property system. Public-sector activity also produces unintended consequences but may be even more difficult to correct. Finally, the argument fails to make the distinction between personal choice and coerced choice.

EIGHT

COMBATING WEALTH'S NEGATIVE EFFECTS

Riches are a good handmaid, but the worst mistress.
—Francis Bacon, *De dignitate et augmentis scientiarum*

If affluence has contributed to the problems discussed over the preceding chapters, what can we do about it? Will the problems correct themselves, or will concerted efforts be necessary both in the public and private sector to turn them around? If public policy changes are required, where should we begin? These are the questions we try to address in this chapter.

In considering the effects of affluence on society in Chapters 5–7, we have attempted to play the role of detached analysts, looking for insights without engaging in very much moral or political philosophy. As we now turn to making suggestions for dealing with the problems, we attempt to maintain that same perspective as much as possible. If nothing else, heavy-handed attempts in the past to improve society through the public sector should stir fear in the hearts of would-be reformers. The contributions of public policy solutions to the rise of organized crime during Prohibition or to the tremendous growth in illegitimacy and single parenthood in the past quarter century serve as reminders of the difficulty of forecasting the side effects of government policy, even if well-intended. History is replete with well-intended policies that turned into disasters. Even when trying to dissect bad public policy previously enacted, one must always be on the lookout for unintended consequences.[1]

To be sure, not all and maybe not even most of the redirection must start with governmental policies. A few of the potentially negative consequences may even have self-correcting mechanisms. For instance, if educational performance remains flat or drops in the United States enough to place its citizens at a competitive disadvantage, education may become a higher priority, based on the involvement and demands of parents and students. Higher and higher levels of regulatory intervention may eventually stir a citizen backlash once these regulatory costs reach a critical threshold. If crime rates rise high enough or fast enough, everyday citizens may begin to place more value on traditional parenting.

Still, these countervailing forces may or may not offset the problems to a significant degree. Especially in the areas where the costs of behavior do not rest on the shoulders of the individuals engaging in the behavior but spill over onto many others in society, public policy may be a necessity. In the case of illegitimacy, for example, unwed mothers certainly bear a tremendous load for their actions. Yet when these actions lead to long-run implications for poverty, crime, and delinquency, the behavior also affects the lives of many other people.[2]

We do not propose a reduction in living standards as the solution. Perceiving the ill effects of modern culture, counterculture movements of the past have proposed turning the clock back on living standards. In these retro visions, people would be better off by returning to a primarily rural existence where everyone picks nuts and berries, casts aside technology, moves into communes, and lives "in harmony" with nature. If for no other reason, the substantial benefits of higher living standards render such back-to-berry-picking campaigns unpopular with mainstream families. How many people really want to go back to a time when work meant rising before dawn and laboring on backbreaking chores until dusk just to have barely enough food to survive? Only the most radical within our society would long to return to a time when even simple appendicitis brought death and when the infant mortality rate was 20 percent. In fact, most of the berry-picking movements in this country's past have cheated to some extent, choosing to profit from some of mankind's material progress while disavowing allegiance to it. Most have not desired a return to infant mortality rates of 20 percent.

In contrast to these kinds of counterculture proposals, we ask: How can a society reign in wealth's negative consequences while holding on to wealth's benefits? If wealth is responsible for both good and bad results, trying to hold on to the good while excising or reducing the bad effects is no easy task. It would be easy to suggest remedies that would ultimately diminish living standards, not to mention producing immense but unintended negative side effects. In essence, holding on to the higher living standards while slicing off the negative consequences is the same question that has been faced by many individual households for the past few generations in the United States. How can parents allow their children to enjoy the benefits of higher living standards—more toys, more entertainment, less childhood labor—and at the same time instill in them a sense of personal responsibility, a sound work ethic, and an appreciation for the items they have? How does a person reap the benefits of wealth without becoming spoiled by it? These are questions with no perfect answers.

Triage of Affluence Effects

Before making any prescriptions for public policy, we consolidate the diagnosis of the effects of affluence on society that we covered in the preceding chapters. This triage of affluence's effects separates the truly critical effects requiring immediate attention from those for which attention may be needed but the results of putting off treatment may not be disastrous. These are distinguished from those effects that require no attention because they show the health rather than any sickness within the economy.

First, we have identified several areas that need to be left alone. These are the issues where the stagnation writers have interpreted data as displaying negative symptoms, when in reality, they show a healthy economy. Other than promoting accurate information and stifling attempts to use public policy, we would not see the need for any kind of policy response to these phantom problems. Several of the labor-related issues of Chapter 5 fall into this category, including worker compensation, leisure time, job stability, and downsizing. In nearly every case, the forecasters of economic doom have either looked past data that show improvements in total compensation and leisure time or they have failed to understand the effects that rising affluence will have on employment figures. A case in point is the duration of unemployment, where increases may show problems but may also signal the ability to hold out longer for better employment prospects *because of* greater affluence. Even with respect to the job loss rate, where data have shown weaknesses in the past quarter century, the major increases can be traced to the recession of the 1970s and early 1980s. Since that time, the long-term trends have been positive.

Second, we have identified areas in which the effects of affluence could lead to varying degrees of concern and policy response. For example, educational outcomes fit into this category. The data are not nearly as bad as some might profess, but they do not exhibit strong positive signs either—especially in terms of the dollars spent and outcomes achieved. Changes may need to be considered but should be considered in light of the likely connection between affluence and disinterest in education. Another problem fitting into this "mild-response" category would be the anxiety about economic matters, which seems so rampant, according to public opinion polls.

A different example in this category that may require attention from public policymakers is the political consequence of affluence. In terms of the growing number of regulations that cannot be justified by any realistic estimates of costs and benefits and class-driven concerns about the redistribution of income, the economy and society in general may suffer serious long-term consequences if no action is taken. Although these problems require attention, they present lower threats than those in the next category.

Third, we have identified areas in which the effects of affluence along with other contributing factors deserve the full attention of policymakers. The most pressing category of affluence-driven effects comes from family-related matters. The threats to American society posed by illegitimacy and divorce—especially with respect to their combined influence on single parenthood—can hardly be overstated. Charles Murray directs his comments—"Sometimes the sky really is falling"—specifically toward the problem of illegitimacy, and we agree with the seriousness of this issue. As he notes, the movement of child rearing toward this kind of *Lord of the Flies* environment can only spell disaster. Whether that disaster is impending or whether it will hold off for twenty years or much longer is impossible to predict. Still, as John DiIulio has warned us, the time bomb is ticking and many of the consequences have already been felt in terms of enormous increases in criminal activity by youth.

Information as a Solution

Accurate information may be the most important weapon in battling
the negative results of growing affluence. The effects of improved information to citizens are wide-sweeping. Information is the enemy of
lies, partial truth, misrepresentation, special interests, and vested
power. Much of the anxiety and despair in American households and
in political circles is based on ignorance and detachment. Most Americans are detached from the living standard experienced by most of
the world's citizens. Most are ignorant of the vast amount of regulatory burden placed on the economy and of the interest-group-driven
results of much of public policy. In many instances, if consumers or
voters are armed with relevant and accurate information, no further
adjustments are needed. The problem is one of how to overcome the
incentives that have led to ignorance and apathy in the first place so as
to prompt better informed decisions.

An accurate and unwavering look at reality is not always pleasant,
but it can have effects, even if short-lived. For instance, baby boom
children may not have been fond of hearing their mothers prod them
into eating their peas by talking about those poor children in Armenia
or wherever. Still, the argument was bothersome, in large part because its basic premise and logic were so obvious. It takes a truly cal-
lous person to continue whining about supper, lack of job satisfaction, and other matters of daily concern to Americans while watching
a commercial depicting the suffering of Rwandan refugees or starvation among Somalian and Ethiopian children.

More accurate information would also place limits on the ability to
offer utter nonsense with any degree of respectability. If every time a
politician, a newspaper editor, an advocate for some special interest,
or a TV reporter started in on the bad times in America, they were
met with a barrage of scoffs and howls from other journalists, other
politicians, and citizens in general, the politics and anxieties based on
"how bad we've got it" would diminish. Of course, to arrive at a position where Americans and those who provide the bulk of the information to them have a more reality-based conception of their affluence will require a little more than just a snap of the fingers.

Several groups have a role to play in improving information in this
regard. Professional economists have a role to play, especially those
teaching college freshmen and sophomores. These beginning courses
in economics are often the only exposure to these issues that students

ever get. If a future journalist or future eighth-grade teacher is ever going to receive an accurate picture of the influences on long-term economic growth or of the relative affluence and poverty in the United States versus the world, this is the time. Historically, economic educators in basic college classes have dragged students through a maze of terms, theories, and graphs concerning Keynesianism, monetarism, marginal propensity to consume, multipliers, and other concepts that were largely watered-down versions of debates raging at the highest levels within the profession.

As a result, most students exited their economic education with little sense of the kinds of topics necessary to separate fact from fiction in media and political discussions about economic stagnation. Facts about and reasons for growth of household income over long time periods in the United States, cross-national differences in living standards, income differences of households in the United States, poverty, and similar topics have typically been shunted to minor chapters toward the end of books and are often just ignored. Most professors in these classes, much less their students, cannot give "in-the-ballpark" responses to questions about per capita consumption differences across countries or over time in the United States. Yet these are the very topics necessary for students to gain an accurate picture of affluence and the factors behind it. Ironically, these are also the topics that have a much greater degree of agreement about the facts and theories behind them. Improvement is being made in this regard. A new generation of beginning macroeconomics texts is appearing that places more emphasis on the economics of long-term growth and cross-national differences in consumption.

Also, economists engaged in research and graduate-level education also have a role to play in improving the accuracy of information about American affluence. As we pointed out in Chapter 3, economists have known about many of the limitations of measures such as GDP and the CPI ever since their inception. But knowing and doing something about it are different things. Because of conceptual and practical difficulties in making alterations to these measures, economists continue to rely heavily on them, offering just passing and obligatory waves at their limitations. In some respects, at least, this situation is starting to improve. By and large, there seems to be a renewed commitment among many high-level economics researchers to make the accuracy of the basic data of economics a major agenda item in coming years.

Beyond economists, journalists certainly must be held partially accountable for the poor awareness of economic realities. If anything can get the blood of economists boiling, it is the pitiful state of economic journalism. The issue of the journal *Jobs and Capital* cited in earlier chapters focused on this very topic. In it, MIT economist Paul Krugman and ABC reporter John Stossel laid into journalists for their pathetic state of knowledge about economics and risk. In fairness to the journalists, the sad state of economic journalism may be due as much to the shortcomings of economic education as it is to intellectual laziness among journalists.

Nonetheless, the news media are not without their own sins in perpetuating nonsense about economic facts in America. For one thing, journalistic coverage of economic issues and affluence in particular tends to display ignorance of even the most basic economic and statistical concepts. In areas and on topics where seemingly anybody with a pen in hand should have a better grasp of evidence or of economic principles, these principles sometimes escape journalists. Further, journalists do not have a very good appreciation for matters of legitimate debate and disagreement between economists or, for that matter, any evidence-based discipline. Journalists give too much credence and respectability to the views of nonprofessionals on matters that may require a great deal of economic expertise. Whether on *Nightline* or the McNeil-Lehrer news program, a Nobel Prize–winning economist is just as likely to be paired with an interest-group lawyer or celebrity as with another respected economist. Finally, journalists dabble around the edges of complex issues, looking for sound bites and quotes that tend to confirm whatever point of view they already have in mind rather than truly investigating alternative views from respected professionals.

These problems in economic journalism reflect underlying weaknesses in the training of journalists that extend far beyond economics. Journalists typically lack an appreciation for the nature of or the history of science and the evaluation of evidence. Science, regardless of the discipline, contains facts, near-facts, working hypotheses, and wild guesses, but these nuances seem to escape the attention of journalists. This lack of appreciation leads journalists to spurn serious input from economists (and other professionals) on occasion or to treat disagreements between economists as evidence that their own ideas or those of anyone off the street are just as good as anybody else's. Being unable to separate matters of wide consensus from matters of ongoing

serious debate, they tend to view all disagreements between economists as an indictment of the whole discipline. Even though professional economists might disagree about certain aspects of income inequality and how to correct them, for example, these economists
might be able to rule out other interpretations that are appealing to
journalists.

The benefits for political debate of improved reporting might be
large. Instead of trying to one-up each other with demagoguery or
catchy sound bites, these politicians might actually have to engage in
a reasonable dialogue about the pros and cons of their positions. One
candidate might well claim that Americans would be made better off
because of a particular proposal, but it would become much more difficult to sell political agendas based merely on ridiculous claims of despair about living standards. Of course the question arises, will this
sell to the public?

The government itself could play a much more valuable role in providing information to consumers and voters than it does now. Federal
and state governments publish reams of statistics and studies, most of
which collect dust in government-document sections of libraries. In
contrast, governments spend only a minuscule fraction of taxpayers'
money in the disseminating of important information in ways that
can reach mass audiences. In fact, in important ways, governments
have often helped to blockade the dissemination of relevant information as a means of promoting a special interest. For example, information about medical care services—prices, mortality rates of hospitals,
and so on—have historically been held by medical boards and bodies
usually holding government-sponsored authority. These kinds of restrictions have only recently diminished.

As one specific and relatively radical means of securing a greater
amount of information in political dialogue in America, we might
propose an end to the *Federal Register*. The *Federal Register* is the official forum in which newly proposed regulations are announced to
the public for comment and discussion before the proposals find their
way into the *Code of Federal Regulations*. In place of the *Federal Register*, we might suggest a rule that forces the federal government to
purchase prominent space in metropolitan newspapers, devoted to
announcing proposed regulations in bold print and giving realistic
ranges for the expected costs and benefits of the new regulations. We
would imagine that if the second page of the front section or of the
sports section of major newspapers announced restriction on the vol-

ume of toilet or shower water flow, this information would lead to a much greater public outcry than the same announcements buried in a publication like the *Federal Register,* which is inaccessible to most Americans.

Although we believe that improving the dissemination of information to citizens is paramount in limiting the pessimistic view of national wealth in the United States, the problem is this: How do we get teachers, journalists, politicians, and so forth to spend time and energy delving into the numbers? It may not be in the interest of various politicians or others with a particular agenda to discuss the negative consequences of unwed motherhood or corporate welfare.

Specific Remedies: Between a Rock and a Hard Place

Beyond recommending improved information to the public—hardly a controversial proposal—contemplating additional remedies for the ills created by growing affluence puts most would-be reformers with any degree of hesitancy about public policy, including us, in an uneasy position. The difficulty of this problem was recognized long ago by John Adams, in a letter written to Thomas Jefferson: "Will you tell me how to prevent riches from being the effects of industry? Will you tell me how to prevent luxury from producing effeminacy, intoxication, extravagance, vice and folly?"[3]

As economists, we can identify a few overriding principles for the operation of efficient public policy that pertain to the negative consequences of affluence. A key principle is making individuals bear the full costs of their actions as much as is feasible. Using this simple principle, if sexual behavior resulting in rising illegitimacy imposes costs on society by increasing crime rates, then males and females responsible for the rising illegitimacy must "pay" for these costs, on top of whatever personal burdens they bear because of the illegitimacy. The enhancement of and effective enforcement of laws regarding child support would fall under this general principle of making people fully responsible for their actions.

Of course, economic efficiency is not the only reason people support "pay-for-your-actions" principles. In legal and moral philosophy, the idea of holding people strictly liable for their actions leads to similar—though not necessarily identical—principles for guiding public policy.

Whether efficiency-based or as a philosophical stance, a "pay-for-your-actions" principle to guide public policy might be easy to state in theory. Making application in consistent and useful ways is another matter. In some cases, the principle of responsibility for behavior presents few practical problems—charging someone for a fishing license, placing a toll on highway use, or imposing stiff penalties on drunk drivers. In other settings, the implementation of this principle raises many thorny issues. The complexity of many issues makes practical use of this very simple principle difficult, if not impossible.

Again, we can use illegitimacy and the associated costs as an example of the practical problems of implementation. Which parents are charged for the costs to society? Ideally, only the parents whose children impose costs on society because of the parental actions would be charged. The information required to target accurately the taxes, fines, and so on that would affect behavior would be enormous. Parents whose children were upstanding would need to be separated from those whose children were not. Then, what about children whose behavior became degrading only after parental control was lost, which is usually the case? In a society in which we seemingly have difficulty in making fathers pay child support to their own families, how could such a plan ever work on seemingly more complicated problems?

If the policy could work flawlessly, then many people might be willing to support the universal application of these kinds of principles, whether they supported it purely on grounds of efficiency or on grounds of morality. However, whether because of the complexity of implementation or the strong moral overtones or the combination of them both, even social conservatives often shy away from proposing public policies that attempt to fully integrate the "pay-for-your-actions" idea. At most, these authors would try to make governmental policy—whether through taxes or subsidies—"neutral" toward single parenthood or other such problems. By "neutral," they mean eliminating the incentives through which public policy amplifies the negative effects of affluence, as in the case of subsidizing illegitimacy or penalizing marriage. But the idea of going on to the next level and actually imposing penalties on unwed parents or other offenders makes them feel uneasy.

What headway can be made on developing concrete remedies to problems when these remedies must not only deal with complex behavior and its consequences but also walk a tightrope between simple but hard-to-enforce principles and moral philosophy? Rather than providing specific remedies, we suggest that the first order of business in addressing the negative consequences of affluence is to consider the best method for arriving at the solutions. For the most part, the problems created by affluence are too complex and morally charged to leave up to typical majority-rule mechanisms, much less to bureaucrats. As we discussed in Chapter 7, simple democratic majority rule is subject to tremendous influence from special interests and often underrepresents the views of the vast majority of people. Arriving at effective solutions to the kinds of problems under consideration here while ensuring widespread support requires broad public awareness of the items under discussion as well as a consensus that extends well beyond a simple majority of voters or of a legislative body.

What we have in mind is a "rules-of-the-game," or constitutional-level, decisionmaking. By a "rules-of-the game," or constitutional-level, approach, we mean one in which general rules of governance are determined only after substantial public debate and based on the support of "supermajorities" of, say, 65 to 75 percent of the population.[4] The method of amending the U.S. Constitution would be an example of implementing such an approach, though not the exclusive means.

Under idealized conditions, citizens would have to decide on fundamental rules without knowing what their own particular relative position—in regard to income, wealth, status, occupation, and so on—would be in the society. The use of this conceptual device for considering fundamental rules for society was first espoused by philosopher John Rawls.[5] Nobel Prize–winning economist James Buchanan and others have extended these ideas and developed alternative ideas along the same lines in dealing with fundamental questions about how to structure the most basic rules of society.[6] The various applications of the idea differ on what knowledge individuals possess about the consequences of their decisions for society as a whole, on the specifics that drive their decision rules, and other items. We do not attempt to get into all of these issues here. Instead, we will proceed with illustrative examples of the general idea and assume that individuals are well aware of the important consequences of the rules chosen for society as a whole but not for them individually.

As an example of this kind of conceptual approach, we consider the contribution of affluence to the problems of excessive regulation and redistribution politics discussed in Chapter 7. As affluence has increased, more individuals and groups have sought to indulge their special interests and have been able to secure the financial backing to pursue their objectives. This has created a regulatory maze of 150,000 pages, bred an incredibly complex tax code, and fostered one transfer of income after another across and within income classes. In addressing these problems, day-to-day majority politics in Congress usually winds up creating additional problems—more regulatory pages, more tax rules, and more transfers. These incremental attempts at "reform" have proven futile. For example, lobbying to increase the safety of automobile passengers led to regulations regarding mandatory use of seat belts and child safety seats and air bags. As technology developed, front-dash air bags were mandated as a regulatory device to increase passenger safety. However, the use of air bags endangered small children seated in front seats or in child safety seats in the front seat. This prompted public officials to try to "educate" people about seating their children in the back seat as well as another round of regulation to permit the disengagement, under certain conditions, of the front-passenger air-bag feature.

Taking taxes as the topic for the moment, suppose we ask this question: What general rules for the federal tax code would be developed if no one knew what income, wealth, occupation, or living arrangements they would hold in society and if 70 percent of the people had to agree before a rule could be adopted? With this kind of process selecting the broad rules governing taxation, many things about federal taxation would likely change. It would not be hard to imagine that almost everyone would select a simpler tax code over a more complex code. Without knowing income or living arrangements, the preference given to home owners who hold home mortgages might well disappear. As to whether these people would opt for a regressive tax structure, a flat-tax schedule, or a progressive scheme, we might be hard pressed to accurately predict. But if people did select a progressive schedule without knowing what their income would be, this would give more credibility to the idea that progressive schemes promote fairness. People might place limits on the total amount of income that government could take. This kind of provision would specifically address the tendency for government revenue shares to grow as incomes grow. As for items left up to the day-to-day discretion of legislators, the legislators might have the ability to adjust the collection process based on technological changes. Also, special provision might be made for wars, allowing emergency funding, and so forth.

We can also direct this kind of mental exercise about tax code rules toward our central concern—the role of affluence. Would people who knew that median family income would be $2,000 per year choose the same basic rules of the game as people who knew that median family income would be $40,000 per year? If preferences are linked to affluence, then they would not. John Rawls thought that desire for liberty rises with affluence. Although Rawls may be correct for countries with very low income levels, evidence from wealthier countries would seem to suggest just the opposite: Societies have a greater preference for "meddling" as incomes rise very high. If we suppose that people do prefer a greater role for government as average incomes rise very high, a constitutional-level decision to cap the share of government at, say, 30 percent versus 10 percent still places restraints on the ability of special interests to use day-to-day politics to increase the level of government expenditure. A recent contribution to this kind of analysis has tried to further define these boundaries for day-to-day majority politics.[7] One key limitation placed on everyday majority politics would be that rules passed must be nondiscriminatory. For instance, legislatures might have the authority to raise more tax revenue, but they would have to do so in a way in which each household bears the same proportion of the burden as before the increase. This feature reduces the incentive for policymakers to bow to special interests.

The same kind of mental exercise could be applied to problems like illegitimacy, criminal justice, or any other topics involving either critical issues with sweeping consequences for society or those where leaving decisions up to day-to-day politics would merely lead to a struggle for power. What kinds of rules regarding illegitimacy would emerge if no one knew what their income, wealth, occupation, sex, or household status would be? We might suppose the people making the decision understand that illegitimacy contributes substantially to violent crime, relative poverty, and other family troubles but do not know all of the unintended effects of a particular policy. In this kind of mental experiment, what would 70 percent or so of the population agree upon?

As with tax policy, the answer might depend on the average level of income of the population. For very poor societies, people might well choose very harsh penalties for this behavior. If median family income were in the $40,000-plus range, as in the late 1990s, it is very difficult to imagine that people would select rules that would allow children born out of wedlock and their mothers to starve without any aid. However, the ability to choose "up front," as well as the knowledge of the severe problems to which illegitimacy contributes, might allow for widespread agreement to impose much tougher sanctions or much lower subsidies on this behavior than would ever be selected by routine political mechanisms.

Steering away from these mental exercises and toward more practical situations, constitutional-level choice is not without its problems. Foremost among them, the idea of people choosing rules without explicit knowledge of their position in society is, obviously, nothing more than a mental device. It is an option available only to authors contemplating various rules. In reality, constitutional framers and amenders do know their situation or have a general idea of their future status. For example, had none of the members of the Constitutional Convention in 1789 known whether they would be freemen or slaves after the ratification of the Constitution, the issue of slavery would have very likely been settled then and not seventy years later. But, the framers were real men with a keen knowledge of their position in society. Even the ones without a strong personal interest in maintaining slavery or an interest in eliminating it knew people who owned slaves and were also cognizant of the political upheaval that the abolition of slavery would and ultimately did create.[8] In the idealized setting, no such dilemma exists, because the choice is made before the fact. How to make real-world constitutional choices approximate the idealized setting has not been adequately resolved.

A second knowledge problem can also arise in constitutional choice. People cannot always anticipate the indirect consequences of the rules and, as a result, underestimate the downside to a policy—even one that originally attracted broad support. Prohibition is the prime and most disturbing example. Here was a rule pushed through as a constitutional measure—not just a law based on a simple majority. Yet Prohibition was not only ineffective in stemming the consumption of alcohol in many locations but helped to spark growth in organized criminal activity and produced other negative consequences.

Still, even with the limitations on constitutional choice in real-world settings, the idea of considering public policy at this level from time to time rather than simply relying on daily politics could yield benefits. It is a choice mechanism probably utilized too infrequently. The rapid rise in affluence since the Great Depression has created many problems that neither the founders who wrote the Constitution in 1789 nor even people of the early part of the twentieth century could barely have imagined. Who in the 1950s could have predicted that out-of-wedlock births would account for one-third of all births in the United States within forty years? Who could have predicted that violent crime rates would jump by three times, even as living standards rose to new heights? These problems have come upon us so rapidly and unexpectedly that the basic rules of society have been left in the dust. The time may have come for these rules to be addressed at a high level of debate.

Religion's Role

The mere mention of a role for religion in offsetting the negative consequences of affluence sends tremors through many people. The practice of religion, especially in very zealous forms, can have negative spillovers in society. As we mentioned in Chapter 6, the mingling of church and state has led to many oppressive government policies throughout history. Even without full control over the state, the traditional role of religion in opposing various kinds of behavior that has gained more acceptance, for example, gay and lesbian sexuality, causes discomfort about discussing religion's role. Additionally, the constitutional separation of church and state suggests that religion's role is quite limited in addressing the negative consequences of affluence—not to mention that affluence itself may reduce interest in religion.

Because of these fears and objections, we should make several points clear about our views on the role of religion. First, given the historical precedents concerning the curtailing of basic civil liberties when church and state have intermingled, we view the restriction on direct intervention by religious organizations into government activity as a good thing. Whatever religion's benefits may be, we think that their most appropriate avenue is through voluntary restraints on behavior rather than through political means. Those in the politico-religious movements in this country who might like to set up very strict and expansive codes of moral conduct would do well to remember that the original European settlers in New England came to America to escape the burden of religious intolerance sanctioned or even sponsored by the state, yet sometimes they used the coercive powers of the state to practice intolerance themselves once established in America. Very restrictive and expansive codes of conduct can be and historically have been turned into battering rams against civil liberties when religion has been allowed to influence state policy, often restricting alternative religious views.

Second, and in contrast, fears of religion's intrusion into U.S. politics are frequently overstated. Critics of religious fundamentalism will point toward Salem witch-hunts or the excesses of Islamic radicals as evidence of the dangers posed by people who are intensely religious. In a country that has taken appropriate and substantial constitutional means of securing individual rights and limiting organized religion's ability to run affairs of state, the threat of religious extremism to civil liberty would seem to be much less than suggested by these historical episodes where civil liberties were not so protected. By and large, the religious faithful are not the perpetrators of horrendous acts of violence in American cities; rather, independent of political agendas, they are among the kinds of people important to restoring American families.

Third, it is not the case that religious individuals hold on to moral norms of behavior but that nonreligious people do not. Almost everyone supports laws that reflect basic moral norms. Disagreements may exist on which of these norms to place into law and which to hold as purely voluntary social norms, but still, most people agree with state sanctions against murder, theft, fraud, and many other actions. At the core, the main difference between religious people, especially those with intense, traditional views about religion, and nonreligious people is in how expansive and restrictive their norms are. For many Christian traditionalists, homosexuality is unacceptable and divorce is frowned upon. For people outside this group, these behaviors may be seen as more or less acceptable or even worthy of support. By contrast, most nonreligious or nominally religious people are not put off by religious opposition to pedophilia and even support laws against it. Yet there would be and there are many people—even among the religious—who are put off by the views of religious zealots who disdain the celebration of holidays with pagan origins such as Halloween.

It is not at the polar extremes of things like pedophilia or Halloween celebrations, however, where the political views of religious advocates and the nonreligious or nominally religious clash. The supporters of the minority positions on these kinds of issues are so tiny in number that no big battleground appears. The major clashes take place on issues such as homosexuality and abortion, where the number of people holding a minority viewpoint is large enough to stir vociferous debates about acceptable behavior and the extent of public power.

Because of these flash points, the positive spillover effects of religion onto society, even for the nonreligious, are often forgotten. No doubt, religion can foment dangerous levels of intolerance for viewpoints or lifestyles of others even when religion does not possess powers of the state. The bombings of abortion clinics are a recent example. Yet, because religion—especially among the more traditional adherents—establishes voluntary norms of behavior that are relatively inflexible and that can be quite restrictive, religion limits many of the activities that lead to social decay. Basic moral codes like the Ten Commandments, which discourage theft, murder, lying, and sexual promiscuity while encouraging respect for parents, have for centuries composed an important part of the stable foundation for society. Without these kinds of voluntary norms and the influence they exert on behaviors dealing with sexuality, parenting, and divorce, Americans are left only with a secular moral compass, directed most prominently by academics, politicians, and journalists—hardly a source of moral stability.

The upshot here is that voluntary social norms backed by religious conviction play a very important role even in a society determined to maintain broad civil liberties. Those not inclined toward strong traditional religious viewpoints should be able to recognize the positive influence that religion-backed norms can exert even if they would not be willing to adopt some of these norms as law. A truly "judgment-free" society would likely not be a very habitable place. If political liberals and Libertarians see many of these norms as too restrictive and do not want to adopt specific pieces of the agenda of religious evangelicals and fundamentalists as matters of personal choice or public law, that is their business. Yet limiting the extent to which certain moral judgments are included in laws is different from discrediting the people who hold on to strict moral codes as crazed lunatics. The rank and file of these movements is made up largely of people devoted to family and hard work and to living peaceful, law-abiding lives.

Our point also presents implications for those with very restrictive moral ideas based on religious convictions. They must recognize the importance of influence that is exercised through voluntary social norms and personal pressure rather than through legal coercion. In order to maintain a society with broad protections of personal liberty—including religious liberty—a society's legal code must permit certain activities that some people with strong religious convictions disdain. Examples could include alcohol or cigarette consumption, extramarital sexual relationships, lying, and many other matters. These practices have both direct and indirect effects on the people who engage in them as well as on others who do not. A society that protects personal liberty may choose to impose legal sanctions on the most serious and definable effects of these actions, such as deaths caused by a drunk driver. In general, though, the time and energy of the very religious would probably be better spent on attempts to persuade, cajole, plead, and otherwise influence behavior through means that do not require changes in laws. Exactly where the line is drawn to determine when some act is deemed so reprehensible as to require legal sanctions is, no doubt, disputable. Our main point is that those with strong religious views recognize that imposing legal sanctions on behavior in a free society necessitates a much higher standard than deeming a practice to be unacceptable and attempting to influence its practice through purely voluntary means.

Fourth, because of the lack of religion's ability to directly manipulate affairs of state as well as its own dependence on affluence, it is not altogether clear how or whether religion will rectify America's social problems. To play much of a role, growth in religious commitment will have to pick up despite growing affluence, and these people will have to exert influence on others, either through personal contacts or grassroots political movements. On this front, Robert Fogel, a Nobel Prize–winning economic historian, thinks that the United States is already entering a fourth "Great Awakening" of religious fervor.[9]

A Cynical Outlook

As for the willingness of Americans to adopt workable strategies to address potentially disastrous social decay, only time will tell. If one were cynical, one might expect the results of such remedies to be about as successful as the flower children of the 1960s were in enticing large numbers to try communal living. Even if citizens and policymakers seriously devote themselves to assessing policy options that would stem the negative behavior, arriving at solutions that effectively separate out the bad aspects of economic growth while holding on to the good aspects is by no means easy. More discouraging is the idea that turning the problems around will not be effortless; rather, it will require difficult and perhaps unattainable choices for households and policymakers. Once a generation has been reared in broken homes or in violent surroundings, those experiences can never be completely reversed. Further, turning around the factors that have led to these breakdowns is by no means simple, even if one accepts the link between wealth and social decay.

In affluent twentieth-century America, one of the most appealing remedies for any apparent problem is to "throw money" at it and hope for the best. It is less time-consuming to write a check and hope the problem will go away. This lower opportunity cost of detached assistance helps explain the growth and persistence of such programs much better than just the persuasiveness of liberal legislators and advocates of the programs. Although many voters may complain about the chunk taken out of their paychecks, working on society's problems in this way seems more efficient than many alternatives. To reiterate, only a rich society like ours can afford to "throw money" at problems.

Unfortunately, this kind of easy solution just has not worked. One would think that Americans who have witnessed the explosion and implosion of the Great Society programs could well understand that merely increasing spending on social programs is not sufficient to improve every kind of social problem. It may be possible to argue that more money is a necessary condition for improvement, but it can hardly be said that more money alone is sufficient for improvement. Even some of the staunchest believers in massive social programs are now willing to admit this obvious point. Chapters 5–7 drummed home the point that it is just not possible for an affluent society to merely buy its way out of its problems—when many of those problems are exacerbated by affluence.

But if we search for more fundamental means of addressing these problems, one question that arises is this: Why would large numbers of people be interested in changing outcomes that are now intimately tied to affluence? Maybe these bad outcomes, in a perverse sort of way, are exactly what Americans with all of their affluence really want. Most people would prefer lower crime rates and fewer births to teenagers if they could be achieved without cost, but they may not want to adopt policies that begin to infringe on their affluence-riddled tastes. Many people do not really like the fifteen extra pounds they are carrying, but they may like the idea of cutting back on their Doritos and soft drinks even less. Alcoholics may understand the deterioration in life they are causing with their drinking, but they also know that they enjoy the feeling they get from drinking. If Johnny likes being spoiled rotten, why would we think Johnny is going to support politicians who will infringe on his behavior?

The dilemma America faces in this respect is akin to the overweight person putting a combination lock on the refrigerator. If restraining one's behavior were as simple as that, then those twenty pounds hanging over the belt might never have appeared. Nonetheless, surprisingly, such self-restraining attempts occasionally work.

At its core, handling affluence effects is most fundamentally a family problem. As we noted in Chapter 1, many individual families have had to address the question that now sits before society as a whole: How can we and our children enjoy the benefits of affluence without becoming spoiled by it? If individual families do not successfully address these problems in the years in which children form the basis for their values and preferences, it is not at all clear how successful public policy of any label or design will be. What means does society have to turn a delinquent eighteen-year-old into a responsible, hardworking thirty-year-old? What policies could ever be enacted to improve relationships between spouses or between parents and children?

It is not our intent to arrive at an entirely nihilistic conclusion. Although the current trends in family life, work, and politics leave us fairly cynical about prospects, we do not view America as being on a deterministic, downward spiral that will end in its demise. We do not have a crystal ball. The factors contributing to the social decay, including affluence, may be offset by countervailing events and forces that we cannot foresee. For the near term, however, we are not very confident about the direction in which the United States is heading.

NOTES

Chapter One

1. Jack Germond, *Mad as Hell: Revolt at the Ballot Box* (New York: Warner Books, 1992).

2. Buchanan has summarized his economic analysis in *The Great Betrayal: How American Sovereignty and Social Justice Are Being Sacrificed to the Gods of the Global Economy* (New York: Little, Brown, 1998).

3. The data here come from Karl Zinmeister, "Pay Day Mayday," *American Enterprise* (September–October 1995):44–48, and from data discussed in Chapter 3.

4. The baseball statistics are from Sean Luhman's Baseball Archive, available: www.baseball.com.

5. Robert Samuelson, *The Good Life and Its Discontents* (New York: Times Books, 1995).

6. Ibid.

7. John Kenneth Galbraith, *The Affluent Society* (Cambridge: Riverside Press, 1958).

8. Ben Wattenberg, *The Good News Is the Bad News Is Wrong* (New York: Simon and Schuster, 1984).

9. Some of Julian Simon's works include *The State of Humanity* (ed.) (Cambridge: Cambridge University Press, 1995), *Population Matters* (New Brunswick, N.J.: Transaction Publishers, 1990), *Economics of Population Growth* (Princeton: Princeton University Press, 1977), and *Ultimate Resource* (Princeton: Princeton University Press, 1998).

10. Robert Bartley, *The Seven Fat Years* (New York: Free Press, 1992).

11. These three reports are W. Michael Cox and Richard Alm, "Time Well Spent: The Declining Real Cost of Living in America," *Federal Reserve Bank of Dallas Annual Report, 1997*; "By Our Own Bootstraps: Economic Opportunity and the Dynamics of Income Distribution," *Federal Reserve Bank of Dallas Annual Report, 1995*; and "These Are the Good Old Days: A Report on Living Standards," *Federal Reserve Bank of Dallas Annual Report, 1994*.

12. Richard McKenzie, *Paradox of Progress* (New York: Oxford University Press, 1996). McKenzie authored an earlier book about economic progress

in the alleged stagnation era, entitled *What Went Right in the 1980s* (San Francisco: Pacific Research Institute, 1994).

13. See, for example, Karl Zinmeister's editorial, "Coming This Year: Marx for Dummies," *Wall Street Journal*, January 25, 1996, where he discusses the fallacy of the despair message, dismissing it as mere rhetoric, overblown expectations, and war-period economic statistics.

14. Daniel Bell, *The Cultural Contradictions of Capitalism* (New York: Basic Books, 1996). The 1996 volume is the twentieth-anniversary edition of Bell's original work. The article most closely in alignment with our argument is probably Nicholas Eberstadt, "Prosperous Paupers and Affluent Savages," *Society* (January–February 1996):17–25.

15. Nobel Prize–winning economist Milton Friedman developed these ideas in the 1950s, and they came to be known as the Permanent Income Hypothesis.

16. George Stigler and Gary Becker, "De Gustibus Non Est Disputandum," *American Economic Review* (March 1977):76–90.

17. The idea that rising wealth increases the importance of economic and societal factors on preferences is discussed by Gary Becker in *Accounting for Tastes* (Cambridge: Harvard University Press, 1996). This book consolidates Becker's many extensions of his basic article on tastes with Stigler ("De Gustibus"). These include pricing anomalies, addictive behavior, advertising, and other social interactions.

Chapter Two

1. David Wessel and Gerald Seib, "Americans, Especially Baby Boomers, Voice Pessimism for Their Kids' Future," *Wall Street Journal*, January 19, 1996.

2. See George Judson, "Most Residents See Drop in Standard of Living, Study Finds," *New York Times*, December 11, 1995.

3. Lynn Smith and Bob Sipchen, "Two-Career Families Face Dilemma," *Los Angeles Times*, August 12, 1990.

4. Christina Duff, "America's Bad Mood Finally Turns Upbeat Years After Economy," *Wall Street Journal*, October 16, 1996.

5. In Richard McKenzie, *Paradox of Progress* (New York: Oxford University Press, 1996), McKenzie documents that negative stories about the economy in the press outnumber positive stories on the order of four to one.

6. Readers can also consult Richard McKenzie, *What Went Right in the 1980s* (San Francisco: Pacific Research Institute, 1994), for additional detail on the message of decay.

7. Kuttner had earlier devoted an entire book to this subject: Robert Kuttner, *The Economic Illusion* (Boston: Houghton-Mifflin, 1984).

8. Robert Kuttner, "Fewer Fruits for Our Labors," *Washington Post*, September 4, 1994.

9. Robert Kuttner, "The Rewards of Our Labors Are Increasingly Unequal," *Boston Globe*, September 4, 1995. See also Robert Kuttner, "Search for Elusive Candidate X," *Washington Post*, August 27, 1995.

10. George Melloan and Guy Molyneaux, "It's the Economy, Stupid," *Wall Street Journal*, January 29, 1996, and Guy Molyneaux, "It's the Economy, Stupid," *Los Angeles Times*, March 3, 1996.

11. Roger Lowenstein, "Intrinsic Value: Why Primary Voters Are So Angry," *Wall Street Journal*, February 22, 1996.

12. "Real Buchanan Alternatives," *Atlanta Constitution*, March 4, 1996.

13. John Yang, "Hill Picks Up Buchanan's Economic Anxiety Issue," *Washington Post*, February 28, 1996.

14. Ronald Yates, "In Larger Picture, U.S. Not So Competitive," *Chicago Tribune*, September 29, 1995.

15. Carolyn Bell Shaw, "Productivity Grew at a Modest 1.1% in 1995," *Los Angeles Times*, March 7, 1996.

16. Carolyn Bell Shaw, "Bridging the Income Gap," *Boston Globe*, March 12, 1996.

17. Rick Bragg, "Big Holes Where Dignity Used to Be," *New York Times*, March 5, 1996.

18. Charles Stein, "For Workers, It's the Age of Anxiety," *Boston Globe*, January 21, 1996.

19. This quotation is from Peter Passell and Leonard Ross, *The Retreat from Riches: Affluence and Its Enemies* (New York: Viking Press, 1973), p. 10.

20. David Wessel, "Budget Seeks to Raise U.S. Living Standards and Reduce Inequality," *Wall Street Journal*, February 7, 1997.

21. Jacob Schlesinger, "UPS Pact Fails to Shift Balance of Power Back to U.S. Workers," *Wall Street Journal*, August 20, 1997.

22. Sue Schellenberger, "Work and Family: Do We Work More or Not? Either Way We Feel Frazzled," *Wall Street Journal*, July 30, 1997.

23. Jonathan Rowe, "Major Growing Pains: The Economy Is Rosy but People Are Not," *U.S. News and World Report*, October 21, 1996, pp. 62–64.

24. Clifford Cobb, Ted Halstead, and Jonathan Rowe, "If the GDP Is Up, Why Is America Down?" *Atlantic* (October 1995):59–78.

25. Then Stanford economist Paul Krugman covered these events in "How the Press Miscovers Economics," *Jobs and Capital* (Summer 1996):9–11.

26. CNN has also made contributions. See *Downsizing the Dream*, hosted by Frank Sesno, Turner Learning Video, 1997.

27. Kevin Phillips, *Boiling Point: Democrats, Republicans, and the Decline in the Middle Class* (New York: HarperPerennial, 1994).

28. Kevin Phillips, *The Politics of Rich and Poor: Wealth and the American Electorate in the Reagan Aftermath* (New York: Random House, 1990).

29. Jeffrey Madrick, *The End of Affluence* (New York: Random House, 1995).

30. Friedman had earlier contributed a volume of his own on the topic: Benjamin Friedman, *Day of Reckoning* (New York: Random House, 1988).

31. Jeffrey Madrick, "If We're So Tired, Why Aren't We Rich?" *New York Times*, January 16, 1996.

32. Robert Frank and Phillip Cook, *The Winner-Take-All Society* (New York: Free Press, 1995).

33. New York Times, *The Downsizing of America* (New York: Times Books, 1996).

34. Paul Ehrlich, *The Population Bomb* (New York: Ballantine Books, 1968). For an update on these views, see Paul Ehrlich, *The Population Explosion* (New York: Simon and Schuster, 1990), p. xi.

35. This quotation is from Paul Ehrlich and Ann Ehrlich, *The End of Affluence* (Rivercity, NH: Rivercity Press, 1975), as cited in Alan Stockman, *Introduction to Macroeconomics* (Forth Worth, Tex.: Dryden, 1996), p. 238.

36. Ravi Batra, *The Coming Depression of 1990* (New York: Simon and Schuster, 1987).

37. Ravi Batra, *Surviving the Great Depression of 1990* (New York: Simon and Schuster, 1988).

38. Charles Murray, *Losing Ground* (New York: Basic Books, 1984), p. 26.

39. Just a small sampling includes Joel Kurtzman, *The Decline and Crash of the American Economy* (New York: Norton, 1988), Bennet Harrison and Barry Bluestone, *The Great U-Turn* (New York: Basic Books, 1988), Haynes Johnson, *Sleepwalking Through History* (New York: Norton, 1991), and Katherine Newman, *Declining Fortunes* (New York: Basic Books, 1993), in addition to the other books cited within this chapter.

40. Bill Clinton and Al Gore, *Putting People First* (New York: Times Books, 1992).

41. Ibid., pp. 5, 7.

42. Ibid., p. 5.

43. Ibid., p. 100.

44. Robert Reich, "Out of the Loop," *Chicago Tribune*, April 18, 1995.

45. The books by Robert Reich are *The Next American Frontier* (New York: Times Books, 1983) and *The Work of Nations* (New York: Vintage Books, 1992).

46. Sylvia Nasar, "An Unorthodox Choice for Economic Advisor," *New York Times*, December 12, 1992.

47. See James Bennett, "Exultant Buchanan Pushes Economic Insecurity Theme," *New York Times*, February 22, 1996. Most recently, Buchanan consolidated his views in *The Great Betrayal: How American Sovereignty and Social Justice Are Being Sacrificed to the Gods of the Global Economy* (Boston: Little, Brown, 1998).

48. Kenneth Boulding, *Beyond Economics* (Ann Arbor: University of Michigan Press, 1968), p. 281.

49. Nicholas Georgescu-Roegen, *The Entropy Law and the Economic Progress* (Cambridge: Harvard University Press, 1971).

50. Herman Daly, *Beyond Growth: The Economics of Sustainable Development* (Boston: Beacon Press, 1996) and *Steady State Economics* (Washington, D.C.: Island Press, 1977).

51. Robert Heilbroner, *The Economic Problem* (Englewood Cliffs, N.J.: Prentice-Hall, 1972), and Robert Heilbroner and Lester Thurow, *Five Economic Challenges* (Englewood Cliffs, N.J.: Prentice-Hall, 1981), p. 127.

52. See Paul Samuelson, "The Optimum Rate of Economic Growth for Population," *International Economic Review* (October 1975):531–538, and Nicholas Kaldor, "A Model of Economic Growth," *Economic Journal* (December 1957):591–624.

53. See Julian Simon, *The Theory of Population and Economic Growth* (Oxford: Basil Blackwell, 1986), *Population Matters* (New Brunswick, N.J.: Transaction Publishers, 1990), *The State of Humanity* (ed.) (London: Blackwell, 1995), and *Ultimate Resource* (Princeton: Princeton University Press, 1996).

54. Lester Thurow, *The Zero-Sum Society* (New York: Basic Books, 1980).

55. Ibid., pp. 5–6.

56. Paul Krugman, *The Age of Diminished Expectations: U.S. Economic Policy in the 1990s* (Cambridge: MIT Press, 1990), p. 1. Krugman has received the John Bates Clark Award, handed out annually by the American Economic Association to the economist under forty making the most significant contributions to the discipline.

57. Juliet Schor, *The Overworked American: The Unexpected Decline of Leisure* (New York: Basic Books, 1991).

58. Ibid., p. 47.

59. Juliet Schor, *The Overspent American: Upscaling, Downshifting, and the New Consumer* (New York: Basic Books, 1998).

60. The report is Lawrence Mishel and Jared Bernstein, "State of Working America 1994–95," Economic Policy Institute, Washington, D.C., 1994, and is cited in Barbara Vobejda, "Education Is No Protection from Wage Squeeze, Report Says," *Washington Post*, September 4, 1994.

61. Center for Labor Market Studies, "The State of the American Dream in New England," Northeastern University, Boston, 1995, as cited in Ronald Yates, "In Larger Picture, U.S. Not So Competitive," *Chicago Tribune*, September 29, 1995.

62. Cited in Yates, "In Larger Picture, U.S. Not So Competitive."

63. Alan Blinder, *Hard Heads, Soft Hearts* (Reading, Mass.: Addison-Wesley, 1987).

64. "A Valuable Economics Seminar," *New York Times*, December 16, 1996.

65. John Taylor, "The Path to Growth," *Wall Street Journal*, October 18, 1996.

Chapter Three

1. Anne Rice, *The Vampire Lestat* (New York: Ballantine Books, 1985).

2. The facts about this high-school basketball team were related to us by a resident of this central Kentucky county.

3. The source is the U.S. Bureau of Economic Analysis, as cited in Karl Zinsmeister, "Wages," *American Enterprise* (July–August 1996):18–19.

4. Juliet Schor, *The Overworked American: The Unexpected Decline of Leisure* (New York: Basic Books, 1991).

5. These data are drawn from research by Stanley Lebergott, *Pursuing Happiness* (Princeton: Princeton University Press, 1993).

6. Alan Stockman, *Introduction to Macroeconomics* (Fort Worth, Tex.: Dryden, 1996) discusses several of these episodes in his chapter on economic growth.

7. Charles Maurice and Charles Smithson, *Doomsday Myth: 10,000 Years of Economic Crisis* (Stanford: Hoover Institution Press, 1984).

8. "Environmental Scares," *Economist*, January 2, 1998, pp. 19–21.

9. Julian Simon, ed., *The State of Humanity* (London: Blackwell, 1995).

10. Jonathon Rowe, "Major Growing Pains: The Economy Is Rosy but People Are Not," *U.S. News and World Report*, October 21, 1996, pp. 62–64, and Clifford Cobb, Ted Halstead, and Jonathon Rowe, "If the GDP Is Up, Why Is America Down?" *Atlantic* (October 1995):59–78.

11. Stanford economist Paul Krugman, mentioned in Chapter 2 as one of the stagnation messengers, takes the press to task for this particular point in "How the Press Miscovers Economics," *Jobs and Capital* (Summer 1996):9–11.

12. The measure created in the 1940s was called gross national product (GNP). This measure was used through the 1980s. During the 1980s, GDP was developed to more accurately reflect domestic production and now has become the measure of choice. However, the conceptual differences between GDP and GNP are slight, and the actual differences between them using contemporary U.S. data are trivial in comparison to their levels.

13. The recent move to "chain-weighted price indexes" represents such improvements. For a readable summary of this improvement, see Kevin

Kliesen, "Chained, Rested, and Ready: The New and Improved GDP," *St. Louis Federal Reserve Bank Regional Economist* (January 1996):10–11.

14. A good overview of measuring the underground economy is provided by Edward Feige, ed., *The Underground Economy* (Cambridge: Cambridge University Press, 1989).

15. For example, see Jonathon Rowe, "Major Growing Pains: The Economy Is Rosy But People Are Not," *U.S. News and World Report,* October 21, 1996.

16. The GDP-implicit price deflator is the main alternative and is made up of many more subindexes than the CPI, and the weights for categories of goods and services are changed more frequently, making it a somewhat more reliable indicator of average prices.

17. See Adam Smith, *The Wealth of Nations* (New York: Penguin Books, 1981), p. 351.

18. Quoted in Michael Mandel, "The Truth About the Economy," *Business Week,* November 7, 1994, p. 111.

19. The figures cited here are from Charles Hulten, "Quality Change in the CPI," *Federal Reserve Bank of St. Louis Review* (May–June 1997): 87–100. This issue contains an interesting discussion among several of the experts in this area. It provides valuable insight into the details of the quality–price level problems. Also, the chief of the Division of Price Index Number Research at the Bureau of Labor Research gives an overview of CPI bias issues in Brent Moulton, "Bias in the Consumer Price Index: What Is the Evidence?" *Journal of Economic Perspectives* (Fall 1996):159–178.

20. Charles Hulten, "Quality Change in the CPI," p. 96.

21. See U.S. Bureau of the Census, *Statistical Abstract of the U.S.* (Washington, D.C.: USGPO, various years).

22. The most advanced methods, "hedonic pricing models," estimate algebraic equations that estimate the willingness of consumers to pay for quality variation. Implicitly, the accuracy of these equations relies on small, continuous changes rather than large, discrete changes, although they are often used where big changes are under investigation.

23. Henry Simons, an influential economics teacher at the University of Chicago around the middle of the twentieth century, is credited with emphasizing this simple yet underappreciated definition of income as the sum of consumption plus changes in wealth.

24. These data are taken from two studies that are representative of many similar ones. They are Winfred Gibbs, *The Minimum Cost of Living: A Study of Families on Limited Income in New York City* (New York: Macmillan, 1917), and Frank Streighthoff, *The Standard of Living Among the Industrial People of America* (Boston: Houghton-Mifflin, 1911).

25. George Stigler, "The Cost of Subsistence," *Journal of Farm Economics* (May 1945):303–314.

26. Victor Smith, "Linear Programming Models for the Determination of Palatable Human Diets," *Journal of Farm Economics* (May 1959): 272–283.

27. Angus Deaton is an eminent economist who has continued to contribute to the analysis of household consumption patterns and their information on living standards. Leonard Nakumura, "Is the U.S. Economy Really Growing Too Slowly? Maybe We're Measuring the Wrong Thing," *Federal Reserve Bank of Philadelphia Business Review* (March–April 1997):3–14, is a recent overview of the importance of assessing living standards by referring to consumer expenditure patterns. Some economists within the Department of Agriculture continue to monitor these kinds of statistics and report them in journals such as *Family Economics Review* and *Food Review*.

28. Hendrik Houthakker, "Engel's Law," in *The New Palgrave: A Dictionary of Economics*, ed. J. Eatwell, M. Milgate, and P. Newman (London: Macmillan, 1987), p. 143.

29. The foods and their quantities included in these diets are taken from Victor Smith, *Journal of Farm Economics* (May 1959):272–283. We then computed expenditures per family by multiplying these quantities by 1970 and 1994 prices for each of the goods, which we obtained from several different government publications, including U.S. Bureau of the Census, *Statistical Abstract of the U.S.* (Washington, D.C.: USGPO, various years), U.S. Bureau of the Census, *Historical Statistics of the U.S.* (Washington, D.C.: USGPO, 1975), and U.S. Department of Agriculture, *Agricultural Statistics* (Washington, D.C.: USGPO, various years).

30. These data were compiled and reported in Bureau of Economic Analysis, "The Improved Estimates of the National Income and Product Accounts for 1959–95," *Survey of Current Business* (January–February 1996):1–27. See also Leonard Nakamura, *Federal Reserve Bank of Philadelphia Business Review* (March–April 1997).

31. Additional examples are included in Michael Cox and Richard Alm, "Time Well Spent: The Declining Real Cost of Living in America," *Federal Reserve Bank of Dallas Annual Report, 1997*; "These Are the Good Old Days: A Report on Living Standards," *Federal Reserve Bank of Dallas Annual Report, 1995*; and "By Our Own Bootstraps: Economic Opportunity and the Dynamics of Income Distribution," *Federal Reserve Bank of Dallas Annual Report, 1994*.

32. See James Quirk and Rodney Fort, *Pay Dirt* (Princeton: Princeton University Press, 1997).

33. John Weicher, "Wealth and Its Distribution," *Federal Reserve Bank of St. Louis Review* (January–February 1997):3–23, provides a more detailed discussion of these biases.

34. Kevin Phillips, *Boiling Point: Democrats, Republicans, and the Decline of the Middle Class* (New York: Random House, 1994).

35. A recent book representative of this way of thinking is Juliet Schor, *The Overspent American: Upscaling, Downshifting, and the New Consumer* (New York: Basic Books, 1998).

Chapter Four

1. Robert Frank and Phillip Cook, *The Winner-Take-All Society* (New York: Free Press, 1995), p. 5.

2. Ibid.

3. See U.S. Bureau of the Census, *Statistical Abstract of the U.S.* (Washington, D.C.: USGPO, various issues).

4. Kevin Phillips, *Boiling Point: Democrats, Republicans, and the Decline of the Middle Class* (New York: HarperPerennial, 1994), p. 160.

5. Also see Daniel Slesnick, "Gaining Ground: Poverty in the Postwar United States," *Journal of Political Economy* (February 1993):1–38.

6. See Karl Zinsmeister, "Income vs. Consumption," *American Enterprise* (July/August):21.

7. We could not locate expenditure data based on the poverty line for 1971.

8. See W. Michael Cox and Richard Alm, "Time Well Spent: The Declining Real Cost of Living in America," *Federal Reserve Bank of Dallas Annual Report, 1997*, pp. 2–24.

9. These statements are based on data reported in Central Intelligence Agency, *Handbook of International Economic Statistics, 1997* (Washington, D.C.: USGPO, 1997), and Robert Summers and Alan Heston, "The Penn World Table: An Expanded Set of International Comparisons, 1950–1988," *Quarterly Journal of Economics* (May 1991):327–368.

10. Office of Tax Analysis, "Household Income Mobility During the 1980s: A Statistical Analysis Based on Tax Return Data," U.S. Department of the Treasury, 1992.

11. Isabel Sawhill and David McMurrer, "How Much Do Americans Move Up or Down the Economic Ladder?" Urban Institute, Washington, D.C., November 1996, and Isabel Sawhill and David McMurrer, "Economic Mobility in the United States," Urban Institute, Washington, D.C., December 1996.

12. W. Michael Cox and Richard Alm, "By Our Own Bootstraps: Economic Opportunity and the Dynamics of Income Distribution," *Federal Reserve Bank of Dallas Annual Report, 1995*.

13. These figures were collected by Richard Easterlin, Christine Schaeffer, and Diane Macunovich and are cited in Karl Zinsmeister, "Mobility," *American Enterprise* (July–August 1996):20. See also Benjamin Zycher, "The Rich and the Poor," *Jobs and Capital* (Summer 1996):30–31.

14. To be accurate, colder water sinks except at temperatures very close to freezing.

15. For these and other top income figures, see Robert LaFranco, "The Forbes Top 40," *Forbes,* September 22, 1997.

16. Robert Haveman, *Earnings Inequality: The Influence of Changing Opportunities and Choice* (Washington, D.C.: American Enterprise Institute, 1996).

17. Robert Lerman, "Is Earnings Inequality Really Increasing?" Urban Institute, Washington, D.C., March 1997.

18. Sarah Anderson and John Cavanagh, "The Top 10 List," *Nation,* December 8, 1997, p. 8.

19. See Executive Office of the President, *Economic Report of the President* (Washington, D.C.: USGPO, 1997), p. 338.

20. These figures are based on our calculations using data from U.S. Bureau of the Census, *Historical Statistics of the U.S.* (Washington, D.C.: USGPO, 1975), and U.S. Bureau of the Census, *Statistical Abstract of the U.S.* (Washington, D.C.: USGPO, 1997).

21. The figures here are from Peter Lynch, "The Upsizing of America," *Wall Street Journal*, September 20, 1996.

22. Ibid.

23. Rick Bragg, "Big Holes Where Dignity Used to Be," *New York Times*, March 5, 1996.

24. We believe this quote to be attributable to the late Nobel Prize–winning economist George Stigler, but we do not know its source exactly.

25. Cox and Alm, "By Our Own Bootstraps."

26. Lester Thurow, *The Zero-Sum Society* (New York: Basic Books, 1980), p. 3.

27. Robert Heilbroner and Lester Thurow, *Five Economic Challenges* (Englewood Cliffs, N.J.: Prentice-Hall, 1981), p. 39.

28. Paul Krugman, *Diminished Expectations* (Cambridge: MIT Press, 1990), p. 116.

29. Julian Simon, *The State of Humanity* (London: Blackwell, 1994), p. 242.

30. Data on these comparisons for middle- and lower-income countries can be found in U.S. Bureau of the Census, *Statistical Abstract of the U.S.* (Washington, D.C.: USGPO), various issues.

31. These ownership rates are from U.S. Bureau of the Census, *Statistical Abstract of the U.S.* (Washington, D.C.: USGPO, 1997), p. 842.

32. These figures are from the U.S. Health Care Financing Administration, as cited in Ronald Alsop, ed., *The Wall Street Journal Almanac 1998* (New York: Ballantine Books, 1997), p. 731.

33. See ibid., p. 732.

34. Other than China, the figures are for 1993 and from U.S. Bureau of the Census, *Statistical Abstract of the U.S.* (Washington, D.C.: USGPO, 1997).

35. Ibid., p. 483.

36. U.S. Bureau of the Census, *Statistical Abstract of the U.S.* (Washington, D.C.: USGPO, various issues).

Chapter Five

1. Juliet Schor, *The Overworked American: The Unexpected Decline of Leisure* (New York: Basic Books, 1991).

2. John Robinson is a sociologist and director of the Americans' Use of Time Project; Geoffrey Godbey is a professor of leisure studies. The data cited here are based on John Robinson and Geoffrey Godbey, "Are Average Americans Really Overworked?" *American Enterprise* (September–October 1995):45.

3. Robert Browning, "The Glove," in Geoffrey Cumberlege, ed., *The Poetical Works of Robert Browning* (London: Oxford University Press, 1940), p. 23.

4. A full discussion of compensating differentials can be found in Ronald Ehrenberg and Robert Smith, *Modern Labor Economics* (Reading, Mass.: Addison-Wesley, 1998).

5. The salary figure for UPS was provided by an MBA student who works for UPS.

6. See U.S. Department of Labor, *Report on the American Workforce* (Washington, D.C.: USGPO, 1995).

7. Henry Farber, "Are Lifetime Jobs Disappearing? Job Duration in the United States" (Princeton: National Bureau of Economic Research, 1995, Working Paper No. 5814).

8. See John Cassidy, "All Worked Up," *New Yorker*, April 22, 1996.

9. For data on the job-loser rate, see Bureau of Labor Statistics, *Employment and Earnings* (Washington, D.C.: USGPO, monthly).

10. For these data, see Marvin Kosters, ed., "Relative Wage Trends, Women's Work, and Family Income," *American Enterprise Institute*, Washington, D.C., conference summaries, January 1997.

11. These figures are from U.S. Department of Education, National Center for Education Statistics, *Digest of Education Statistics, 1996* (Washington, D.C.: USGPO, 1996).

12. For more on this point of view, see Eric Hanushek, review of *What Money Can't Buy*, by Susan Mayer, *Journal of Policy Analysis and Management* (3) (1998):535–538.

13. For more on this point about the rewards to mediocrity, see Robert Lerman, "Economic Restructuring and the Job Market," Urban Institute, Washington, D.C., September 1997.

Chapter Six

1. For perspective on these events, see Barbara Dafoe Whitehead, "Dan Quayle Was Right," *Atlantic* (April 1993):47–84.

2. Hillary Clinton, *It Takes a Village* (New York: Simon and Schuster, 1996).

3. "The National Prospect: A Symposium," *Commentary* (November 1995). See also articles such as Nicholas Eberstadt, "Prosperous Paupers and Affluent Savages, *Society* (January–February 1996):17–25, and Lionel Tiger, "Nasty Turns in Family Life," *U.S. News and World Report,* July 1, 1996, p. 57.

4. See U.S. Bureau of the Census, *Statistical Abstract of the U.S.* (Washington, D.C.: USGPO, 1997), p. 834.

5. See Charles Murray, "The Coming White Underclass," *Wall Street Journal,* October 29, 1993.

6. See Ronald Alsop, ed., *The Wall Street Journal Almanac* (New York: Ballantine Books, 1997), p. 789.

7. These figures are taken from Ronald Alsop, ed., *The Wall Street Journal Almanac* (New York: Ballantine Books, 1998), p. 711.

8. U.S. Bureau of the Census, *Statistical Abstract of the U.S.* (Washington, D.C.: USGPO, 1997), p. 834.

9. Ron Haskins, "Does Welfare Encourage Illegitimacy?" *American Enterprise* (July–August 1996):48–49, cites a University of Pennsylvania study showing that a 10-percent rise in welfare benefits causes a 12-percent increase in illegitimate births.

10. See Gay Kitson and H. Raschke, "Divorce Research: What We Know; What We Don't Know," *Journal of Divorce* (1981):1–37.

11. Gary Becker, *The Economic Approach to Human Behavior* (Chicago: University of Chicago Press, 1976) consolidates many of his important contributions to topics such as marriage, fertility discrimination, crime, and others. A very readable popularization of these ideas is Richard McKenzie and Gordon Tullock, *The Best of the New World of Economics* (Boston: Irwin, 1989). Another contribution in this vein is Mariano Tommasi and Kathryn Ierulli, *The New Economics of Human Behavior* (New York: Cambridge University Press, 1995).

12. In addition to Gary Becker's work, another work about the economic influences on the decision to have children is Julian Simon, *Effects of Income on Fertility* (N.p.: Carolina Population Center, 1974).

13. Desmond Morris, *The Human Animal* (New Brunswick, N.J.: Transaction Publishers, 1995).

14. Ibid.

15. See Greg J. Duncan and Saul D. Hoffman, "Economic Consequences of Marital Instability," in Martin David and Timothy Smeeling, eds., *Horizontal Equity, Uncertainty, and Economic Well-Being* (Chicago: University of Chicago Press, 1985). See also Robert Haveman and Barbara Wolfe, "The Determinants of Children's Attainment: A Review of Methods and Findings," *Journal of Economic Literature* (December 1995):1829–1878.

16. See Charles Murray, "What to Do About Welfare," *Commentary* (December 1994):26–34, and Ron Haskins, *The American Enterprise* (July–August 1996):48–49.

17. See J. G. Bachman, L. D. Johnson, and P. M. O'Malley, *Monitoring the Future* (Ann Arbor: University of Michigan Survey Research Center, 1993).

18. Melvin Borland and Robert Pulsinelli, "Household Commodity Production and Social Harassment Costs," *Southern Economic Journal* (October 1989):291–301, discuss social harassment effects at length.

19. Robert Bork, *Slouching Towards Gomorrah* (New York: Regan Books, 1996).

20. See Jody Lipford, Robert McCormick, and Robert Tollison, "Preaching Matters," *Journal of Economic Behavior and Organization* (August 1993):235–250.

21. This quotation comes from a comprehensive study showing the link between deviancy and single parenting after controlling for most other relevant factors. See S. M. Dornbusch et al., "Single Parents, Extended Households, and the Control of Adolescents," *Child Development* (April 1985):326–341.

22. See William Comaner and Llad Phillips, "Best Crime Stopper: A Father in the Home," *Wall Street Journal*, March 10, 1998.

23. For a discussion, see John Lott, "Can Government Crime Data Be Trusted?" *Investor Business Daily*, July 16, 1998.

24. See U.S. Bureau of the Census, *Statistical Abstract of the U.S.* (Washington, D.C.: USGPO, 1997), p. 204.

25. John DiIulio Jr., "Rescue the Young from Barbarism," *American Enterprise* (May–June 1995):22–23. See also John DiIulio Jr., "Defining Criminality Up," *Wall Street Journal*, July 3, 1996.

26. Daniel Patrick Moynihan, "Defining Deviancy Downward," *American Scholar* (Winter 1993):17–30.

27. John DiIulio Jr., "A More Gated Community," *Weekly Standard*, July 7, 1997.

28. These figures are from U.S. Department of Justice, *Sourcebook of Criminal Justice Statistics* (Washington, D.C.: USGPO, 1991), p. 626.

29. Again, see Comaner and Phillips, "Best Crime Stopper."

30. Murray, "The Coming White Underclass."

31. For a detailed perspective on the overextension of due process, see George Dentes, "Radically Narrow the Exclusionary Rule," *American Enterprise* (May–June 1995):42–45, and Jagdish Bhagwati, "Or Get Rid of It Altogether," *American Enterprise* (May–June 1995):42–45.

32. See U.S. Department of Justice, *Sentencing Reform in the U.S.* (Washington, D.C.: USGPO, 1985).

33. See ibid., and U.S. Department of Justice, *National Assessment of Structured Sentencing* (Washington, D.C.: USGPO, 1996) for a more detailed review of these efforts.

34. See Morgan Reynolds, "Crime and Punishment in America," National Center for Policy Analysis Policy Report No. 193, Dallas, Tex., June 1995.

35. See ibid., Table 4.

36. State requirements are summarized in Council of State Governments, *Book of the States* (Lexington, Ky.: Council of State Governments, 1994), pp. 536–537.

37. The figures here are taken from John DiIulio Jr., "Abolish the Death Penalty, Officially," *Wall Street Journal,* December 15, 1997.

38. We computed the average reduction in life expectancy by taking the likelihood of execution (0.001) and multiplying it by the difference between the remaining given life expectancy of a murderer at the time of the murder (we assumed fifty years, on average, at the upper end and forty, on average, at the lower end) and the average time until execution (nine years).

39. These data are from Federal Bureau of Prisons, *Prisoners Released from State and Federal Institutions* (Washington, D.C.: USGPO), various volumes, and from U.S. Department of Justice, *Sourcebook of Criminal Justice Statistics* (Washington, D.C.: USGPO), various volumes.

40. For a detailed discussion of this problem, see George Kelling and Catherine Coles, *Fixing Broken Windows: Restoring Order and Reducing Crime in Our Communities* (New York: Free Press, 1996).

41. As evidence of the maxim that a little crime leads to a lot of crime, Peter Greenwood, "Selective Incapacitation," Report R-2815-NIJ, Rand Corporation, Santa Monica, Calif., 1982, found that an average inmate had committed 187 crimes the year previous to incarceration.

42. See Gary Becker and George Stigler, "De Gustibus Non Est Disputandum," *American Economic Review* (March 1977):76–90, and Gary Becker, *Accounting for Tastes* (Cambridge: Harvard University Press, 1996).

43. See U.S. Bureau of the Census, *Statistical Abstract of the U.S.* (Washington, D.C.: USGPO, 1997), Table 645.

44. Lisa Verrico, "What's Your Problem? Mark E. Smith—Hippies," *Vox* (March 1994):18.

Chapter Seven

1. John Kenneth Galbraith, *The Affluent Society* (Cambridge: Riverside Press, 1958), pp. 328–329.

2. See Cheryl Holsey and Thomas Borcherding, "Why Does Government's Share of National Income Grow? An Assessment of the Recent Literature on the U.S. Experience," in *Perspectives on Public Choice: A Handbook,* ed. Dennis Mueller (Cambridge: Cambridge University Press, 1997).

3. Chapter 17 in Dennis Mueller, *Public Choice II* (Cambridge: Cambridge University Press, 1989), provides a good overview of this literature.

4. See Robert Higgs, *Crisis and Leviathan: Critical Episodes in the Growth of American Government* (New York: Oxford University Press, 1987).

5. Murray Weidenbaum, "A New Approach to Regulatory Reform," Center for Study of American Business, St. Louis, Mo., Policy Report No. 147, August 1998.

6. Thomas Hopkins, "Regulatory Costs in Profile," Center for Study of American Business, St. Louis, Mo., Policy Report No. 132, August 1996.

7. This statement is based on the relationship of the regulatory index cited above and GDP since 1950, as reported in Brian Goff, *Regulation and Macroeconomic Performance* (Boston: Kluwer Academic Press, 1996).

8. This statement is from an 1811 letter written by de Maistre.

9. This section relies on and extends the scholarly contributions of James Buchanan, Gordon Tullock, Mancur Olsen, Duncan Black, William Riker, Peter Ordeshook, and others influential in the "public choice" field of economics and its counterpart in political science, called "positive political economy." These contributions are diverse, incorporating insights about majority voting and its effects, interest group activity, federalism, bureaucracy, income transfers, and other politically related topics.

10. See Gordon Tullock, *The Social Dilemma: The Economics of War and Revolution* (Blacksburg, Va.: University Publications, 1974), and Samuel Popkin, *Rational Peasant: The Political Economy of Rural Society in Vietnam* (Berkeley: University of California Press, 1979).

11. Cited in Indur Gokleny, "Richer Is Cleaner," in *The True State of the Planet*, ed. Ronald Bailey (New York: Free Press, 1995).

12. For an overview, see Morris Fiorina, "Voting Behavior," in *Perspectives in Public Choice: A Handbook*, ed. Dennis Mueller (Cambridge: Cambridge University Press, 1997).

13. See Marcia Angell, *Science on Trial: The Clash of Medical Evidence and the Law in the Breast Implant Case* (New York: W. W. Norton, 1996).

14. See John Stossel, "Pandering to Fear," *Jobs and Capital* (Summer 1996):16–21.

15. The defendant, who had no prior criminal record, later sued the federal government and CNN for unreasonable search and seizure, including the presence of the CNN reporters, which was not mentioned in the search warrant. See Kevin Helliker, "CNN Got Its Story, but Rancher Cries Foul," *Wall Street Journal*, September 25, 1997.

16. This figure is simply the total pages in the *Federal Register* per year divided by 365.

17. For example, see Albert Hunt, "Congress's Scandalous Money Machine," *Wall Street Journal*, March 7, 1996.

18. To our knowledge, Gordon Tullock was the first person to emphasize this question.

19. See Brian Goff, *Regulation and Macroeconomic Performance* (Boston: Kluwer Academic Press, 1996), p. 39. `

20. For these and other examples of cost-benefit analysis of governmental regulation, see W. Kip Viscusi, John Vernon, and Joseph Harrington, *Economics of Regulation and Antitrust* (Cambridge: MIT Press, 1995).

21. These figures are from Wayne Brough, "The EPA's Proposed Air Quality Standards: First, Do No Harm," *Citizens for a Sound Economy*, June 1997.

22. From Kenneth Chilton and Stephen Huebner, "Sound Standards Require Cost-Benefit Analysis," *Regulation* (Winter 1997), p. 14.

23. See U.S. Bureau of the Census, *Statistical Abstract of the U.S.* (Washington, D.C.: USGPO, 1997), p. 228.

24. For numerous case studies on the effects of private conservation efforts and the negative effects of government stewardship, see publications from the Center for Private Conservation. See also Fred Smith, "Hoarding the Nation's Wealth," *CEI Update*, October 1996.

25. See U.S. Bureau of the Census, *Statistical Abstract of the U.S.* (Washington, D.C.: USGPO, 1997), p. 375.

26. This is from Harvey Rosen, *Public Finance* (New York: Irwin/McGraw-Hill, 1997), p. 162. Daniel Slesnick, "Gaining Ground: Poverty in the Postwar United States," *Journal of Political Economy* (February 1993):1–38, provides an overview of the improvements in the material living standards of the poor in America.

27. In addition to the sources cited in the figures, additional data on the poor can be found in U.S. Bureau of the Census, "Characteristics of the Population Below the Poverty Level," *Current Population Reports*, Series P-60, various years.

28. Harry Jaffa, "The Party of Lincoln vs. the Party of Bureaucrats," *Wall Street Journal*, September 12, 1996.

29. For an analysis of these efforts, see Paul Krugman, "A Raspberry for Free Trade: Protectionists Serve Up Tainted Fruit," available: slate.com, November 20, 1997.

30. The reference to the ten-year-old is not just hypothetical. One of the author's own fathers not only picked cotton at this age but worked behind a team of mules as well as performing many other farm chores. A seven-year-old sister joined in the cotton picking—very efficiently because of her small hands. As an additional note, both these children viewed their parents as loving and caring—then and now.

31. Lucy Martinez-Mont, "Sweatshops Are Better Than No Shops," *Wall Street Journal*, June 25, 1996. Ms. Martinez-Mont is a professor of economics at Fransisco-Marroquin University in Guatemala City.

32. Paul Krugman, "In Praise of Cheap Labor: Bad Jobs at Bad Wages Are Better Than No Jobs at All," available: slate.com, March 20, 1997.

33. Jagdish Bhagwati, "Does Free Trade Harm the Environment? The Case for Free Trade," *Scientific American* (November 1993):41–57.

34. Karl Hess, "Environmentalists v. Wildlife," *Wall Street Journal*, June 5, 1997.

35. These figures are from Bruce Ames, "Pesticides, Cancer, and Misconception," and Elizabeth Whelan, "The Carcinogen or Toxin of the Week," both from *The State of Humanity*, ed. Julian Simon (Cambridge: Cambridge University Press, 1995).

36. Ibid.

37. P. J. O'Rourke, *Parliament of Whores* (New York: Vintage Books, 1991), p. 197.

Chapter Eight

1. For a classic discussion of the unintended consequences and public policy, see Friedrich Hayek, *The Road to Serfdom* (Chicago: University of Chicago Press, 1944).

2. Several of the articles in Chapter 6 bolster this point, including William Comaner and Llad Phillips, "Best Crime Stopper: A Father in the Home," *Wall Street Journal*, March 10, 1998, and John DiIulio Jr., "Rescue the Young from Barbarism," *American Enterprise* (May–June 1995):22–23.

3. This quotation is cited in George Will, *The Woven Figure* (New York: Scribner, 1997), p. 102.

4. The optimal size of the majority depends on several factors, including the degree of similarity of the constituents. See Andrew Caplan and Barry Nalebuff, "On the 64%-Majority Rule," *Econometrica* (July 1988):787–814, and "Aggregation and Social Choice: A Mean Voter Theorem," *Econometrica* (January 1991):1–24.

5. John Rawls's main work is *A Theory of Justice* (Cambridge, Mass.: Belknap Press, 1971).

6. This area of economics has come to be known as "constitutional economics" or "constitutional political economy." Some of the seminal contributions include James Buchanan and Gordon Tullock, *The Calculus of Consent* (Ann Arbor: University of Michigan Press, 1962), John Harsanyi, *Rational Behavior and Bargaining Equilibrium in Games and Social-Situations* (Cambridge: Cambridge University Press, 1986), and Geoffrey Brennan and James Buchanan, *The Power to Tax: Analytical Foundations of a Fiscal Constitution* (Cambridge: Cambridge University Press, 1980).

7. James Buchanan and Roger Congleton, *Politics by Principle, Not Interest: Toward Nondiscriminatory Democracy* (Cambridge: Cambridge University Press, 1998).

8. A very interesting analysis of the slavery dilemma for constitutional de-cisionmaking is presented in Thomas West, *Vindicating the Founders* (Lan-ham, Md.: Rowman and Littlefield, 1997).

9. See Robert Fogel, "The Fourth Great Awakening," *Wall Street Journal*, January 9, 1996.

SELECTED BIBLIOGRAPHY

Alsop, Ronald, ed. 1997. *Wall Street Journal Almanac*. New York: Ballantine Books.

Ames, Bruce. 1995. "Pesticides, Cancer, and Misconception." In Julian Simon, ed., *The State of Humanity*. Cambridge: Cambridge University Press.

Anderson, Sarah, and John Cavanagh. 1997. "The Top 10 List." *Nation*, December 8.

Angell, Marcia. 1996. *Science on Trial: The Clash of Medical Evidence and the Law in the Breast Implant Case*. New York: W. W. Norton.

Bachman, J. G., L. D. Johnson, and P. M. O'Malley. 1993. *Monitoring the Future*. Ann Arbor: University of Michigan Survey Research Center.

Bartley, Robert. 1992. *The Seven Fat Years*. New York: Free Press.

Batra, Ravi. 1987. *The Coming Depression of 1990*. New York: Simon and Schuster.

_____. 1988. *Surviving the Great Depression of 1990*. New York: Simon and Schuster.

Becker, Gary. 1976. *The Economic Approach to Human Behavior*. Chicago: University of Chicago Press.

_____. 1996. *Accounting for Tastes*. Cambridge: Harvard University Press.

Bell, Daniel. 1996. *The Cultural Contradictions of Capitalism*. New York: Basic Books.

Bennett, James. 1996. "Exultant Buchanan Pushes Economic Insecurity Theme." *New York Times*, February 22.

Bhagwati, Jagdish. 1993. "Does Free Trade Harm the Environment?: The Case for Free Trade." *Scientific American* (November):41–57.

_____. 1995. "Or Get Rid of It Altogether." *American Enterprise* (May/June):42–45.

Blinder, Alan. 1987. *Hard Heads, Soft Hearts*. Reading, Mass.: Addison-Wesley.

Bork, Robert. 1996. *Slouching Towards Gomorrah*. New York: Regan Books.

Borland, Melvin, and Robert Pulsinelli. 1989. "Household Commodity Production and Social Harassment Costs." *Southern Economic Journal* (October):291–301.

Boulding, Kenneth. 1968. *Beyond Economics.* Ann Arbor: University of Michigan Press.

Bragg, Rick. 1996. "Big Holes Where Dignity Used to Be." *New York Times,* March 5.

Brennan, Geoffrey, and James Buchanan. 1980. *The Power to Tax: Analytical Foundations of a Fiscal Constitution.* Cambridge: Cambridge University Press.

Brough, Wayne. 1997. "The EPA's Proposed Air Quality Standards: First, Do No Harm." *Citizens for a Sound Economy* (Washington, D.C.), June.

Buchanan, James, and Gordon Tullock. 1962. *The Calculus of Consent.* Ann Arbor: University of Michigan Press.

Buchanan, James, and Roger Congleton. 1998. *Politics by Principle, Not Interest: Toward Nondiscriminatory Democracy.* Cambridge: Cambridge University Press.

Buchanan, Patrick. 1998. *The Great Betrayal: How American Sovereignty and Social Justice Are Being Sacrificed to the Gods of the Global Economy.* New York: Little Brown.

Caplan, Andrew, and Barry Nalebuff. 1988. "On the 64-Percent-Majority Rule." *Econometrica* (July):787–814.

——— 1991. "Aggregation and Social Choice: A Mean Voter Theorem." *Econometrica* (January):1–24.

Cassidy, John. 1996. "All Worked Up." *New Yorker,* April 22.

Center for Labor Market Studies. 1995. "The State of the American Dream in New England." Boston: Northeastern University.

Central Intelligence Agency. 1997. *Handbook of International Economic Statistics, 1997.* Washington, D.C.: USGPO.

Chilton, Kenneth, and Stephen Huebner. 1997. "Sound Standards Require Cost-Benefit Analysis." *Regulation* (Winter):14–15.

Clinton, Bill, and Al Gore. 1992. *Putting People First.* New York: Times Books.

Clinton, Hillary. 1996. *It Takes a Village.* New York: Simon and Schuster.

Cobb, Clifford, Ted Halstead, and Jonathan Rowe. 1995. "If the GDP Is Up, Why Is America Down?" *Atlantic* (October):59–78.

Comaner, William, and Llad Phillips. 1998. "Best Crime Stopper: A Father in the Home." *Wall Street Journal,* March 10.

Cox, W. Michael, and Richard Alm. 1994. "These Are the Good Old Days: A Report on Living Standards." *Federal Reserve Bank of Dallas Annual Report.*

———. 1995. "By Our Own Bootstraps: Economic Opportunity and the Dynamics of Income Distribution." *Federal Reserve Bank of Dallas Annual Report.*

———. 1997. "Time Well Spent: The Declining Real Cost of Living in America." *Federal Reserve Bank of Dallas Annual Report.*

Daly, Herman. 1991. *Steady State Economics*. Washington, D.C.: Island Press.

_____. 1996. *Beyond Growth: The Economics of Sustainable Development*. Boston: Beacon Press.

Dentes, George. 1995. "Radically Narrow the Exclusionary Rule." *American Enterprise* (May/June):42–45.

DiIulio, John, Jr. 1995. "Rescue the Young from Barbarism." *American Enterprise* (May/June):22–23.

_____. 1996. "Defining Criminality Up." *Wall Street Journal,* July 3.

_____. 1997. "A More Gated Community." *Weekly Standard,* July 7.

_____. 1997. "Abolish the Death Penalty, Officially." *Wall Street Journal,* December 15.

Dornbusch, S. M., J. M. Carlsmith, S. J. Bushwall, R. L. Ritter, H. Leiderman, A. H. Hastof, and R. T. Gross. 1985. "Single Parents, Extended Households, and the Control of Adolescents." *Child Development* (April):326–341.

Duff, Christina. 1996. "America's Bad Mood Finally Turns Upbeat Years After Economy." *Wall Street Journal,* October 16.

Duncan, J. G., and S. D. Hoffman. 1985. "Economic Consequences of Marital Instability." In Martin David and Timothy Smeeling, eds., *Horizontal Equity, Uncertainty, and Economic Well-Being*. Chicago: University of Chicago Press.

Eberstadt, Nicholas. 1996. "Prosperous Paupers and Affluent Savages." *Society* (January/February):17–25.

Ehrenberg, Ronald, and Robert Smith. 1998. *Modern Labor Economics*. Reading, Mass.: Addison-Wesley.

Ehrlich, Paul. 1968. *The Population Bomb*. New York: Ballantine Books.

_____. 1990. *The Population Explosion*. New York: Simon and Schuster.

Executive Office of the President. 1997. *Economic Report of the President*. Washington, D.C.: USGPO.

Farber, Henry. 1995. "Are Lifetime Jobs Disappearing? Job Duration in the United States." Princeton: NBER Working Paper No. 5814.

Federal Bureau of Prisons. Various volumes. *Prisoners Released from State and Federal Institutions*. Washington, D.C.: USGPO.

Feige, Edward, ed. 1989. *The Underground Economy*. Cambridge: Cambridge University Press.

Fiorina, Morris. 1997. "Voting Behavior." In Dennis Mueller, ed., *Perspectives in Public Choice: A Handbook*. Cambridge: Cambridge University Press.

Fogel, Robert. 1996. "The Fourth Great Awakening." *Wall Street Journal,* January 9.

Frank, Robert, and Phillip Cook. 1995. *The Winner-Take-All Society*. New York: Free Press.

Friedman, Benjamin. 1988. *Day of Reckoning.* New York: Random House.

Galbraith, John Kenneth. 1958. *The Affluent Society.* Cambridge: Riverside Press.

Georgescu-Roegen, Nicholas. 1971. *The Entropy Law and the Economic Progress.* Cambridge: Harvard University Press.

Germond, Jack. 1992. *Mad as Hell: Revolt at the Ballot Box.* New York: Warner Books.

Gibbs, Winfred. 1917. *The Minimum Cost of Living: A Study of Families on Limited Income in New York City.* New York: Macmillan.

Goff, Brian. 1996. *Regulation and Macroeconomic Performance.* Boston: Kluwer Academic Press.

Gokleny, Indur. 1995. "Richer Is Cleaner." In Ronald Bailey, ed., *The True State of the Planet.* New York: Free Press.

Greenwood, Peter. 1982. "Selective Incapacitation." Santa Monica, CA: Rand Corporation, Report R-2815-NIJ.

Hanushek, Eric. 1998. "Review of What Money Can't Buy." *Journal of Policy Analysis and Management* 3:535–538.

Harrison, Bennett, and Barry Bluestone. 1988. *The Great U-Turn.* New York: Basic Books.

Harsanyi, John. 1986. *Rational Behavior and Bargaining Equilibrium in Games and Social Situations.* Cambridge: Cambridge University Press.

Haskins, Ron. 1996. "Does Welfare Encourage Illegitimacy?" *American Enterprise* (July/August):48–49.

Haveman, Robert, and Barbara Wolfe. 1995. "The Determinants of Children's Attainment: A Review of Methods and Findings." *Journal of Economic Literature* (December):1829–1878.

Hayek, Friedrich. 1944. *The Road to Serfdom.* Chicago: University of Chicago Press.

Heilbroner, Robert, and Lester Thurow. 1981. *Five Economic Challenges.* Englewood Cliffs, N.J.: Prentice-Hall.

Helliker, Kevin. 1997. "CNN Got Its Story, But Rancher Cries Foul." *Wall Street Journal,* September 25.

Hess, Karl. 1997. "Environmentalists v. Wildlife." *Wall Street Journal,* June 5.

Higgs, Robert. 1987. *Crisis and Leviathan: Critical Episodes in the Growth of American Government.* New York: Oxford University Press.

Holsey, Cheryl, and Thomas Borcherding. 1997. "Why Does Government's Share of National Income Grow? An Assessment of the Recent Literature on the U.S. Experience." In Dennis Mueller, ed., *Perspectives on Public Choice: A Handbook.* Cambridge: Cambridge University Press.

Hopkins, Thomas. 1996. "Regulatory Costs in Profile." St. Louis: Center for Study of American Business, Policy Report No. 132.

Houthakker, Hendrik. 1987. "Engel's Law." In J. Eatwell, M. Milgate, and P. Newman, eds., *The New Palgrave: A Dictionary of Economics.* London: Macmillan.

Hulten, Charles. 1997. "Quality Change in the CPI." *Federal Reserve Bank of St. Louis Review* (May/June):87–100.

Hunt, Albert. 1996. "Congress's Scandalous Money Machine." *Wall Street Journal,* March 7.

Jaffa, Harry. 1996. "The Party of Lincoln vs. the Party of Bureaucrats." *Wall Street Journal,* September 12.

Johnson, Haynes. 1991. *Sleepwalking Through History.* New York: Norton.

Judson, George. 1995. "Most Residents See Drop in Standard of Living, Study Finds." *New York Times,* December 11.

Kaldor, Nicholas. 1957. "A Model of Economic Growth." *Economic Journal* (December):591–624.

Kelling, George, and Catherine Coles. 1996. *Fixing Broken Windows: Restoring Order and Reducing Crime in Our Communities.* New York: Free Press.

Kitson, Gay, and H. Raschke. 1981. "Divorce Research: What We Know; What We Don't Know." *Journal of Divorce* 4:1–37.

Kliesen, Kevin. "Chained, Rested, and Ready: The New and Improved GDP." *St. Louis Federal Reserve Bank Regional Economist* (January):10–11.

Kosters, Marvin, ed. 1997. "Relative Wage Trends, Women's Work, and Family Income." Washington, D.C.: AEI Conference Summaries, January.

Krugman, Paul. 1990. *The Age of Diminished Expectations: U.S. Economic Policy in the 1990s.* Cambridge: MIT Press.

_____. 1996. "How the Press Miscovers Economics." *Jobs and Capital* (Summer):9–11.

_____. 1997. "A Raspberry for Free Trade: Protectionists Serve Up Tainted Fruit." Available: *Slate.com.* November 20.

_____. 1997. "In Praise of Cheap Labor: Bad Jobs at Bad Wages Are Better Than No Jobs at All." Available: *Slate.com.* March 20.

Kurtzman, Joel. 1988. *The Decline and Crash of the American Economy.* New York: Norton.

Kuttner, Robert. 1984. *The Economic Illusion.* Boston: Houghton-Mifflin.

_____. 1994. "Fewer Fruits for Our Labors." *Washington Post,* September 4.

_____. 1995. "Search for Elusive Candidate X." *Washington Post,* August 27.

_____. 1995. "The Rewards of Our Labors Are Increasingly Unequal." *Boston Globe,* September 4.

LaFranco, Robert. 1997. "The Forbes Top 40." *Forbes,* September 22.

Lebergott, Stanley. 1993. *Pursuing Happiness.* Princeton: Princeton University Press.

Lerman, Robert. 1997. "Economic Restructuring and the Job Market." *Urban Institute*, September.

Lipford, Jody, Robert McCormick, and Robert Tollison. 1993. "Preaching Matters." *Journal of Economic Behavior and Organization* (August): 235–250.

Lott, John. 1997. "Can Government Crime Data Be Trusted?" *Investor Business Daily,* July 16.

Lowenstein, Roger. 1996. "Intrinsic Value: Why Primary Voters Are So Angry." *Wall Street Journal,* February 22.

Lynch, Peter. 1996. "The Upsizing of America." *Wall Street Journal,* September 20.

Madrick, Jeffrey. 1995. *The End of Affluence.* New York: Random House.

_____. 1996. "If We're So Tired, Why Aren't We Rich?" *New York Times,* January 16.

Mandel, Michael. 1994. "The Truth About the Economy." *Business Week,* November 7.

Martinez-Mont, Lucy. 1996. "Sweatshops Are Better Than No Shops." *Wall Street Journal,* June 25.

Maurice, Charles, and Charles Smithson. 1984. *Doomsday Myth: 10,000 Years of Economic Crisis.* Stanford: Hoover Institution Press.

McKenzie, Richard. 1994. *What Went Right in the 1980s.* San Francisco: Pacific Research Institute.

_____. 1996. *Paradox of Progress.* New York: Oxford University Press.

McKenzie, Richard, and Gordon Tullock. 1989. *The Best of the New World of Economics.* Boston: Irwin.

Melloan, George, and Guy Molyneaux. 1996. "It's the Economy, Stupid." *Wall Street Journal,* January 29.

Mishel, Lawrence, and Jared Bernstein. 1995. "State of Working America 1994–95." Washington, D.C.: Economic Policy Institute.

Molyneaux, Guy. 1996. "It's the Economy Stupid." *Los Angeles Times,* March 3.

Moulton, Brent. 1996. "Bias in the Consumer Price Index: What Is the Evidence?" *Journal of Economic Perspectives* (Fall):159–178.

Moynihan, Daniel Patrick. 1993. "Defining Deviancy Down." *American Scholar* (Winter):17–30.

Mueller, Dennis. 1989. *Public Choice II.* Cambridge: Cambridge University Press.

Murray, Charles. 1993. "The Coming White Underclass." *Wall Street Journal,* October 29.

_____. 1994. "What to Do About Welfare." *Commentary* (December): 26–34.

Nakumura, Leonard. 1997. "Is the U.S. Economy Really Growing Too Slowly? Maybe We're Measuring the Wrong Thing." *Federal Reserve Bank of Philadelphia Business Review* (March/April):3–14.

Nasar, Sylvia. 1992. "An Unorthodox Choice for Economic Advisor." *New York Times,* December 12.

National Center for Health Statistics. Annual. *Vital Statistics of the U.S.* Washington, D.C.: USGPO.

Newman, Katherine. 1993. *Declining Fortunes.* New York: Basic Books.

New York Times. 1996. *The Downsizing of America.* New York: Times Books.

Office of Tax Analysis. 1992. "Household Income Mobility During the 1980s: A Statistical Analysis Based on Tax Return Data." Washington, D.C.: U.S. Department of the Treasury.

O'Rourke, P. J. 1992. *Parliament of Whores.* New York: Vintage Books.

Passell, Peter, and Leonard Ross. 1973. *The Retreat from Riches: Affluence and Its Enemies.* New York: Viking Press.

Phillips, Kevin. 1990. *The Politics of Rich and Poor: Wealth and the American Electorate in the Reagan Aftermath.* New York: Random House.

_____. 1994. *Boiling Point: Democrats, Republicans, and the Decline in the Middle Class.* New York: HarperPerennial.

Podhoretz, Norman, ed. 1995. "The National Prospect: A Symposium." *Commentary* (November).

Popkin, Samuel. 1979. *Rational Peasant: The Political Economy of Rural Society in Vietnam.* Berkeley: University of California Press.

Rawls, John. 1971. *A Theory of Justice.* Cambridge, Mass.: Belknap Press.

"Real Buchanan Alternatives." 1996. *Atlanta Constitution,* March 4.

Reich, Robert. 1983. *The Next American Frontier.* New York: Times Books.

_____. 1992. *The Work of Nations.* New York: Vintage Books.

_____. 1995. "Out of the Loop." *Chicago Tribune,* April 18.

Reynolds, Morgan. 1995. "Crime and Punishment in America." Washington, D.C.: National Center for Policy Analysis, Policy Report No. 193, June.

Robinson, John, and Geoffrey Godbey. 1995. "Are Average Americans Really Overworked?" *American Enterprise* (September/October):45.

Rowe, Jonathon. 1996. "Major Growing Pains: The Economy Is Rosy but People Are Not." *U.S. News and World Report,* October 21.

Samuelson, Paul. 1975. "The Optimum Rate of Economic Growth for Population." *International Economic Review* (October):531–538.

Samuelson, Robert. 1995. *The Good Life and Its Discontents.* New York: Times Books.

Sawhill, Isabel, and David McMurrer. 1996. "How Much Do Americans Move Up or Down the Economic Ladder?" Washington, D.C.: Urban Institute, November.

_____. 1996. "Economic Mobility in the United States." Washington, D.C.: Urban Institute, December.

Schellenberger, Sue. 1997. "Work and Family: Do We Work More or Not? Either Way We Feel Frazzled." *Wall Street Journal,* July 30.

Schlesinger, Jacob. 1997. "UPS Pact Fails to Shift Balance of Power Back to U.S. Workers." *Wall Street Journal,* August 20.

Schor, Juliet. 1991. *The Overworked American: The Unexpected Decline of Leisure.* New York: Basic Books.

_____. 1998. *The Overspent American: Upscaling, Downshifting, and the New Consumer.* New York: Basic Books.

Selby, Henry, Arthur Murphy, and Stephen Lorenzen. 1990. *The Mexican Urban Household.* Austin: University of Texas Press.

Shaw, Carolyn Bell. 1996. "Productivity Grew at a Modest 1.1 Percent in 1995." *Los Angeles Times,* March 7.

_____. 1996. "Bridging the Income Gap." *Boston Globe,* March 12.

Simon, Julian. 1974. *Effects of Income on Fertility.* N.p.: Carolina Population Center.

_____. 1977. *Economics of Population Growth.* Princeton: Princeton University Press.

_____. 1986. *The Theory of Population and Economic Growth.* Oxford: Basil Blackwell.

_____. 1988. *Ultimate Resource.* Princeton: Princeton University Press.

_____. 1990. *Population Matters.* New Brunswick, N.J.: Transactions Publishers.

_____, ed. 1995. *The State of Humanity.* London: Basil Blackwell, 1995.

Slesnick, Daniel. 1993. "Gaining Ground: Poverty in the Postwar United States." *Journal of Political Economy* (February):1–38.

Smith, Adam. 1981. *The Wealth of Nations.* New York: Penguin Books.

Smith, Fred. 1996. "Hoarding the Nation's Wealth." *CEI Update* (October).

Smith, Lynn, and Bob Sipchen. 1990. "Two-Career Families Face Dilemma." *Los Angeles Times,* August 12.

Smith, Victor. 1959. "Linear Programming Models for the Determination of Palatable Human Diets." *Journal of Farm Economics* (May):272–283.

State Statistical Bureau. 1985. *A Survey of Income and Expenditure in Households in China, 1985.* Beijing: People's Republic of China.

Stein, Charles. 1996. "For Workers, It's the Age of Anxiety." *Boston Globe,* January 21.

Stigler, George. 1945. "The Cost of Subsistence." *Journal of Farm Economics* (May):303–314.

Stigler, George, and Gary Becker. 1977. "De Gustibus Non Est Disputandum." *American Economic Review* (March):76–90.

Stockman, Alan. 1996. *Introduction to Macroeconomics.* Fort Worth, Tex.: Dryden.

Stossel, John. 1996. "Pandering to Fear." *Jobs and Capital* (Summer): 16–21.

Streighthoff, Frank. 1911. *The Standard of Living Among the Industrial People of America.* Boston: Houghton-Mifflin.

Summers, Robert, and Alan Heston. 1991. "The Penn World Table: An Expanded Set of International Comparisons, 1950–1988." *Quarterly Journal of Economics* (May):327–368.

Taylor, John. 1996. "The Path to Growth." *Wall Street Journal,* October 18.

Thurow, Lester. 1980. *The Zero-Sum Society.* New York: Basic Books.

Tiger, Lionel. 1996. "Nasty Turns in Family Life." *U.S. News and World Report,* July 1.

Tommasi, Mariano, and Kathryn Ierulli. 1995. *The New Economics of Human Behavior.* New York: Cambridge University Press.

Tullock, Gordon. 1974. *The Social Dilemma: The Economics of War and Revolution.* Blacksburg, Va.: University Publications.

Turner Broadcasting. 1997. *Downsizing the Dream.* Hosted by Frank Sesno. Turner Learning Video.

U.S. Bureau of the Census. 1975. *Historical Statistics of the U.S.* Washington, D.C.: USGPO.

_____. 1990. *Census of Housing and Population, 1990.* Washington, D.C.: USGPO.

_____. 1990. *Children's Well-Being: An International Comparison.* Washington, D.C.: USGPO.

_____. Various issues. "Characteristics of the Population Below the Poverty Level." *Current Population Reports,* Series P-60. Washington, D.C.: USGPO.

_____. Various issues. "Geographic Mobility." *Current Population Reports,* Series P-20. Washington, D.C.: USGPO.

_____. Various issues. "Marital Status and Living Arrangements." *Current Population Reports.* Washington, D.C.: USGPO.

_____. Annual. *Statistical Abstract of the U.S.* Washington, D.C.: USGPO.

_____. Available: www.census.gov.

U.S. Department of Agriculture. Annual. *Agricultural Statistics.* Washington, D.C.: USGPO.

U.S. Department of Commerce. 1975. *American Housing Survey, 1975.* Washington, D.C.: USGPO.

_____. 1995. *American Housing Survey for the U.S. in 1995.* Washington, D.C.: USGPO.

_____. Monthly. *Current Construction Reports.* Washington, D.C.: USGPO.

U.S. Department of Education. National Center for Education Statistics. 1996. *Digest of Education Statistics.* Washington, D.C.: USGPO.

U.S. Department of Justice. 1985. *Sentencing Reform in the U.S.* Washington, D.C.: USGPO.

_____. 1989. *National Assessment of Structured Sentencing.* Washington, D.C.: USGPO.

_____. Annual. *Sourcebook of Criminal Justice Statistics.* Washington, D.C.: USGPO.

U.S. Department of Labor. Monthly. *Employment and Earnings.* Washington, D.C.: USGPO.

_____. 1995. *Report on the American Workforce.* Washington, D.C.: USGPO.

_____. Bureau of Labor Statistics. Available: stats.bls.gov.

U.S. Immigration and Naturalization Service. Annual. *Annual Report of the Immigration and Naturalization Service.* Washington, D.C.: USGPO.

"A Valuable Economics Seminar." 1992. *New York Times,* December 16.

Verrico, Lisa. "What's Your Problem? Mark E. Smith—Hippies." *Vox* (March):18.

Viscusi, W. Kip, John Vernon, and Joseph Harrington. 1995. *Economics of Regulation and Antitrust.* Cambridge: MIT Press.

Vobejda, Barbara. 1994. "Education Is No Protection from Wage Squeeze, Report Says." *Washington Post,* September 4.

Wattenberg, Ben. 1984. *The Good News Is the Bad News Is Wrong.* New York: Simon and Schuster.

Weicher, John. 1997. "Wealth and Its Distribution." *Federal Reserve Bank of St. Louis Review* (January/February):3–23.

Wessel, David. 1997. "Budget Seeks to Raise U.S. Living Standards and Reduce Inequality." *Wall Street Journal,* February 7.

Wessel, David, and Gerald Seib. 1996. "Americans, Especially Baby Boomers, Voice Pessimism for Their Kids' Future." *Wall Street Journal,* January 19.

West, Thomas. 1997. *Vindicating the Founders.* Lanham, Md.: Rowman and Littlefield.

Whelan, Elizabeth. "The Carcinogen or Toxin of the Week." In Julian Simon, ed., *The State of Humanity.* Cambridge: Cambridge University Press.

Whitehead, Barbara Dafoe. 1993. "Dan Quayle Was Right." *Atlantic* (April):47–84.

Will, George. 1997. *The Woven Figure.* New York: Scribner.

Yang, John. 1996. "Hill Picks Up Buchanan's Economic Anxiety Issue." *Washington Post,* February 28.

Yates, Ronald. 1995. "In Larger Picture, U.S. Not So Competitive." *Chicago Tribune,* September 29.

Zinsmeister, Karl. 1995. "Pay Day Mayday." *American Enterprise* (September/October):44–48.

_____. 1996. "Coming This Year: Marx for Dummies." *Wall Street Journal,* January 25.

_____. 1996. "Income vs. Consumption." *American Enterprise* (July/August).

_____. 1996. "Mobility." *American Enterprise* (July/August):20.

_____. 1996. "Wages." *American Enterprise* (July/August):18–19.

Zycher, Benjamin. 1996. "The Rich and the Poor." *Jobs and Capital* (Summer):30–31.

INDEX